The Pluralist Philosophies Of England And America

Jean Wahl

THE PLURALIST PHILOSOPHIES
OF ENGLAND AND AMERICA

WILLIAM JAMES.

1842–1910.

[To face title-page.

THE
PLURALIST PHILOSOPHIES
OF ENGLAND & AMERICA

BY

JEAN WAHL
AGRÉGÉ DE PHILOSOPHIE, DOCTEUR ÈS LETTRES,
PROFESSEUR AU LYCÉE DE MANS

AUTHORISED TRANSLATION BY FRED ROTHWELL

LONDON
THE OPEN COURT COMPANY
149 STRAND, W.C. 2
1925

Printed in Great Britain by
NYHI & Co, Ltd, EDINBURGH.

À
MONSIEUR ÉMILE BOUTROUX

TABLE OF CONTENTS

BOOK I

MONISM IN ENGLAND AND IN AMERICA

BOOK II

THE FORMATION OF PLURALISM

CHAPTER I

GERMAN INFLUENCES

BOOK IV

FROM PERSONAL IDEALISM TO NEO-REALISM

CHAPTER I

THE OXFORD SCHOOL AND SCHILLER

Personal Idealism

The Pluralism of Schiller

CHAPTER II

HOWISON AND THE CALIFORNIAN SCHOOL : SOME PLURALIST IDEALISTS

CHAPTER III

SOME TENDENCIES OF PSYCHOLOGISTS AND LOGICIANS

CHAPTER IV

NEO-REALISM

The Cambridge School

THE
PLURALIST PHILOSOPHIES
OF ENGLAND & AMERICA

BOOK I

MONISM IN ENGLAND AND AMERICA

It was mainly after the year 1870 that philosophical teaching in British Universities came under the influence of the idealistic monism of German metaphysics, though this influence had made itself felt from the very beginning of the century. Coleridge, following Schelling, sang of the " miraculous all," the " omnific " spirit, the unity apprehended by reason and imagination, the human soul annihilated in God. De Quincey had studied Kant and Herder. Later on, Carlyle advised British youths to " open their Goethe " and offered for their silent admiration the indivisible nature of German philosophy.

German ideas—which were at first adopted by poets and writers—increasingly gained ground in philosophical circles. Caird became a follower of Carlyle. Stirling sang the praises of Hegel in two volumes, irregular and obscure in style. According to this writer, Hegelianism alone could successfully oppose the reaction against transcendentalist tendencies, the path to which was being paved by Buckle and his friends. Reason alone could restore the English to Christianity. He believed in a sole necessity, an eternal must-be, and summed up his belief as follows :

> "One absolute proportion is the whole,
> One sole relation, whose correlatives
> Are at once the multitudinous vast
> And Unity—finite and infinite—
> Matter and mind—the creature and its God."

The influence of Stirling was a real one. Green recommended the *Secret of Hegel* as a true and thorough exposition of the development of German philosophy. In America, too, Harris spoke of Stirling as a writer "who has power to awaken in the student of philosophy that immense faith which is indispensable to the one who will master the speculative thinking."

Jowett, the Greek scholar, inspired a few souls with the idea of a philosophy capable of combating successfully the empiricism of Mill and especially "Spencerian monism."

In 1874 and 1875 T. H. Green and his friends contrasted materialistic monism with an idealistic monism. Green was mainly concerned to show the unity of the thinking subject in the slightest perception, and the unity of universal consciousness in the smallest living being : given a fact, he could only regard it in its relation to the whole of which it is a part. In him, both the need and the sense of totality are very pronounced. He cannot conceive of the existence of relations between things without admitting the existence of one subject only, the spiritual bond between these relations. Every idea is envisaged in terms of the whole.

Books on philosophy, journals and periodicals, even the *Journal of Mental Science*, were at that time crammed with Hegelian ideas. By the aid of these ideas, it was hoped that it would be possible to overcome agnosticism

in metaphysics, associationism in psychology, and utilitarianism in morals.   As Eucken wrote in 1897, speaking
of England, "More and more the Hegelian system is
becoming the rallying-point of all who stand in need
of a comprehensive scheme for combating scepticism,
dualism, and unitarianism."

Metaphysical, moral, and religious needs all seemed to
acknowledge that the Neo-Kantian and the Neo-Hegelian
philosophy was bringing salvation in its train.

Soon, however, the monism that had developed under
the influence of religious needs came to be looked upon
by certain philosophers as the negation of religion.   Is
not religion, they said, regarded by Bradley as a stage
in thought which must be transcended ?   Do not the
monists tell us that the universe must not be looked
upon as under the governance of an omnipotent moral
person ?

Thus monism seemed to have undergone a transformation : in its first aspect—as interpreted by Green
and by his friends and disciples—it would not allow
philosophy to be reduced to a sort of phase of absolute
thought.   Jowett wished there to be " harmonious
proportion " between man and divinity.   Jones and
Haldane conceived the Absolute as an individuality
or an ensemble of individualities, and at times their
philosophy was more akin to that of Lotze than to that
of Hegel ; on the whole, they remained faithful to the
thought of Coleridge, regarding as one the Absolute of
the thinkers and the God of the believers.   Their
absolutism was opposed to scepticism and, in a measure,
also to Spinozism ; [1] it was an absolutism with theistic
tendencies.   But a few years afterwards there appeared

---

[1] And yet Nettleship wrote : " I think that I shall end my days as
something like a Spinozist," *Philosophical Lectures*, p. xlvii.

a doctrine, the pragmatist, the pluralist doctrine, which in the name of religious thought—the religious thought of naturally and simply believing souls—took up arms against absolutist ideas. The pragmatists showed that these contained both a withering dogmatism and an even more withering scepticism, an enervating optimism and an incurable pessimism ; in a word, that they constituted the very negation of religion and faith.

Bradley seemed to have given idealistic monism a new form. At the outset, he had set forth ideas which might seem purely Hegelian, but in his *Logic* (1883) and above all in *Appearance and Reality*, he presents a form of monism and of absolutism which, at first at all events, is very clearly distinguished from the preceding aspects of the Neo-Hegelian doctrine.

The idea of Absolute Reality towards which Bradley's metaphysic tends, the idea of experience with which it starts, the idea of the method it employs, may be found in the *Ethica* of Spinoza, in the *Treatise on Human Nature* of Hume, in the *Logic* of Hegel, as well as in the thoughts of the Sophists of old ; none the less all the doctrines are transformed, transmuted, as he would say, in his system, which is comprehensive, precise, abounding in deeps and steeped in the unknowable ; at one time we feel ourselves approaching the thought of James, at another, that of Hegel. Faith and experience, totality and diversity, pragmatism and anti-pragmatism, transcendence and immanence seem blended in this idea ; this union of uncompromising absolutism, ironical scepticism, and eagerness for experience and for individual facts, constitutes the difficulty and originality of this philosophy, the profundity of which is not to be denied.

Under the influence of this idea of the diversity of tendencies found in Bradley, we must take care not to lose the thread of his doctrine or neglect his fundamental conceptions. We will briefly state them so as to understand the strictures made upon them by the pluralists and to see what an effort is needed to interpret the teaching aright. In our study we shall use especially *Appearance and Reality*, referring occasionally, however, to *Essays on Truth and Reality*.

In the first part of *Appearance and Reality*, Bradley shows how the concepts we generally use to account for experience, how the distinctions we make, the wholes we form, are finally unsatisfying to the reason, contradictory, and consequently incapable of being anything but appearances. The distinctions between primary and secondary qualities, between substantives and adjectives, the notions of relations and qualities, of time and space, of causality and activity, of thing and self, of body and soul, are all criticised.

Everywhere we find things and terms breaking up, and relations taking their place, which relations in their turn, vainly seeking for their terms, elude our grasp.

The illusion of separating things into relations and qualities is the origin of all other illusions ; this it is which makes reality unintelligible ; for on the one hand qualities are nothing without relations, since qualities exist only because of distinctions and connections ; and on the other hand they cannot be understood if we admit the idea of relation. Besides, quality appears both as a condition and as a result of relations : a dual affirmation which is a contradiction.

A " relational " thought can give us only appearance —not truth. In practice it simply constitutes a compromise and separates what ought not to be separated. Bradley says that what he repudiates is the separation of feeling and its object, or of desire and its object, or of thought and its object, or indeed of anything whatsoever and anything else.

All these criticisms are therefore based on the idea of the internality of relations. Any relation apart from its terms is an illusion; "A relation between A and B really implies a substantial foundation within these terms." Consequently there must everywhere be a totality which contains that which is in relation.

The idea of the externality of relations is thus no more than a relative point of view necessary for our action. There is no absolute difference between an "inner relation" and an "outer relation." To affirm pure externality is to set up our own ignorance as a reality. Will it be alleged that position in space, on the one hand, and comparison on the other hand, offer us relations which in no way change their terms ? This is a question which Bradley studies at length in an appendix to *Appearance and Reality*. If comparison between two terms has nothing to do with the terms, does not transform them, then with what has it to do ? If it is external to the terms, how can it be said to apply to them ? If we are really the creators of judgment, is not judgment purely arbitrary ? What, at bottom, is a truth external to things ? An external relation cannot be true. There is neither identity nor resemblance, says Bradley, except within a totality ; consequently, if the totality becomes different, if a new synthesis is created, the terms must become different, from the very fact that they enter into this new totality.

Let us now look at space relations : shall we admit that there is no reason at all why terms should change the relations which exist between them ? If we do, we shall be admitting a purely irrational process. To represent points in space as capable of being arranged otherwise than they are is to take them as they are not. Bradley arrives at the same conclusion as Leibniz regarding space, and for the same reasons ; space is an abstraction, there is nothing purely spatial, and the appearance of externality is the very sign that here we have nothing but appearance. "There must somewhere be a reason why A and B appear at the same time." He also arrives at the same general affirmation that there is no such thing as chance, that everything is determined

Hence Bradley is able to reject two theories : that of phenomena *per se* on the one hand, and that of substances *per se* on the other : phenomenalism and substantialism.

The reason we have criticised appearances is that we have made use of a certain positive criterion, have determined to satisfy certain rational requirements within ourselves. If we have judged our different concepts to be unsatisfactory because they contradicted themselves and one another, it was owing to the idea of the non-contradictory character of ultimate reality. Therefore we may now say that everywhere the evidence of Absolute Reality is manifest.

It is useless to attempt to deny or to doubt this criterion ; our very negations and our doubts only affirm its importance. The real is coherent. And this coherency will be shown both by its harmony and by its comprehensiveness ; harmony and comprehensiveness are indeed ideas which imply one another ; whatever is not absolutely comprehensive must thereby contradict itself internally.

The real is coherent, individual, unique, and total, since every relation implies a basis of unity and external relations are essentially contradictory.

If unity were not present at the outset, it would never be attained, and experience and knowledge would be impossible. By the fact that we know things, there is but one reality. "To suppose that the universe is plural" is to contradict oneself; at bottom, this is to suppose that it is one. The formula beloved of many Hegelians, "the many in one," is dismissed.

The real is experience (sentience—sentient experience). In addition, it must contain a surplus of pleasure: on the one hand, in the Absolute there can be no unsatisfied desire; and on the other hand, the Absolute must satisfy the whole of our nature. "A result which does not succeed in satisfying the whole of our nature is not perfect. Our principal needs must all find their satisfaction."

Thus, first of all a pragmatist, in the sense that our main concepts are but practical compromises—Bradley is also a pragmatist, in the sense that the ideas we form of the Absolute must satisfy the whole of our nature.

Reservations are made, however, in certain passages: it must not be imagined that our satisfaction can be complete. "There is no reason why we should have all we desire and just in the way we desire it."

But, if we may now speak of connections, what connections will there be between the Absolute and the ideas we first criticised? Gradually, in the course of the first chapter of Book II, the thought of Bradley is revealed. Appearances have an undoubted human value; and not only that, but appearance exists, it "belongs" to reality. In our appearance we can discover the essential nature of reality. On the other hand, there is no reality outside of appearance. Without appearances, the real would be indeterminate, and where would appearances be if not within the real itself? Thus there is a reality of appearance; first because appearance exists somehow, and also because the Absolute must somehow be as rich as the relative. The world of reality, as Bosanquet says, is the world of appearances itself.

No doubt the reality of appearance can be obtained only by a transmutation of appearance, for if it were thought to be such as it is, it would involve contradictions. Nothing is real in itself; but, on the other hand, nothing is lost in the Absolute, everything is therein transmuted, and by this transmutation assumes fresh significance. No particular unity, no difference disappears; these very differences and discordances form the exuberant wealth of the Absolute.

It is in immediate experience itself that the finite centre, through appearances, is drawn beyond them, and in these very appearances is conscious of the presence of the Absolute. Hence we shall now be able to fix the starting-point, the method and the direction of human thought, beginning with the theory of the " finite centre."

Bradley, in his study of immediate experience, shows himself as radical an anti-intellectualist as James or as Bergson. What he regards as primitive is feeling, an experience without distinction, wherein being and knowing are one and yet infinitely diverse; it is this perceived substratum which constitutes the unity of our life. Behind self and the world, behind terms and relations, is an indefinite mass of perceived things to which the name of object cannot be given. Again, between object and subject there are finally no relations; the presence of the subject before the object is a fact, an indescribable and inexplicable fact. It is a fact that the Absolute appears in and for the finite centres, uniting them in a single experience. Moreover, what Bradley means by finite centre is neither the self nor the soul; for the self and the soul presuppose, the one, a non-self opposed to the self, the other, a before and an after, as well as phenomena distinct from substance. My self and my soul depend on what can in no way become an object, on the finite centre which is an experience united with its reality; an experience of itself and at the same time of the universe. The finite centre is, for itself, the whole world. It is not in time, it is a presence; it is not contrasted with other objects, it is everything.

In this immediate experience there seems at first to be mutual implication, complete unity of existence and of content or character, of what we may call the *that* and the *what*. The facts of immediate experience, however, says Bradley in *Essays on Truth and Reality*, cannot be accepted, for these also are appearances; that is to say, if we observe them, we see that their character supersedes their existence, that there is in them lack of adaptation between their character and their existence. Ideally things go beyond themselves. Things are ideal in the sense that they change and that the change consists in successively assuming different characters.

Thought consists essentially in distinguishing the *that* and the *what* which at first seemed to imply one another in immediate experience; it is ideal, it continues this movement, this ideality which is immanent in the world, since all movement is itself ideality, that is to say, a separation of existence and character, an assumption by the *that* of a new *what*.

The incessant effort of thought towards truth consists in the will to make equivalent the subject and the predicate, the *that* and the *what*, in uniting things with themselves, in seeking the inner basis of the connection between terms; it tries to reconstruct the totality, the union between fact and quality. And it is only because of the destructions, the dissociations effected by ideas, that we can approach this concrete knowledge. This will be the task of philosophy. And now we understand the place that rational thought occupies between immediate synthesis and absolute synthesis.

Thus immediate experience is transcended; from the outset, it is transcended seeing that it transcends itself, that it contains within itself a world which goes beyond itself. In another sense, however, it is never transcended, for it contains the developments which transcend it, and it judges them. It is this unanalysable background that makes analysis possible and is finally the judge of analysis. True, the force of Bradley's dialectic, especially in *Appearance and Reality*, lay in the principle of non-contradiction, the idea of totality; but in the *Essays* it is rather primitive experience itself, both harmonious and comprehensive, a multiplicity and a unity, that invokes or inspires within us this idea of totality. There we find that union of the multiple and the one which no rational thought can reconstruct and no rational thought can ignore.

Bradley, while saying that God or the Absolute is " also my state," can justifiably profess to be no panpsychist: the *that* is external to thought; thought does not contain the whole of the real; thought is always found with another, and the existence of this term external to thought is revealed by the effort of the subject towards an infinite whole, and by the immediate character of perception, by the absence in this perception of any division between the *that* and the *what*. Consequently thought cannot completely absorb the object, it has always in front of it something other than itself.

Reality is therefore something else than thought, and yet in a sense it is thought. Thought tends essentially to supersede itself, and ideality is the motor of the world ; that is, reality makes use of thought to realise itself. Thus, according to Bradley, idealism and realism can be reconciled. The judgment seeks a higher form of "immediacy" than it can reach, and this effort of thought cannot come to anything, for if it did, we should leave the realm of thought altogether, we should have attained—more than truth—reality itself. Never will ideas be coherent, they will always be a denial of themselves. How a predicate applies to a subject ; how the world is both one and diverse : these are problems we cannot solve.

Thus, so long as subject and predicate are not identified, thought has not reached its goal, but if it did, terms and relations would have ceased to be. Subject and predicate ought to be and cannot be identified with each other.

The reason is that the world of relations remains an inadequate and essentially false expression of primitive reality. We can now put back into the whole development of thought the relations we have criticised ; they form a compromise whereby thought would reconcile and harmonise the character both of plurality and of unity in the world, a compromise, however, which never can be fully satisfactory.

Primitive reality is infra-relational, ultimate reality is supra-relational : relations are the necessary though contradictory expression of non-relational unity. If we think of them as external, we deny the immediate unity of our experience and we cannot think of them completely as internal.

Separating and uniting its subject and its attribute, separating them both from the rest of the universe, presenting them as unconditioned and implying a multitude of conditions, judgment is an inadequate form of thought. The form of thought which will satisfy alike our feeling, our sensation, and our intellect must be found somewhere beyond judgment and intellect.

And so we again come to the idea of an Absolute, in which Thought finds its " Other " without there being any contradiction, in which each element attains to self-fruition while at the same time blending with the other elements.

No doubt we are unable fully to realise the existence of the Absolute, but at all events we can know it by making use of the feelings and the relations themselves now that they have been criticised, and also of our ideas of the good and the beautiful, degrees of reality that enable us to approach the one Reality.

Differences do not disappear, but they are all contained in the whole after having been transmuted ; each element, Bradley tells us, is able to retain its special character. Within the experience which absorbs the particular, this latter may retain its individual consciousness.

We are always coming back to the Absolute. But certain problems are bound to present themselves to us : first, how can error and evil be contained in the Absolute ? and then, how can these particular determinations, " the here " and " the mine," nature, body and soul, belong to it ? In a general way, we can prove neither how nor why the universe possesses these characteristics of finite existence. We cannot understand how relational form is included in the Absolute. But what we can do —and what it will be sufficient to do—is to show that these particular determinations are not incompatible with it, that they increase its wealth ; now, that which is possible, that which by a general principle we are forced to acknowledge must be, necessarily is. Here, possibility suffices to prove reality.

Bradley affirms that error is but partial truth and is compatible with absolute perfection. And are not these partial truths necessary in the interests of the different individuals ?

In attempting to solve the problem of evil, Bradley makes distinctions between suffering, failure, and moral evil. As regards suffering, we may observe that slight sufferings are frequently swallowed up in a greater pleasure. If we are able to conceive that there is a surplus of pleasure in the universe, we ought to do so. Even admitting—a very debatable point—that in the world as we see it pleasure does not outweigh suffering, this world is but a small part of the whole universe ; now we are in possession of a principle which compels us to acknowledge that, as regards the whole of the universe, that which can be, and at the same time ought to be, really is. In respect of evil as a failure, the results we reach, if we regard it as within a vaster whole, can no longer be looked upon as failures. Dealing with the problem of moral evil, morality *qua* morality must not be attributed to the Absolute ; moral evil exists only within moral experience, and this experience is essentially very incoherent. The higher end of man is above morality. And evil plays its part within the vaster good.

If, after the problem of the negative—meaning thereby the problem of error and evil—we approach the problem of the particular, we find ourselves confronted with spatial and temporal appearances. But time, to some extent, presupposes something permanent, science endeavours to make of reality something outside of time, association and memory are negations of time ; we are brought to see that time endeavours to transcend itself and tends towards the eternal, that space strives to lose itself in a more rational and more unified form of perception. Nor have we any reason whatsoever to conceive of time as a single succession. Temporal series may not have temporal relations with one another. We construct a single time which we call real time, starting with the identity of our own existence and neglecting first the creations of imagination and then all those series of phenomena with which we are unacquainted. Direction of time, distinction between past and future, depend on our particular experience. In so far as we can affirm anything in this connection, there may be in the Absolute a multitude of temporal series without any temporal bond with one another. The bond between them may be quite other than temporal. Bradley makes similar observations on the nature of space ; there may be an indefinite number of material worlds unconnected in space, and Nature is only the extended world in so far as it is in rapport with my body.

We are thus led to examine the appearances of *this* and *mine*, seeing that time and space depend on them. They have both a positive and a negative aspect. Their positive aspect, *i.e.* the *this* and the *mine* as simple feelings, is compatible with the Absolute. True, we cannot explain why experience must take place within finite centres ; what we can be certain of is that all the divisions and differences we find within the universe can only contribute to make it richer But the *this* and the *mine* appear also as negations ; now, negations can be but false appearances, Bradley tells us, for all negation is determination with reference to something or other ; all external relation, as we have seen, is self-contradictory. Even the exclusive character of these relations of the *mine* and the *here* implies the idea of a unity which contains them, *i.e.* through them the *mine* and the *here* are related to something else than themselves, something beyond themselves. Their exclusive character is thus a proof of their necessary absorption within the inclusive absolute. The *this* essentially transcends itself. Nothing *per se* is "opposed," nothing refuses to unite, says Bradley in the Appendix to *Appearance and Reality*. The *this* and the *mine* seem to have form and matter; but their form, that burning sense of personality which characterises them, comes from "their union with the central fire"; their matter is simply that which does not succeed in becoming one with the other contexts, it comes from the failure of our attempts at integration; it is essentially chance. To rely on this negative character in criticising the idea of the Absolute is to transform into a positive objection the simple fact of our ignorance. In reality everything that seems to belong to the *mine* and to the *this* is capable of becoming one element of a vaster whole, and our mental life actually consists in efforts of this kind for transcending the particular, for revealing by association and generalisation those characters with which such or such a datum appears, but which are not fully possessed by it alone.

There remains nothing individual except the Absolute. The Absolute is a superabundance; containing all distinctions, it yet exists superior to them. Is it personal? Assuredly. Containing all, it contains the individual, but it is something else, it is many other things besides the individual. "To call it personal would be as absurd as to inquire if it is moral." The Absolute is above time, above the individual.

Still, we must not see on the one side error and on the

other side truth; neither error nor truth is absolute.
Thus Bradley reaches what he calls his doctrine of degrees
of truth or reality. Of two given appearances, that
which is the more comprehensive or harmonious will be
the more real, the one which will least need to be
transformed.

That which gives us the richest and most concrete
notion of the real is spirit. Reality is spiritual; the more
spiritual a thing is, the more truly real it is.

Thus all appearance may be positively regarded as
bearing upon reality; reality is not an abstraction, it is
present in the midst of its appearances. Such are the
two affirmations at the centre of all true philosophy.

In the *Essays on Truth and Reality*, Bradley attempts
more than he had previously done to assimilate his
doctrine to concrete reality, to show its concrete value.
Even in the experience of each of us, the whole is partially
attained, although no doubt it is in absolute reality that
we really attain to it in a way our senses cannot perceive.

Everything is immanent and transcendent. On the
one hand, both my entire knowledge and reality itself
imply transcendence. I exist only in so far as I am
" beyond." On the other hand there is no separation
within the universe, and the real presence of the Absolute,
including God, is felt and experienced within the finite
centre.

Appearance, as it now seems to us, is the fact that in
the finite is present something that carries the finite
beyond itself. Thus it is the Absolute which constitutes
appearance. In one sense, absolute reality is the given
fact; in order to find it, we have no need to transcend
fact. We remain in the Absolute and transcend the
lower forms in which it appears in order to proceed
towards the more real forms; but from the first moment

2

the finite centre is transcended; from the first moment it is one with the universe.

Bradley concludes his *Essays* by affirming the importance of the finite conditions through which the ideal may be realised; on this point his ideas coincide with those of Bosanquet. The Good, the Beautiful, and the True, he says, live in the immortal paradise which is here, which is wherever any finite being is lifted to that higher life which alone is waking reality. "Whether it is a sign of weakness or of old age, I now regard more and more as literal truth what in childhood I admired and loved as poetry."

At the same time, he insists more strongly on what the effort of philosophic thought should be, an effort which consists in retaining simultaneously ideas which seem contradictory. Man may believe at the same time that there is perfect goodness and that nothing is more intensely real than action undertaken with a view to the good, and that these two beliefs are connected. My will must count, and, on the other hand, Good is already realised. We must believe simultaneously in the struggle in the world and in the peace of God, and endeavour not to allow either of these two ideas to disappear. God must be within us and beyond us. Bradley accuses pragmatism of being too eager in seeking after coherence; absolutism, "a hard doctrine," attempts to teach us to dispense with it sometimes. Philosophy, as he would have it, is an heroic philosophy.

Such a doctrine, Bradley tells us, supplies us with knowledge adequate to satisfy the main interests of our nature, but on the other hand it does not allow us to outstrip the limits of what we are capable of knowing. It does not make us believe, in spite of the reproaches of its critics, that we are in the midst of a world of illusions;

it affirms, thanks to the doctrine of degrees of reality, that what we think most true, most beautiful, and most good, really *is* most true, most beautiful, and most good. It refutes alike that kind of transcendentalism which sees reality everywhere, and that agnosticism which sees it nowhere; it is reality itself which, in different degrees, appears in its appearances.

Bradley makes a cult of the particular, the exact fact. He regards experience as incapable of taking place except in " finite centres." Ever thirsting after the concrete, he would dispense with categories and " their immaterial ballet." He does not regard the intelligible and the real as identical; such a proposition would convert the world into a cold phantasmal appearance, like the world of the materialist. As regards the Absolute, he asks himself the same question as James did with reference to each of the finite details of experience: " Can we then say anything about the concrete nature of the system ? " And do we not find in Bradley that sobriety and reserve in induction and deduction which is a part of the ideal of the pragmatist method ? Affirming both the Absolute and certain things about it, he nevertheless refuses to say that it can be really understood.

On the other hand he agrees with pragmatism that every idea necessary for the satisfaction of a human need is true, that the ideas adopted by our sense of value, even if they seem contradictory in themselves, possess some truth. For practical needs, he says, there is something higher than theoretical coherency. His doctrine of the criterion of truth—as well as his section on Nature and the Real World—is closely akin to pragmatism.

Bradley insists that life should retain the whole of its tragic worth. We said just now that he worships the particular fact; we might even say that his universe, in one sense, is full of diversity ; just as absolutism leads to relativism, so one might say that his monism allows him to make certain pluralist affirmations. As though the whole could alone have the prerogative of unity and harmony, he likes to distinguish, to dissolve all things, to break beings and qualities alike. Pragmatists have been known to defend experience against what they called the " pluralising " attacks of Bradley. James was heard to declare that " Mr Bradley's understanding shows the most extraordinary power of perceiving separation and the most extraordinary impotence in comprehending conjunctions."

In the eyes of Bradley, everything becomes loose and separate. His very absolutism enables him to make these separations. His Absolute reigns only over an infinite dust of facts. Why should there be one single time ? Things unite in the Absolute, apart from time. In the world of appearances, why should there not be pluralities of directions, seeing that in the Absolute no direction exists ? The very bonds between causes and effects may be undone ; the unity of the Absolute is above causes and effects.

Let the worlds multiply. " Nature, strictly speaking, cannot be called a single world." Like James, Bradley conceives of " physical systems as numerous as you please, without spatial relations with one another," " incoherent worlds," worlds varied with experiences, independent of one another.

There is nothing to prove, he says in *Essays on Truth*, that the dream-world is unreal, although this restricted world of ours must be accepted for all practical purposes. Quality and qualities reappear like times and spaces.

He comes to wonder why the world should remain the same, why there should not be " indefinite variations in the plurality of worlds," and he recognises only a certain average of identity.

No doubt he regards Nature, thus defined, as that which is most strongly contrasted with the autonomy and unity of the Absolute. All the same, it exists. And so, following inversely the trend of his thought, setting the theory of appearance after the theory of reality, as Parmenides his predecessor had done in ancient times, we can discover what distinctions and diversities he retains behind his Absolute. From the standpoint of his one immutable Absolute, he sees all things transformed and unified; but if we place ourselves at the heart of appearances, we everywhere come in contact with the partial and the fragmentary. As Bradley well says : the man who wants to act in the world must believe in finite personality, in the succession of things in time : if he fails, he must believe that the whole world undergoes defeat with himself; if he is victorious, he feels himself the cause of a triumph of the universe.

And yet it is not difficult to see what irritates the pluralists in Bradley's philosophy : first, this intellectual hedonism which seems at moments to consider only the exigencies of thought, then this negation of the idea of relations and the agnosticism which would appear to make it inevitable that we should know nothing of the Absolute, the idea that all experiences will be transmuted in the Absolute, and, finally, that kind of optimistic quietism which they imagine it implies, and the negation of time and finality, of individual teleology, of human liberty. They have emphasised what we have called the dogmatic scepticism of the doctrine. Certain passages, in which Bradley insists on the diversity and opulence of things, they have for the most part regarded as mere contradictions in terms. A distinction must be made between the reality of Bradley's philosophy and what it appeared to be in the eyes of several of his followers and many of his opponents.

Of all the philosophers who come nearest to Bradley, Bosanquet is unquestionably the most important.

In spite of identity of fundamental conception, we must note certain shades of thought that distinguish these two men. Scepticism is less pronounced in Bosanquet. Relying on the theory of degrees of reality as we see it in Bradley, Bosanquet emphasises the positive element in Nature, in the creations of imagination and reason. The contradictory character of appearance does not make an illusion of appearance; it characterises it without destroying it.

Appearance becomes a revelation: time, says Bosanquet, is an appearance inseparable from the fact that the finite is part of the infinite, and consequently inseparable from the fact that a reality, which, *qua* totality, is outside of time, is self-revealing.

Hence it comes about that it is possible to supply suggestions—which would appear to be more concrete than those of Bradley—as to the nature of the real; human experiences, especially the sublimest, are presentiments and manifestations of the Absolute and may thus serve as examples enabling us to understand its nature, which is that of a " world."

Bradley had insisted above all—at least this is the first impression we receive of his doctrine—on the work of separation effected by the mind; Bosanquet emphasises the unifying activity of reason, " the active form of totality," an activity whereby thought, instead of separating us from the concrete, vivifies things and endows them with richer meanings. In one sentence, which appears to express a totally different idea from that of Bradley, he tells us that by drifting away from original experience we by no means do away with its direct and significant character.

In works of art we discover worlds which may serve us as instances to enable us to understand the meaning of the universal concrete. "Here thought is at ease in reality and assumes the attitude of intuitive intelligence." Bosanquet maintains that there are concrete modes of thought by which we return to the fullness of experience.

Another difference, connected with the same conception of the concrete, may be seen in Bosanquet's theory of externality as necessary for the development of the soul, a sort of concentration of externality, and in his conception of the part played by the body, in his idea of the magnificent contrast and reconciliation of body and soul. He insists on incorporation and tradition, on body and history, on continuity with matter and with other souls.

Whilst Bosanquet and younger disciples—Joachim, Taylor—were developing the logical and ontological consequences of this philosophy, others had recourse to the formula of the " many in the one " or the " one in the many " which Bradley had determined to banish. Schiller's pluralism in his *Riddles of the Sphinx* (1893) appeared as forming part of a widespread reaction against radical monism.

There was a group of thinkers who, whilst remaining monists, were classed as " critics of Hegelianism." We may regard the Seth brothers as representative of this movement. Andrew Seth (Pringle-Pattison) contrasted Scotch philosophy with the Hegelianism imported from abroad. James compared *Hegelianism and Personality* with *Riddles of the Sphinx* as representing " revolts against the tendency to reduce reality to thought."

No doubt Seth retains many Neo-Hegelian beliefs : he believes in a world system and denies pluralism altogether. " I thought I had sufficiently guarded against the faintest suspicion of ontological pluralism," he writes. In his opinion, there is an experience or a being that embraces all things, that sustains and explains our fragmentary and contradictory experience while completing it. He shares with Bradley the thought that truth belongs to God alone. He declared that there was no clash, no contradiction between his new opinions and his former conception. All the same, the consideration of the possible moral consequences of monism and perhaps also the study of the two doctrines that contributed so largely to the development of pluralism, those of Lotze and Renouvier, induced Andrew and James Seth to modify their opinions considerably.

A pragmatist up to a certain point, Andrew Seth sees in the Hegelian doctrine a " paralysing" conception of existence ; it " contradicts our best established standards" ; it is an unreasonable philosophy, one that, in the final analysis, destroys the reality of both the divine and the human subject. He reproaches Hegel for suppressing the concrete reality of individuals. He affirms that " the processus of the world is a real processus in time."

" At each moment, there is but one stage that is real." God himself is in time, for abstractions alone are outside of time. Thus Andrew Seth unites himself with the pluralists, since he believes in the profound reality of duration and of the individual. Each self, he says, is an impenetrable existence, and material impenetrability is but a feeble image of that of the mind. The individual is individual down to the deepest fibre of his being.

James Seth perhaps even more deliberately accepts

personality as an ultimate metaphysical concept. If we would approve in their entirety all the demands of consciousness, he declares, we must not look upon metaphysics as a complete whole. The reality of the moral life implies the independence of man as regards God, and imposes on us rather a pluralistic than a monistic view of the universe.

Thus there came about a reaction against monism, and the pages of English and American philosophical reviews were never more filled with controversial articles on the one and the many. "The pluralist movement," said Ritchie, "will but make explicit theories that are only implicit in the anti-Hegelian arguments of Professor Seth."

It was also about this period that the followers of James Martineau developed his ethical personalism, based on the ideas of God, freedom, and immortality.

Even amongst the most faithful Hegelians the sense of individuality was more clearly apparent. Taylor, one of the most uncompromising followers of Bradley on certain points—partly, it may be, influenced by American philosophy and especially by that of Royce—shows how experience is both one and multiple. "The entire system forms an experience, and its constituent factors are in their turn single experiences." Consequently his philosophy is neither monism nor pluralism altogether. He declares himself in profound sympathy with the tendencies of Sturt to insist on the reality of human freedom, on the importance which the teleological categories of the personal life must assume in a final interpretation of the universe. He insists on the plurality of terms in logic and on our psychological experience which makes us apprehend the self, that is to say, a substance. This philosophy, which Schiller frequently attacked, is at bottom fairly akin to the pluralist philosophies.

Nevertheless, Taylor and the monists regard the fundamental category as one of inclusion. This is not the case with McTaggart, who proceeds rather by juxtaposition. He claims, however, to remain faithful to the spirit of Hegelianism : as an exegete and interpreter of the thought of Hegel, he aims—in restoring the idea of plurality in the Absolute—not at correcting Hegel as Seth does, but at making a thoroughly critical study of his philosophy.

From orthodox Hegelianism he retains the idea of the impersonal Absolute, the idea of the imperfection of everything temporal. He regards, however, the unity of the world as being no more profoundly real than its diversity. He is led to drift farther away from Neo-Hegelian orthodoxy by a keen sense of individuality and a strong desire after immortality. In his thought this question of immortality, in which after all James often seems but slightly interested, is persistently present. According to the reply given to this question, we are either the supreme end of reality or else reduced to the passive state of instruments. Thus it is this idea of immortality that leads him to metaphysical individualism. The influence of pluralists like Lowes Dickinson emphasises these tendencies.

McTaggart maintains that " the element of differentiation and multiplicity occupies a far larger place in Hegel's system than is generally believed." His object is to show that in this system the world is a society of souls, an assemblage of minds, and that divinity is but one of these minds amongst all the rest. All individualities are eternal. A society of minds does exist, the Absolute lives only in and through individuals. There can exist

only persons, conscious beings who know, will, and feel.
" Each of the parts of the whole is thoroughly individual,"
and it is for that reason, according to himself as well as
to Royce, that the whole is a perfect unity. Individuals
have an absolute reality. No doubt McTaggart frequently seems to conceive of individuals as regulated in
such fashion that, from the knowledge of one, we may
arrive at the knowledge of all. The nature of each
mind would be no more than the expression of its relations
with the Absolute; each self exists only through its
relations with other selves. It is true, nevertheless, to
state that the Hegelian universe is a patchwork universe.

In his *Dogmas of Religion* McTaggart discusses at length
the idea of an omnipotent and creative God, and he
concludes that the idea of absolute power possessed by
God would contradict the absolute individuality of persons. His power over us is limited, we can oppose him
to some extent. If God exists, he is a finite person
fighting on the side of good, and the victory of God
is not an inevitable one. Thus McTaggart is here at
one with James. He admits even the possibility of a
polytheism.

Without including McTaggart, as has been done,
amongst the pluralists, he must be accorded a special
place amongst the monists. The philosophies of Taylor
and McTaggart consist of attempts to exhibit, in the
Neo-Hegelian doctrine, such elements of diversity as
it may contain.

But though there be multiplicity, there is no development in duration in these philosophies of Taylor and
McTaggart; what prevents them, especially that of
McTaggart, from being pluralist doctrines is the absence of the idea of the mobility of things and beings,
the idea of time.

An original system of metaphysics was also developed in the Scottish Universities where Scotus Novanticus (Professor Laurie) wrote in succession *Metaphysica Nova et Vetusta, Ethica*, and *Synthetica*. He created a kind of pluralistic monism wherein subject and object mutually deny each other, man opposes God, and the individual possesses absolute rights. There is irrationality, disharmony, and contingency in the universe. This element of irrationality finds its explanation in a cosmic sin whereby God has denied himself. Without this element of irrationality, however, the world would not be free. Thus, God must now strive for the triumph of the good, and this negation, this irrationality present in the world, is so strong that, but for our help, God might be overcome in the struggle. Let us believe loyally in him, co-operate in his work and sympathise with him, for we must be not only God's companions in work, but his companions in distress, retaining all the time throughout our sadness the irresistible instinct of hope.[2]

In Laurie, as in certain of the Oxford philosophers, it is no longer simply a static pluralism that we perceive, it is also the sense of imperfection, of the incomplete character of the world and the endless human possibilities whereby the world may be redeemed. These are two of the deepest feelings of the future pluralist metaphysics of James and Schiller.

*   *   *   *   *   *

On the other side of the Atlantic, the philosophical ideas originating in Germany at first assumed a particular form, a form at once transcendental and unitarian.

[2] We find a similar theory in certain conceptions of Sir Oliver Lodge; in order to found and develop the human race, the Deity has had—and still has—to endure infinite suffering. But this race must know that in itself lie endless possibilities; when it makes an effort it is of a cosmic nature; in it the whole world is in travail.

But the philosophies of Channing, Henry James, and Emerson were not pure monisms either ; we shall have to endeavour to find in them the germs of pluralism as well as the affirmations of monism.

Whereas William James was rather suspicious of German philosophical importations, his father has been regarded as " Anglo-German in mind." His metaphysic was " half-Swedenborgian, half-Hegelian." His son shows a religious respect for the particular ; the religion of Henry James is that of the Universal. The Universal may be attained by the reason. He reproaches Emerson for despising intellect ; to him there is nothing in life that was not first in the intellect, there is nothing in creation that cannot be apprehended by it. Through intellect combined with feeling, through the communion of beings by heart and reason united, we are enabled to grasp the Universal.

In the doctrine of Henry James, the self which prevents the union of soul with soul, with God, cannot be other than harmful. There can be no private relation whatsoever between God and the individual. " Renounce thyself " is the lesson he teaches. The true nature of the individual is that which universalises him. *E pluribus unum* is the motto of Nature as well as of the United States.

All things lose their independence, they exist only with reference to other things ; their semblance of existence *per se* is but a gross illusion.

Material things are but the symbols of spiritual beings. Philosophy deals with the finite only in so far as the finite overlays the infinite.

May freedom exist in the world as thus conceived ? Henry James believes in a freedom devoid of free-will, in energy without tension, " in a will made up of non-voluntary stirrings." " The life to which I aspire," he writes, " is a life of goodness that is free, spontaneous, and without constraint." He considers that the better springs from the less good by a slow and quiet development. Henry James, the novelist, explains the optimism of his father by his power to see the hidden possibilities whereby things may become, from moment to moment, wholly different, and as beautiful as they were discouraging and gloomy the previous instant. Accordingly there dominates both in Henry James and in William James what might be called the sense of infinite possibilities and incessant changes ; but whereas this is to produce in William James a sort of pessimism where freedom of action is conceived in effort and trembling, it is found at the origin of his father's optimism. Henry James regards the idea that freedom means the power to be good or wicked at one's pleasure, as both dangerous and diabolical. But it is in this hell that his son will wish to live ; rather this dangerous world than a paradise where all effort is meaningless.

Henry James occupies an important place in the evolution of religion in America. While it is true that America is less inclined than in the difficult times of the early settlers " to conceive of heaven as entered by a strait gate and salvation as confined to the few," as one of her historians expresses it,[3] Henry James has thrown more widely open the heavenly portal which Jonathan Edwards would have closed after a few elect had been admitted. He has done something towards this expansion of view, this alleviation of dogma mentioned by the same historian ; instead of fatality there reigns sweet freedom, and pessimism is replaced by confident optimism.

Emerson occupies an even more important place than Henry James in the evolution of American thought.

[3] Boutmy, *Psychologie du peuple américain*, pp. 305 and 306.

Emerson's friends and disciples discovered in the splendour of day and night, in moments of joy and of sorrow, behind sound and more especially behind silence, the inexpressible unity of the higher soul of God, telling us of divine truths that appear through the symbols and parables of every phenomenon of Nature. If they did not create, at all events they popularised, one particular feeling—that of the infinite mysterious profundity of phenomena, the sense of a permanent miracle which reveals itself in flashes. Everything conceals from the vulgar and reveals to initiates the one higher soul. Transcendentalism is essentially a unitary or monistic philosophy. The resemblance between creatures is greater than their differences, Emerson tells us. Behind the ultimate envelope of Nature, in the depths of being, dwells unity. Hence each truth appears only as absolute, being seen under a single aspect. "Within man is the soul of the whole, the wise silence, the universal beauty to which every part and particle is equally related: the eternal ONE." Edgar Allan Poe, giving an ironical recipe for the imitation of transcendentalist works, writes: "Put in something about the Supernal Oneness. Don't say a syllable about the Infernal Twoness."

Emerson, the philosopher of democracy, is succeeded by the poet of democracy, Walt Whitman, the poet who chants as he says the " Song of the Universal," the song of the One formed of everything ; in each man he sees the whole of mankind, the entire world. James calls him "our national ontological poet." We see from his poetry what American ontology was at the beginning of the second half of the nineteenth century and how ardent was the belief in cosmic unity.[4]

[4] *Specimen Days* states that Hegel should be considered as " both the truest cosmical devotee or religioso and the profoundest philosopher."

Though we have insisted on the monistic tendencies of all these writers, we must now unfold the aspirations with which they are filled in the direction of a philosophy of action and diversity. And indeed, in spite of appearances, their doctrine in certain ways resembles the doctrines of the pragmatists. Men like Channing, James, and Emerson, base their philosophy on the necessities of morality and action. Their method is concrete, almost experimental. And finally, their tendency to regard the world as a great association of persons offers some analogy with the tendencies of the pluralists.

Channing declines to give way to abstract speculations. Things must be judged from the standpoint of the man of action ; consequently he is led to accept truths which seem self-contradictory, to combine optimism and pessimism in a way somewhat analogous to that we find in James. To him, religious life is one of solidarity and mutuality ; but at the same time he believes that collective salvation comes about through the personal efforts of each.

Henry James, though influenced by the Hegelian philosophy, had a very keen sense of the concrete. This must have caused perpetual conflict in his soul. " He abhorred his abstractions as much as the most positivist of his readers. No sooner had he expressed each of his formulas than he detested it." It appears to him that the Hegelian dialectic is valid only in the abstract. He writes that " the affirmative spirit " immediately recognises truth and seeks after those particular cases of this truth that are fruitful. Is not this actually a formula of what is to be the principle of Peirce ? Is it not, perhaps, from Henry James that his son, though he was not always quite conscious of this origin of his ideas, was enabled to learn that truth is true only in so far as it is at the service of the good, that truth must serve? Henry James reproached Emerson for the vague character of his precepts; truth must not be separated from life; like life itself, it is individual. " It is a fact that a vital truth can never be transferred, simply and purely, from one mind to another, for life alone is the test of the value of truths." Life does something more than judge truths; it reveals and produces them.

Universalist as he was, did he not contribute to the development of his son's individualism by teaching him that man works out his own salvation and is only what he does? The individual must be self-sufficing. And freedom then appears to him as quite other than that ease in action by which he first defined it; he prays for the time when each man's freedom will be "respected as the luminous star of Divinity," when " every man is enabled to be the living spirit of God," when relations with one another will consist of independence towards one another.

Everywhere there is life; everywhere change. He says that the universes are destined for life made up of such surprising changes that the sequence of their events is a constant disavowal of their birth, and that their complete ripening consists in denying their origin. Thus the idea of life and the conception of contradiction are united in the mind of Henry James in a somewhat romantic and Hegelian fashion: we shall find something similar in *A Pluralistic Universe*. To succeed in understanding this incessant movement, this life, we have not to learn but rather to unlearn; there is such a thing as spiritual architecture, the splendid perfection of which can never be attained by a natural construction but only by a natural demolition.

In this world of changes and efforts, individuals must

3

help one another ; Henry James insists on " human comradeship " ; even more, the world to him is the result of co-operation between man and God, he would not venerate a self-sufficing God ; God must behave " like an honest workman," collaborating in the common task.

As Margaret Fuller received inspiration from the precepts of Emerson, so Mary Temple remained faithful to the ideal of Henry James. She dreams of losing her self in a vaster self, and at the same time she believes in the absolute worth of the individual, in the value of effort, the solitary effort of the individual. " The distant possibility of the best thing is better than the absolute certainty of a thing of slightly less worth." And in our searching she would have us trust in the whole of our nature, she would have man bring the whole of himself into his reasonings. All our needs and aspirations will be reconciled in God ; and whatever incoherencies we have to face, however complicated the labyrinth we have to tread, we should never allow ourselves to give up one of the elements of the problem in the hope of succeeding in solving it in this world. William James affirmed that all his life he retained thoughts of gratitude and fidelity towards Mary Temple.

Similar theories are expounded more profoundly by Emerson and his friends. Precisely because they overlay the eternal One, individuals and moments are infinite. The cult of the moment, imperishable as eternity, and, like eternity, concealing unfathomable depths : such is one of the teachings of Emerson's philosophy. " It is entirely a philosophy of this world," says one of his admirers, a philosophy of the " enveloping now," says William James. " Through the individual fact," he tells us, " there always shone for him the radiance of universal reason."

If the individual is thus the absolute itself, thus opening out on to the infinite, each man must set up his own rule and fashion his own life. Such a nonconformist conviction, linked to a belief in the sacred character of life, is what James regards as the characteristic of Emerson. He teaches us that the world is still new and unexperienced ; that we shall find truth if we look for it with a new vision, not if we listen to others telling us their own visions or endeavour to reconcile our present with our former ideas. The idea he always carries within himself is that of the actual man. Like Longfellow he exhorts us to act " in the living present." We may imagine the influence which Emerson had on James : " those sublime pages," he said, " upheld and encouraged our youth." Emerson taught him that reality is in the present moment, that the present hour is the decisive hour, that every day is the day of judgment.

Moreover, each of these moments is different, and though, as we have seen, it conceals an identical soul, it is none the less separated from all others by endless differences.

In the world imagined by Emerson, as in the world of Carlyle, good does not exist alone ; there is also evil, an evil against which we must struggle. Our life should be a struggle ; and, if we are defeated, we must think nothing of it, but pin our faith in stern and unremitting effort. Emerson, like James, regards these human efforts as the efforts of the world itself. " Build up your own world . . . a like revolution will come about in things, obedient to the influence of spirit."

Men should unite for this struggle. The world may be compared to Hopedale, the colony of the Universalists, " a world-wide association of social reforms," and even more to Brook Farm, that joint-stock company working on lines of co-operative production and consumption, which the transcendentalists had started. The economic law is to Emerson a symbol of the moral law.

Behind Whitman's monism also we shall discover pluralism. " One's self I sing, a simple separate person." Thus he sings the individual. " I, habitant of the Alleghanies, treating of him as he is in himself in his own rights." Thus he sings the self of others. " Pressing the pulse of the life that has seldom exhibited itself. . . ."

He is the singer of personality, because his metaphysic is that of personality : Nothing endures but individual qualities. The self is creative, creative of laws and values. The self is God, for there is not one single God, but a multitude of gods.

The might of the individual and the incessant change of the world : these are his two fundamental conceptions. Ever the procreative urge of the world. Time is the one profound reality. " I accept time absolutely. It alone achieves and completes all ; this mystic and dazzling miracle completes all."

Victory will be slow and halting, but it is certain in the end. Meanwhile, whatever success has been won, from it will come something to " make a greater struggle necessary." " My call is the call of battle," says Whitman ; " I nourish active rebellion." The world's horizon widens.

" (Oh, something pernicious and dread !
Something far away from a puny and pious life !
Something unproved ! something in a trance !
Something escaped from the anchorage and driving free !) "

" Oh, to struggle against great odds, to meet enemies un-
    daunted !
To be entirely alone with them, to find how much one can
    stand !
To look strife, torture, prison, popular odium, face to face ! "

He also tells of vessels in a storm, and the masts cut away, the voyage on which men, possessions, and families embark, the beauty of venturesome persons, the beauty of independence, the American scorn for laws and ceremonies, the man " standing at ease in Nature," the man " aplomb in the midst of irrational things," the man " full of faith." " We must march, my darlings, we must bear the brunt of danger," he cries to the pioneers.

" We debouch upon a newer, mightier world, varied world ;
Fresh and strong the world we seize, world of labor and the
    march,
        Pioneers !   O pioneers !

        We detachments steady throwing,
Down the edges, through the passes, up the mountains steep,
Conquering, holding, daring, venturing as we go the unknown
    ways,
        Pioneers !   O pioneers ! "

What he also sings is the new comradeship born of combat, the friendship of war companions.

Comradeship and individuality are not opposed to each other :

    " One's self I sing, a simple separate person,
    Yet utter the word Democratic, the word En-Masse."

Thus we have discovered in men like Channing, Henry James, Emerson, suggestions of doctrines which later on will naturally fit in with pluralism. For a second time Germanic theories invaded America ; this time they were studied more directly, not in the adaptations of Coleridge, Carlyle, or Cousin, but in the text itself ; not by writers but by university professors. Doubtless it was Henry Brockmeyer, a Prussian emigrant, who imported absolutism into America ; from the group of Hegelians he gathered around him came William T. Harris, who made Saint Louis the centre of Hegelian ideas in America and founded the *Journal of Speculative Philosophy* in 1867. The American universities maintained uninterrupted relations with the German universities. Afterwards, the German influence was felt indirectly in the works of Green, Caird, Bosanquet, and Bradley. America, James tells us, is, along with Scotland, the country in which absolutism developed most rapidly, and in 1904 he bore witness that " in our universities it is the classes in transcendentalism that kindle the most ardent enthusiasm in the students, whilst the classes in English philosophy are committed to a secondary place."

Still, the absolutism of the American philosophers is less intransigent than that of certain English absolutists ; it becomes merged in the tolerant monism of Royce, in his national philosophy of loyalty and his Christian philosophy of interpretation.

Royce was profoundly influenced by Fichte, Schelling, and Hegel. The creative Ego of Fichte and the Self of Hegel, the Ego as spectator of itself, as Royce expresses it, living on the spectacle of its birth and its death : these are all found in his philosophy. But apart from German influence, he is also influenced by the " brilliant cosmological essays of Peirce " and the works of James, as well as by Browning's poems.

The starting-point of his philosophy appears to be in his epistemology. The reason he is a monist is mainly because there can be no knowledge unless diversity stands out from a background of unity. But his monism is also voluntarism and even individualism, for an idea assumes value only if it is individualised, if it possesses a content which cannot be replaced by any other empirical content. " Mere generality always means practical defect." Consequently he affirms that what is real is what appears as the complete incorporation of an idea in a finite reality, and what is the incorporation of the finite reality in the infinite idea.

The progress of his thought is set forth apparently in a somewhat different way in the work to which he gave the title, *The Spirit of Modern Philosophy*. "*If* my world yonder is anything knowable at all, it must be in and for itself essentially a mental world." The outer world is a possibility of experience; now, possibility of experience is for mind alone. From this idealistic affirmation we can pass on to monism. If we think of a thing, it is not enough for us to have within ourselves an image resembling this thing; we must intend to designate the thing; now how can we do this? How can we have present in mind that which is not ourselves? That is impossible. " You designate an object, make an assertion about it—even more, you doubt or are amazed with respect to it—only if your greater self, your deeper personality, actually possesses this object." Thus, when we seek for a name, we already had it. It is the momentary self alone that did not know it. Therefore, in hunting after a lost name or idea, it is my own self that I am pursuing. The thought and its object must consequently form part of a wider thought. And the profoundest self is that which will know, which actually does know, the whole of the truth; it is *this* self whose existence is most certain. The idea of truth can be understood only by the idea of a vaster self which includes both my thought and the object. And there can be only a single self of this kind; for, were there several, their multiplicity and relations would still have to be objects for a self. In this process of reasoning as in the preceding we find the same idea : the union in meaning of subject and object, of the individual and the universal.

By endless inclusions of wholes in ever greater and richer wholes, of meanings in ever loftier meanings, we gradually draw near the cosmic Self, near absolute individuality. But finite individualities are not done away with in the infinite Self, for the Self of the Absolute is a conscious Self; hence its life consists in knowing individualities other than its own. "The notion of an All-Knower," says James, "is the most recent advance, the most refined form of monism." And indeed in this way unity and diversity seem capable of reconciliation. God is consciousness; hence he is unity, a whole. On the other hand, absolute being is the knowledge of particular facts, the more profound meaning of particular facts; while it is the ensemble formed by them, it does not deny, but rather comprehends, individuals. The supreme individual may be actualised in a particular individual, in the same way that we can individualise our ideas by fixing our attention on them. "Just as a cathedral may appear as unique, may not have its like in the entire world of being, and yet all the stones, arches, and carvings of this cathedral are unique, in exactly the same way in the universe, if the whole is the expression of the one absolute will, each fragment of life has its one place within the divine life."

The life of God is a system of contrasted lives, for variety is the best way in which unity of meaning may be effected. Hence the insistence of Royce on diversity. "By this meaning of my life-plan . . . by this intent always to remain another than my fellows despite my divinely planned unity with them—by this and not by the possession of any Soul-Substance I am defined and created a Self." Thus individuality is no longer even defined as a variety, but as a contrast. Each part of the Absolute should be as different as possible from the rest; the Absolute is enriched by these very differences.

Nor are these lives inert; their essence is their will, their meaning, their purpose. The world of Royce is one in which there are objects to be attained and defeats to be made good.

The unique meaning of the individual life, therefore, the meaning of the differences between individuals, is retained in this philosophy of Royce: the Absolute contains the finite without destroying it. Universal life is real through ourselves and through our actions; and each one of us, each pulsation of will in the world, has a "unique relation to this life." The meaning of our personal individuality is necessary to the entire universe. "Rise then," he concludes, "free man, stand upright and go forward into the world. This is God's world, it is also thine."

Moreover, this affirmation of the power of the individual is completed, as we have seen, by the affirmation of the union of individuals. The world is a society. Royce conceives of a sort of cosmic sociology which would constitute true metaphysics.

We see that Royce is distinctly opposed to Bradley, at least as regards the positive and constructive part of his metaphysics. And we also see that sometimes he shows himself a disciple of William James and that at the same time James speaks of him with respect, as of a real master. According to James, in *A Pluralistic Universe* and in several passages of his other works, he is the one contemporary philosopher who has dealt with the Absolute with the greatest wealth and fullness; he compares Royce with Fechner, and tells us that he has filled life with meaning, with successes and defeats, with hopes and efforts, with an inner value. Here the

Absolute is represented as having itself a pluralistic object. "His Individuality," writes McGilvary, "is so admirably elastic that it can stretch itself to envelop all finite individualities without squeezing a drop of individuality out of them. Against such a generous and voluntaristic Absolute, what could the pragmatist have to say save that even pragmatism may be carried to extremes ? "

And yet we find in Royce certain affirmations which make us feel that, in spite of everything, his way of thinking is at bottom anything but a pragmatist and pluralist way of thinking. Thus, he speaks of " our poor, fleeting, finite ideas," and says of the Absolute, " This alone is." Time, to him, often seems to possess no importance, to be only a diminution of eternal reality : no temporal event, no finite fact succeeds in satisfying us entirely. He declares, it is true, that his Absolute is complete at no moment of time. It may be that, by the idea of the infinite such as he imagines it, as a perpetual reduplication of the finite, he is attempting to reconcile these two affirmations. But then they are fused in the idea of a perpetual present, and here again Royce remains an absolutist. And this very idea of transmutation which he criticises is perhaps a part of his doctrine.

BOOK II

THE FORMATION OF PLURALISM

CHAPTER I

GERMAN INFLUENCES

AFTER the development of the systems of Fichte, Schelling, and Hegel, there came into being in Germany various doctrines whose authors insisted on the diversity of things, the personality of men and of God. On the whole, these philosophies were distinctly opposed to the Hegelian philosophy.

Fechner is the most original of these anti-Hegelians. Very general—we may say very vague—ideas lead him to make the most precise studies of physics and psychophysics; on the other hand, by following a method of mingled empiricism and romanticism, he transforms his exact investigations as a physicist and a psycho-physicist into adventurous speculations; it is the blend of these two tendencies, empiricism and romanticism, that fascinates James, who recognises in Fechner a mind akin to his own.

He is the paragon of empiricists, writes James. And his empiricism is essentially a mistrust of abstraction. Abstractions have no existence, consequently his method is not based on distinct and simple ideas and does not proceed by deduction; it is a method of analogy by whose aid very concrete things are united to one another by loose bonds; we have to use the most ordinary type of reasoning to build up our conception of the world. Analogy will enable us both to grasp the resemblances and to preserve the differences; it does not bind like to like but unlike to unlike. The world is always other, and the new cannot be deduced from the old. Whereas abstraction makes things stationary, the method of analogy will permit us to apprehend them as they move forward; whereas the ordinary philosopher kills living things by applying to them his concepts, the empiric philosopher, like Pygmalion, like the true creator, must make things live; whereas the deductive philosopher by employing none but abstract reasonings finds himself faced with nothing but impossibilities and contradictions, the philosopher who starts from the concrete remains all the time within the possible and the real.

This empiricism thus naturally became fused with the romantic tendencies: Fechner is indeed, as Wundt has called him, "the man who revived and completed the romantic *Naturphilosophie*." His thought can be traced back to the romantic metaphysics of Oken, to Schelling, Oken's master; were not Oken, Schubert, and Swedenborg three of his favourite authors, savants like himself, possessed of a bold, romantic imagination?

His philosophy had its origin in a sudden revelation that came to him during a prolonged illness, a revelation which transformed his life; it developed during the entire latter period of his life when, deprived of books, he allowed to expand within himself the vision of a new world, a world peopled with souls.

In spite of his mystical pantheism and his scientific determinism, he sees the world as a place full of movement and animation. Life swarms everywhere, air and ether oscillate to and fro in undulatory motion. His pen finds difficulty in expressing this ferment of life. And as Fechner had parcelled out mind into centres of forces, as each being, from plants to men and from men to stars, surrounds itself with a circle, with a corona of consciousness, each projecting its light into the infinite, these circles cross and intersect ; these various spiritual domains encroach upon one another ; the world becomes in his synechological doctrine " a system which is determined in turn by oscillations and great undulatory movements," a play of various activities. The waves course upon one another, they whirl and fluctuate, advance or recede, or die away.

We may meet with every possible degree of consciousness between the circle of infinite consciousness and the smaller circles. Large consciousnesses, such as the consciousness of the vegetable kingdom or the collective consciousness of humanity, contain thousands of others ; these combined consciousnesses form the great soul of the earth " rolling throughout space like a divine ball of light." This consciousness in turn forms part of the solar system. Finally, along all these steps, we reach God.

The God of Fechner allows individual consciousnesses to live beneath him or by his side. The widest circle contains all the rest, and yet each circle is, as it were, self-contained. The finite mind remains immanent in God though still an individuality ; and even when it appears as though absorbed by the supreme individuality, it still retains its personality. Does a visual sensation cease to be itself because it enters at the same time as other sensations into our greater consciousness ?

Not only do we live an individual life, not only do we act, but our actions influence divinity itself ; each man who is born is a new thought in the Absolute ; indeed, the Absolute lives, it possesses a history and really develops.

Individuality is preserved in Fechner's system, not only the individuality of men but also that of the inferior gods. "Heaven appears as once again inhabited by celestial beings, called gods or angels." To these gods we can offer our prayers. Great is the distance between God and ourselves, but the gods or angels form intermediate stages and man's prayer is more readily addressed to them than to the supreme God ; in Fechner's system, the soul of the earth is there the first to receive our prayers.

Continually, though dimly, we feel ourselves in communication with vaster consciousnesses, surrounded here below by a world of spirits from the Beyond. The waves from this side and from the other intersect. Though Fechner mistrusted spiritism, he was deeply influenced by it. The universe becomes a city of souls.

It was not a causeless antipathy that Fechner experienced for the Hegelian philosophy, as Wundt remarks. His pantheism is distinct from all others. Wundt attempts to define it by saying that it is the pantheism of a savant who recognises the existence of a personal God and of individuals in the world ; and, in the second place, that it is an immanent and phenomenal, not a transcendent and noumenal pantheism. But there are many other characteristics that also distinguish it from pantheism in its classic form, and we well understand why James was so fond of this philosophy based on so broad and romantic an empiricism, so living, encumbered with individualities that cross and clash and are yet arranged in harmonious combinations with one another : a pantheism which ends in a sort of polytheism, a transcendentalism which enables us to perceive the steps of angels and gods on the threshold of our own spiritual life.[5]

Fechner, an exceptional philosopher, scarcely had any influence in Anglo-Saxon countries except upon James: he had few followers in the land of his birth. Lasswitz alone carried on his philosophy, upheld the tradition of atomism, defended a certain individualism somewhat different from that of his master: " This very personality has no beginning and no death, no place in space."

On the other hand, there was perhaps no work, with the exception of that of Hegel and Kant, which met with a wider recognition in England and America than that of Lotze. Bradley and Bosanquet translated some of his works; the monistic idealists, however, were not alone in feeling his influence; almost all the writers of the opposite school read and admire him. F. C. S. Schiller is aware of the immense debt he owes to this philosopher: no one, he says, saw better than did Lotze the disastrous consequences of too rigid systems, no one more constantly kept his eyes fixed on experience; he is a " formidable enemy " of neo-Hegelian monism. In spite of all his efforts to arrive at a monistic philosophy, Lotze largely contributed to the development of a pluralist philosophy. In America, his work has existed in translation ever since the year 1877. Dewey read him and frequently accepted his ideas. James quotes him several times as a precursor of personal idealism and of pragmatism.

Lotze's thought can be traced back to that of Herbart. Herbart decomposes the real into reals, each of which acquires movement and force only from its relation to the rest. The world is a coming and going in space

[5] See James's letter quoted by Flournoy, p. 179: " I have just read the first half of Fechner's *Zend-Avesta*, a wonderful book by a wonderful genius," 3rd January 1908.

(*Kommen und Gehen im Raume*). A qualitative atomism is the name which Lotze gives to Herbart's philosophy, and though he refuses to be called his disciple he yet has the greatest admiration for him. We may say of the philosophy of Lotze—as of Herbart's—that it is a return to Kant, to Kantian phenomenology. "To fill space," was not this for Kant "to oppose whatever tended to enter this space"?

On the other hand, Lotze came under the influence of the Hegelian school, especially the Hegelian right. Weisse, his professor, and I. H. Fichte, one of his friends, had previously attempted to set up a personal God and the freedom of the soul. At first glance, then, his philosophy might be characterised as a reconciliation between the philosophy of Hegel and that of Herbart.

Lotze was helped by the suggestions of two contemporary philosophers. Trendelenburg taught him the importance of movement, the builder alike of things and of categories; he showed him where Hegelian logic invited criticism. To Fechner, perhaps, he is indebted for his atomism, for his idea of centres of forces everywhere in contact throughout the universe.

Lotze was ever on the lookout for concrete and particular facts. "No single particle of truth," he said, "should be sacrificed to deductions." He does not examine the thing in itself, but the thing in its relation to us, in its worth; according to him, the human intellect is not an instrument for representing but one for transforming things; he will have nothing to do with a reality that is cold and unresponsive to our efforts. Consequently the metaphysician must appeal to judgments of value, to human desires, to anticipations of feeling, to suggestions of the æsthetic sense. "The beginning of metaphysics is not in itself, but in ethics." We must not, therefore, leave our logical intellect alone to work ; it ought to be limited by our various needs. Even if it does reason, that will only be in obedience to the first choice, to the option of our freedom.

The problem of unity is that which Lotze first investigates. Under his criticism—a criticism subsequently remembered by Schiller—the idea of substance fades away. " The word *substance* has been used," he says, " to designate a hard and real nucleus which in itself is supposed to possess the solid character of reality." From the nucleus there would appear to emerge, according to the common-sense theory, a sort of solidifying and adhesive matter by means of which phenomena assume consistence ; substance is for the ordinary imagination a sort of glue. But it is not by this strange alchemy, "this amazing phenomenon of crystallisation," that we can succeed in explaining the unity of the world.

On the other hand, the " real " of Herbart, the simple being is inconceivable, and the metaphysician is always forced to diversify substance by means of attributes.

Such, said Lotze, is the torture of the philosophical mind " condemned to seek in things *per se* for the conditions which determine the diversity of phenomenal appearances and to refuse these very things all the determinations of multitude and variety."

If we free ourselves from this passion for logical unity we shall be able to attain to something else than " unsubstantial mythologies."

With substance, with being *per se*, disappear those ideal worlds which more or less Platonic metaphysics had superimposed on the real world. No need of scaffolding to uphold the world of sensations ; sensations uphold themselves. The real alone exists ; it is the real that produces this appearance of a necessity which seems to be interior to it " as the living body builds the skeleton around which it seems to have grown up." The metaphysicians erred in presupposing a mass of abstract principles and endowing them with a kind of legislative power, in separating the being of a thing and its content, time and concrete becoming. Reality is richer than thought; there is, says Lotze in Hegelian language, a union of being and non-being which we cannot build up by concepts and which, *a fortiori*, we could not have guessed. The real construction of things transcends all thought. The ground of the real appears to us as a contradiction. Reality is an interlacing of relations, a subtle play of rapports which we cannot grasp, a moving real which, by processes of composition and decomposition, presents the appearance of substance and unity. A vision of continuous and never completed movement : such was what came first to Lotze. He attempts to make us realise the inner mobility of things; he listens to " that melody of becoming which continues unceasingly." Change is essential to being; we must see all being as it is in the process of becoming, we must liberate it from our fixed categories, we must apprehend its consistence, when it appears, only as a particular form of becoming, as an endlessly renewed birth and disappearance of the similar, not as persistence of the identical.

Being is not identity at rest, it is self-sustained eternal movement ; intertwined relations are ever being woven and unwoven ; there are none but changing actions and reactions, a continuous stream of inner activity developing from phase to phase, a numerous polyphony of voices that rise and fall in endless melody. Often we are unable to catch the rhythm of this melody, and becoming or evolution eludes the rules of our understanding.

After this, substance is no longer anything but a harder mass, a denser vortex carried off in the flux of reality, or else a sort of shadow, a phosphorescence born of the multitude of things and appearing at certain moments, without any one very well knowing why. Strictly speaking, there is no substance separate from phenomena but rather a quality of phenomena, their substantiality, their reflectent power when they offer themselves in a certain harmonious order. Their reflection, then, that ideal law which they project outwards, is their substance. Substance, according to Lotze, might be called a virtual image towards which converge beams of real points, as though obeying an æsthetic need immanent in nature.

Such was the theory of substantiality in Lotze's first *Metaphysik* ; such also, condensed and generalised in the *Metaphysik* of 1879, is the analysis which regards substance as the appearance of appearance, and appearance as the substance of substance. " It is not because of a substance within themselves that things exist ; they exist when they are able to persuade us that they have an appearance of substance." Assuredly, in this second *Metaphysik*, substance is no longer a momentary phosphorescence but a permanent reflection of things ; none the less is it a sort of quality or reflection of these things.

Thus a neo-Heracliteanism takes the place of Herbart's neo-Megarianism, probably under the influence both of an individual *Weltanschauung* and of certain ideas of Hegel.

Nor does this conception do away with the possibility of action ; it is rather the contrary that happens. " To admit that in real becoming there takes place something new that did not previously exist, such to our mind is the profound and indestructible necessity whereby we regulate all our actions in life." The fact is, we must not separate action and movement; becoming is not a mechanical development, it is the result of forces and actions; essence is not a dead point behind action, it is action itself. If there is in the world a plurality of beings, there may come about the creation of new points of application for the forces therein. "We acknowledge the universal value of laws, though holding the secret hope that, in spite of everything, there may yet take place a change of the points of application." Consequently, what we have to do is to find out if there really is a plurality of beings in the world; according to Lotze, pluralism would render freedom possible, the creation of new directions in the universe; we shall now see in what way he affirms plurality.

First of all, the world is a system of relations, a general bringing into relationship. Lotze's philosophy is one of mutual actions and reactions. The wholes are decomposed into multiple and heterogeneous parts which influence one another. A vast multiplicity of different bodies, a multiplicity of simple essences, of strivings: such is the vision offered us by pure perception, such is the conception most convenient for the savant, to whom the idea of one single matter is useless; whilst the unity of things remains inapprehensible, their diversity is ever accessible to science and is never exhausted. Thus continuity is broken up into discontinuities; there remain nothing more than distinct points of departure, foci of actions (*Ausgangpunkte der Wirkungen*).

This vision of the world may be compared with that of Herbart, but Lotze adds to Herbart's ideas that of movement; he introduces, while adapting it to his philosophy, the Hegelian idea of becoming and the Fechnerian idea of intersections (*Durchkreuzungen*) in his

Metaphysik of 1841. His desire is to restore to things " all the determinations of multitude, of variety, of relation, which they would need to condition the varied course of the facts of experience." The similar takes the place of the identical ; the dissimilar acts upon the dissimilar.

After all, what will be the essence of these centres of force ? Let us define them, says Lotze, as consciousness in some degree analogous with our own ; that is what Lotze retains of the idea he held of universal " animation " (*Beseelung*) at the outset of his metaphysical studies, perhaps under Fechner's influence. For things truly to be, he said, they must be more than things ; they can be distinct from their environment only if they become separate from it of themselves, if they are aware of this separation. The world is a system of things *en rapport* ; even more, may we not say that it is a system of consciousnesses in opposition ? Hence, life may have a meaning. What we may momentarily have regarded as an interplay of relations is a struggle of souls developing within time. Therefore the duty of each individual soul is to exert itself and to labour ; individual man should merit his salvation. Moralism or moral earnestness appears as the consequence of the idea of a moving and diverse, an incomplete and many-sided world.

And yet Lotze does not stop at these pluralist conceptions ; like Fechner, led by this idea of a world composed of souls, he advances towards monism. Like Fechner, Lotze, though a precursor of pluralism, remains in spite of everything a confirmed monist. From the idea of substance he had intended to make a shadow of reality ; the shadow now becomes the reality. Essentially, the real is an accident of this apparent substance. He would like, as he expresses it, to bring unity into the world.

Assuredly, in his *Metaphysik* of 1841, it does not appear as though he expected to reach anything but a subjective unity; the unity of the world consists in our way of seeing it as one. But even now there appear traces of the monism which asserts itself in the *Metaphysik* of 1879. The relations of things, he then says, can be explained only by an absolute unity. "The pluralism of our conception at the outset should give way to a monism through which transitive causality, ever incomprehensible, becomes immanent causality."

Still we must not imagine that nothing remains of the original pluralism and that universal substance has done away with the idea of particular facts. Universal being is a living, a qualitative idea, which "clothes itself in varied garb." The parts of this unity may be compared to the formulæ which harmoniously combine to sum up a theory. "These formulæ would mean nothing were they not made up of words with different contents." Thus a multiplicity of varied beings remains. What Lotze refuses to acknowledge, he says, is not pluralism but rather "a pluralism which recognises no limits," a pluralism which "regards the world order as capable of originating in a multitude of elements afterwards united by laws and wholly indifferent to one another."

In the philosophy of religion, Lotze transforms this single substance which he had reached, and which appeared to him impersonal, into a personal God. In the personality of God, pluralism and the temporal character of the world of reality to some extent regain their rationale and their justification.

It would be impossible to mention all the philosophers who uphold the same personalistic tendency. Preyer—whom William James regards as a disciple of Fechner—constructs a theory of pure experience. Sigwart, who

seems to have had a certain influence over James, begins
with the idea of unity, a unity of will, but he intuitively
apprehends individual differences ; he sees the development of an ever incomplete world, the flux of appearances ;
he knows that this flux carries dross and scoria along
with it, that the evil exists. Let us all resist the evil,
whilst God, a personal God, watches over our efforts.
The society of free individuals will win the day.

Teichmüller, who has been regarded as a disciple of
Lotze, insists on the necessity of experience, of " individual
empery." " The one-self," he says, " is not a fleeting
and worthless appearance, but an immortal member
of the whole real world." According to him, the Self
never dies but remains in God, as our thoughts retain
their own individuality within ourselves.

Wundt's influence on philosophic thought was more
prolonged. James places him almost on an equality
with Lotze amongst the precursors of pluralism. Like
Lotze, he was captivated by the problems laid down
in Herbart's philosophy. " Next to Kant," he said,
" it was Herbart who had the greatest influence on
my philosophical development." Wundt's theories are
mainly derived from those of Fechner and Lotze, especially of Lotze, though James regards him as a disciple of
Fechner. While admiring the author of the *Tagesansicht*,
he declares his system to be a fantastic dream. His
intention is to build up a scientific philosophy.

It was science that taught him to consider things in
their movement or flux. Like Lotze he blames all
monadology as being a static philosophy ; substance and
activity, substance and will, substance and becoming are
identical terms. Like Lotze, too, he declares that real
activities are those capable of persuading us of the
existence of a substance, when that substance is but

a sort of phosphorescence projected by them. There is no longer substance, there are only relations, without support.

These relations are the manifestations of individual voluntary units (*Willenseinheiten*); all these units, as in Fechner's system, are harmoniously marshalled, super-imposed, and combined. Thus do mutual actions and reactions, the continuous ceaseless development of the world, become possible. More faithful to pluralism than Lotze, Wundt does not superadd on to it a monism; he will not go beyond relative units. He constructs, as Eisler says, a pluralist metaphysics.

Wundt conceives of the elements of the world as units of will; this constitutes a sealed alliance between voluntarism and pluralism. We do not find this voluntaristic pluralism in Paulsen, though James seems sometimes to place him higher than Wundt in the hierarchy of the prophets of pluralism. Certainly he affirms that everything is volitional; but, like Lotze, he speedily endeavours to free himself of pluralism and return to monism.

To regain this synthesis of pluralism and voluntarism, we must go to the extreme left of German philosophy: to the disciples of Feuerbach, who look upon the world as a godless state, a republic; to Bahnsen, who parcels out the Schopenhauerian will into multiple wills engaged in strife; to Nietzsche, whom Hartmann includes along with Bahnsen among the partisans of " pluralistic and atheistical individualism."

CHAPTER II

THE INFLUENCE OF POLISH PHILOSOPHERS

LIKE Nietzsche in a few passages, so Wartenberg and Lutoslawski boast of being the representatives of Polish thought, of being the philosophers of the nation based on choice, the nation of the *Liberum Veto*. Wartenberg regards the world as an ensemble of dynamic relations between substances finite in number; these substances are wills. While his pluralism owes its origin to Lotze, whom indeed he follows in his evolution towards monism, that of Lutoslawski rather originates in the pluralism of Teichmüller with whose system he deals under the title of Personalism. We shall deal at greater length with Lutoslawski, who was a friend and correspondent of James. According to him, it was neither Teichmüller, nor Struve, nor Fechner, nor Herbart, nor Lotze, nor James who inspired him with his particular pluralism. The thought of the *Liberum Veto*, that of the confederations of lords, forms the centre of his philosophy. It is in the name of "our Polish confraternity" [6] that he speaks. He likes to recall the Polish poets or philosophers who drove individualism to its extreme limits : Liebelt, Mickiewicz who chants before God : "I feel immortality ; I create immortality ; what greater thing hast thou been able to accomplish ? My pinions soar to thee," and who ends with the cry : "My strength came

[6] *The Monist*, 1895–1896, p. 352.

thence whence thou hast taken thine, nor do I fear to lose it."

Lutoslawski's method, a sort of passionate deduction, has no great resemblance to that of the pragmatists; at times, however, he declares that we must not trust to general formulæ, that they cannot tell us whether, at any given moment, unity or diversity dominates the world. Besides, the voluntaristic aspect of his method may allow us to look upon him as an ally of the pragmatists. Pluralism is as incapable of proof or of refutation as is monism. Volition is sufficient.

Starting with the personalism of Teichmüller, Lutoslawski arrives at "that form of individualism called pluralism," as he says, that new "view of the world" which is "its most distinctive property" if we are to believe him. In his opinion, as in that of James, the problem of unity and diversity is the one fundamental problem, that according to which philosophers should be classified.

A voluntarist, he declares that his philosophy is an exaltation of the volition. A spiritualist, he sees in the world an ensemble of immortal souls. His spiritualism is but one form of his individualism; he feels himself a soul, an uncreated immortal soul, recognising according to his Helsingfors thesis, which alone we must here consider, no ruler higher than itself. He adds, and it is not easy to reconcile these statements with a few others, that souls are of various degrees or hierarchies; like Fechner, he imagines there to be stages in this multiplicity of souls. And it is here that spiritualism becomes spiritism: there exist mysterious communications between souls: what we call the unconscious is the mysterious working of other souls upon our own.

There must be in the world a superior being; but

the God of the individualist cannot be an omnipotent
creator, consequently God can but guide the world
without governing it in absolute fashion ; otherwise how
is the existence of evil to be explained ? Besides, the idea
of an eternity of souls prevents us from believing that
God is omnipotent. " I cannot have been created." At
times Lutoslawski affirms the existence of God, though
only to defy him, as it were, just as Mickiewicz did :
" Let the universalists await the coming of this God.
. . . He may work upon millions of servile beings. . . .
I challenge him to become my master." Then again
he imagines this God as a powerful friend : " We have
almost the same object, and therefore numerous enemies
in common."

So far we have studied this conception of Lutoslawski
without introducing the idea of becoming, of the universal
effort which animates and moves the world as he imagines
it. The sense of my freedom, my power of choice, will
set free the world. Through my consciousness of freedom
I can affirm the real development of the universe. " For
the universalist the plan of the world is already completed. The individualist, on the other hand, believes
that all souls advance or retreat freely." Thus the very
idea of the incomplete character of the world is, by
Lutoslawski as by James, connected with a belief in
free-will. A second reason for affirming this growth of
the universe is the hypothesis of interferences between
our universe and the other universes mentioned by
Lutoslawski. Indeed, when we believe the world to be
composed of souls, we can no longer believe in the
regularity of the laws of Nature. Pluralism, indeterminism, and spiritualism are interconnected.

For the very reason that the world appears to him incomplete, a blend of good and evil, the pluralist is

brought to believe that the good will be realised only by our efforts, that our very choice between contrasted moral and metaphysical doctrines possesses a cosmic meaning and importance. The individual soul " gives its free collaboration to the aims of the whole world." The pluralist will run risks, as James said, will stake his earth life, as Lutoslawski said, " when dealing with high ends, on condition these ends require it."

From this individualistic ethics, Lutoslawski proceeds to a social conception of the world. Because of his very individualism, the pluralist will be tolerant : he recognises the rights of the minority. Any person may say to the assembled forces of the universe : *Liberum Veto ;* but the minority must also be willing to sacrifice its rights for the sake of the majority. Love becomes the principal motive of action : " I love mankind, truth, beauty . . . because this is my own free pleasure."

Thus the individual conceives that the ends to which he devotes himself will become the ends common to all beings ; he believes in a cosmic evolution with which individual souls will freely collaborate.

This " metaphysical collectivism " which we have found in most of the predecessors of pluralism and shall almost invariably find in pluralists, appears to us, not as a negation, but rather as a complement of pluralism ; in this collective life the individuals remain individuals. Still, we must clearly distinguish between this idea of a free universal association of beings and certain monistic professions of faith which in reality contradict the essence of pluralism. Does not Lutoslawski tell us at times that souls are something fixed and that things remain identical ? Real movement, then, and time, disappear from the universe as he imagines it : " time and space are within self." Hence we no longer understand how diversity can come about. Can we at least conceive it as an end? Do individuals become increasingly different? Do they live a more and more contrasted life? Rather the contrary takes place, Lutoslawski then tells us. In the centre of things, which all have a certain degree of resemblance, there stand out certain things more similar, more related to one another. These group themselves and make " the totality of the world increasingly one." " The world of souls aims at unity. . . . We indefatigably toil for the unity of the world." True it is that pluralist tendencies suddenly seem to resume mastery, and Lutoslawski declares : " Complete unity is still an ideal that cannot be realised by individualism." None the less does he see this ideal in unity, not in diversity.

Thus, in most of these philosophies, in that of Lutoslawski as in those of Lotze and Fechner, it appears as though pluralism could not stand, could not of itself alone constitute these thinkers' vision of things. After trying to substitute for the one world of the monistic philosophies a multiple and moving world, they seem compelled, as though by a necessity of thought, to reintroduce the idea of unity into this world, and, in reintroducing it, profoundly to transform their conception. Finally, in each of them we witness the resurrection of that thought of unity which we might at first have regarded as vanquished.

CHAPTER III

JAMES graciously acknowledged all the debt he owed to Renouvier and the *Critique Philosophique*. In 1884 he wrote : " I am bound to say that my reasonings are almost wholly those of Renouvier." He calls the *Classification des systèmes philosophiques* an amazing and masterly work. He dedicates his work on psychology to Renouvier, to Pillon, to the *Critique Philosophique*.

Before studying Renouvier's theories and the influence they had on pluralism, we will deal with the influence on his mind of the theories of Fourier, of Proudhon, and especially of Ménard.

Fourier taught Renouvier to conceive of hierarchies of souls as Fechner taught James. There is not one universe, but " universes " ; and he imagines activity in these universes as being produced by a " partnership co-operation " between God and man. God " leaves chances " to man ; he means to play with human reason " a level game " ; man possesses fullness of choice. And this man, possessed of free-will, God takes as a partner ; he sets up a " social code " in the world, and man shares with him " the responsible administration of life." We find these " divine social conceptions·" in the works of many republicans and socialists of this period.

Proudhon, like Fourier, conceived the government of the world as an equalitarian republic : he desires that

" universal harmony " in which each of us may " make himself a sharer and co-operator by free-will." To him, Leibnizianism, with its monadology, is the most rational way of conceiving the universe; there is no longer a " suzerain," but a free democracy of creative liberties wherein justice, of which he gives a definition somewhat like that of Renouvier, reigns alone. But this is still only an ideal; to-day the world is only an " ensemble of struggling forces " in which we cannot hear " that melody of the Great All of which Pythagoras spoke." " Antagonism between beings, independence of substances, causes, wills, and judgments " : such is the universe. But this antagonism will finally become a free harmony. Previous to Renouvier, Proudhon, as a democrat and a republican, criticised the theological and philosophical doctrines which regarded the Absolute as master of the world.

These quotations aid us in understanding how the systems of Renouvier and Ménard sprang from the republican and socialistic struggles of France. From this origin, pluralism has retained certain characteristic features up to the present time; it was as a democrat and a republican that James set forth his philosophy . . . one to which French thought contributed its share.

By nature, Ménard is a pluralist; his pluralism is that of a Latin, of a Hellene. He loves Greece as the land of the Holy Light, where man is inundated with brightness, where the " bright " looks of the citizens are turned towards " inaccessible and luminous heights."

He loves what is clear and definite : forms which seem " cut in marble." Beneath the Grecian sky there are none but " clear lines, pure horizons."

How could the Greek conceive of vague beings ? Everywhere we see form outlined in the sunlight ; everywhere variety. It is form that "limits, makes precise and definite." "Form unites matter to spirit and is the word that gives a body to thought, the mediator between the finite and the infinite." No wonder, says Ménard, that the Greeks regard the finite as the perfect. How can the indefinite be confined within a form ? The entire theology of the Greeks, as well as that of Ménard, is born of their love for the definite and the luminous. Each God, each hero, has "distinctive features," "a special form," "an individual and perfectly-defined physiognomy." Ménard is filled with anger at the religions of the mysteries which confound "the special attributes of the Gods." "When dealing with Dionysos," he writes with mingled sorrow and indignation, "the whole of mythology becomes obscure and uncertain. . . . The God who makes light-headed his enemies seems to have dealt with his worshippers in the same way ; Orphism is the frenzy of intoxication and ecstasy ; human thought, like the whole of nature, is dragged into the great orgy." Beneath ever new forms, he never tires of expounding this idea : "As the shades of evening spread over the sky of the old world, the vision of divine things became less and less distinct." He pursues "vague pantheism," "confused pantheism," right into the precincts of the mysteries of Eleusis and the malodorous cave of Trophonius. "May the divine archer deliver us, both from the umbra and from the penumbra ! "

The universe, for the very reason that its elements are clearly defined, is multiple. We might well apply to Ménard what he says of the Greeks : he "perceives differences everywhere " ; he knows that beings exist only "through the qualities which enable them to be distinguished." Are not forms essentially multiple ? Does not light show outlines in their "endless varieties " ?

Thus Ménard loves to speak of the multiplicity of Greek city-states, to see the " many-sided universe," to base different phenomena on multiple principles, to distinguish " multiple energies " in these principles themselves.

This multiplicity of his is not an abstract one : principles can only be concrete, the offspring of human imagination, and these are Gods. " There is nothing abstract in the universe," " the abstract is always false," and it is always poor. Not without reason did the Greeks believe in living and visible deities, peopling the world with free citizens, who include both men and Gods . . . . Gods not very different from men. In what form can they be imagined, if not in the human form, which is " the divine type of beauty," and in accordance with human consciousness, which conceives of " the divine ideal of justice " ? According to Ménard, there is no religion without anthropomorphism.

He adopts polytheism, as necessary for young and daring nations. He takes into consideration the practical consequences of theologies ; in his own way, Ménard is a pragmatist.

No wonder he opposed all the ideologies that destroy mythologies, all the theories that wither away beneath too crude a light, as he opposed all obscure mysticisms. He opposed Plato's general ideas, born of " theocratic and pantheistic tendencies," the realised abstractions of expiring religions, too perfect, too impassive, and too invisible to be prayed for, too superhuman to be carved by the hands of artists ; above all, he opposed the pantheism whose unity remains " abstract " and " vague," and which " envelops all differences in one uniform sheath." In the penumbra wherein pantheism delights, " law and force, right and action, the ideal and the real " are confounded and fused together. Human freedom no longer exists. Morality disappears, and Ménard devotes an entire book of his *Polythéisme hellénique* to prove how " the influence of the Orient and that of philosophy " here unite. Such is the final reason for which Ménard fights shy of pantheism ; it slays the ideal, morality, activity ; its morality is the morality of castes.

As pantheism is the philosophy of castes, so monotheism is an anti-republican dogma, a " monarchical " dogma. It develops in times of decadence. " When almost all the nations were drowned in the abyss of the Roman Empire, rest became the sole need of souls that had grown old. . . . In heaven, as on earth, the unity of power is recognised." Ever do religious forms correspond to social forms ; and the heaven of the Middle Ages is the " keep " of a feudal God.

Over against the monarchical conception he sets the " republican conception of the world," the great " federation of beings " wherein the Gods are laws and magistrates alike, members of the central council of the world. The world becomes " a great dance chorus, an eternal symphony, a harmony of living laws," and this harmony is a social co-operation.

Ménard creates himself a heaven where " everything is linked together without a hierarchy." He makes jest of the " hierarchical character so beloved of philosophers." The authority of Zeus is the authority of an equal over his equals, he is *primus inter pares*. Ménard proudly writes : " No single vote can be suppressed, for the social law is the sum-total of the rights of each, and man is as necessary as Zeus ; he is one of the citizens of the republic of the Gods ? " " There are neither masters nor slaves in the great family of the universe," he had said in *La Morale avant les Philosophes*, " none but masters, unequal indeed, but independent." All beings are "autonomous." Consequently all beings are immortal. Immortality is necessary, in order that no single vote may be suppressed, no single note muffled.

As we see, Ménard's republicanism and equalitarianism can be traced back to his profound individualism. His individualism, as he expresses it, goes to the point of anarchy: an "organised anarchy," no doubt, according to the definition of the Greek city-states which Ménard gave to de Heredia. He loves "disorderly, anarchical Olympus." This disorder, he says, was in no way shocking to the Greeks.

Beneath Ménard's polytheistic religion is there not concealed something deeper? A pluralist metaphysics? The reason why Ménard's Gods are living and active, the reason why his Olympus is so varied, is because he is aware that "anarchical and multiform" Nature mocks at our systems, "Procrustes' beds of truth," because Nature will not allow herself to be circumscribed and has her centre everywhere. The reason he imagines the Gods as multiple is that a diversity of effects leads him logically to a plurality of causes. "Plurality of causes, independence of forces, harmony of laws," such he regards as the three principles of Greek theology. The Greeks, he tells us, instead of stopping at the unity of eternal substance, distinguish primary qualities creative of forms. For things exist only through differences which enable them to be recognised and named. The world is defined as an ensemble of relations between forces. "This dual series of actions and reactions compels us to conceive of the world of which we form part as an ensemble of forces influencing one another. This is the idea that arises spontaneously from the first impression of Nature on the human mind, the fundamental dogma of primitive

revelation." "These unknown forces," he adds, " are
at the same time laws. . . . Gods are the law-givers."

These laws are living laws, laws that live by their
mutual contrasts. "Zeus, preserver of the balance of
the world, joyfully contemplates the struggle between
the Gods because it is from the opposition of contraries
that arises the universal struggle," and finally harmony.
Thus the entire world becomes a great Troad. Had
Ménard insisted more strongly on this incessant birth,
on the idea of the " perpetual generation of things "
in the Greek religion, he would have given force and
life to his polytheism, which, at times, like a poem of
Leconte de Lisle, gives the impression of immutable
tranquillity. His " people of Gods " is too much of a
people of statues. And pluralism as we shall study it
is frequently allied to a more real sense of the flux, the
ever-incomplete development of things. Ménard's very
love for the complete, the finite, was to render him
averse from that temporalistic pluralism.

Still, it is a true pluralism that we now perceive behind
polytheism. Ménard surmised that polytheism might
perhaps assume new forms. "Physics," he declares at
the end of *Polythéisme hellénique*, "would substitute the
independence of forces for the inertia of matter, it would
replace its mechanistic systems by biological conceptions." The Gods, reincarnated in more modern forms,
will perhaps come again to men to endow them with
courage and activity.

Polytheism indeed leads to definite moral conceptions ;
it enables us to appreciate " energy of action," " resistance to the outer world." Man has a task to fulfil ; not
to remain motionless is the first of his duties. Greek
morality is the " active morality of strife and work."
Indeed, throughout the world it manifests " wills that

are free and conscious of themselves," capable of choosing between possibles, and for which the option between good and evil is a profound reality. Man's life is not a *mêlée* in the dark, it is a fight between persons in the open daylight. But is it really of a fight that we have to speak ? This struggle is a harmony. " Man plays his part in the many-sided drama of life ; he contributes his note to that immense and magnificent concert." Greek morality, the morality of life and action, is antagonistic to that " austere and indifferent " philosophy which " fills souls with a universal abhorrence of the things of earth," to all those passive moralities, those cults of death created by the Oriental soul or the philosophic mind and abounding in the twilight of the ancient world. " The old world, with that prophetic intuition of the dying, felt the approach of a vast darkness, and in the anguish of the coming agony no longer called upon any but the God of the dead." A sorrowful catabasis of man towards the land of Egypt, mother of the cults of the tomb. " On returning to die in that old Egypt which had been his cradle and was about to be his necropolis, he sank silently into the tomb of the past and his last act of worship was to Serapis, the God of Death. The surviving pagan bewails the extinguished light of Greece : " The storm has swept away everything that inspired love of life, inevitable night and hoary winter are about to envelop nature and history, and the world, grown old, can but follow to the tomb its last God."

In the great struggle for life, how are we to dispose harmoniously of the forces at hand ? Order must issue from " the autonomy of forces and the balance of laws," from the autonomy born, say both Ménard and Renouvier, of a voluntary convention which contains both right and duty, law and freedom, a rule for individual forces and a guarantee for public order. Hence set up as free societies, the city-states may boldly plunge into the strife. "Human societies enter as free bodies, as bands of volunteers, whose inner discipline is regulated by mutual agreement"; man contributes "to the social work of the harmony of things."

The Gods, too, advance into the arena as in the days of Troy. M. Bardy assimilates the Greek conception with the American conception, which regards God almost as the servant of man. Ménard does not go so far; he greets the Gods as "benevolent protectors," "friends," "elder brothers." They never give orders, they always give advice. And the reason why man consults oracles is but to "conform his action with that of the collectivity." The Gods leave man entire freedom, they only point out "the direction he has to take." Thus everything combines and unites for the great fight. "Collective action," "the social work of the harmony of things," these expressions manifest in Ménard the ordinary complement of metaphysical individualism: a collective metaphysics in the meaning we have given to the word.

Polytheism is essentially tolerant. Its dogma is supple and diverse; whereas monotheism is "intolerant under penalty of abdication," "the essence of polytheism is the diversity that implies religious tolerance." Symbols may be different, and yet all equally true. Thus is realised not a dry unity, but rather a union, a harmony. The theological teaching of the poets, says Ménard, who takes pleasure in all this diversity, was not more united than Nature herself. From the "bounteous hospitality of Olympus" no God is excluded, as no being is excluded from the "great republic of the world." It is not necessary to conceive of a single sacred mountain—Sinai ; the Himalayas are also the abodes of the Gods. "Why should not faith have several different types reigning in different places and that without offence ?" Ought not revelations to be " multiple as Nature and as the human mind " ?

Thus perhaps we might discover the pathway leading to beauty. Ménard seems to call to mind the laments of Musset. " The world," he writes, " is no longer the abode of a divine life " ; he regrets the time when " the golden stars, the great blue sky, the deep sea, and all the splendours of the vast universe, were the visible forms of eternal laws, the living bodies of the Gods." Semitic monotheism proscribes and repudiates art. The Turks set up an iconoclastic domination over the world. In fact the plastic arts " require the plurality of divine types," of divine forms.

Thus, by an act of faith in a morality of life, of action and tolerance, in an art of light, ends the polytheism which light brought forth.

It is a mistaken idea to think that behind this polytheism may be found a simple dualism between matter and spirit, the worship of the one God. It might be said with greater truth that Ménard did not altogether elude this pantheism, the various forms of which were dear to Leconte de Lisle. Does he not speak of " the intimate and divine activity of nature " in a way that might be even more pantheistic than polytheistic ? We may also remark that whereas he possessed to a far greater extent than did Leconte de Lisle the sentiment of whatever there was of movement and life in the theology of the Greeks, he yet tells us that the superiority of the Gods over men lies in the fact that they *are* ; man, on the contrary, becomes. " The elementary principles of

things " (such is his translation of the word : Gods)
" are unchangeable and incorruptible ; they lend themselves without giving themselves and, lifeless as they are,
maintain all life." He imagines " a sphere of pure
ideas," an " immovable sphere." He loves the light of
summer because it is stationary. To be a temporalistic
pluralist, what he lacks is the sense of time.

Ménard had disciples ; in the periodical, *Candide*,
republicans constituted themselves defenders of polytheism. But, above all, though influenced by Renouvier—
his conception of freedom, of free and rational convention
at the root of all morality, his absolute respect for the
principle of contradiction, are due to neo-criticism—he
in turn exercised considerable influence over Renouvier.

Renouvier, at the beginning of his *Essais de Logique*,
wrote : " I distinctly confess myself a continuer of Kant."
But at the same time he calls himself a disciple of Berkeley
and Hume. From them mainly did he adopt the criticism of the conceptions of substance and cause by which,
according to him, we must proceed to the destruction of
every necessitarian prejudice, to the universal liberating
and loosening of phenomena which is indispensable to
the constitution of a true philosophy. " The Humean
phenomenalism is preserved by neo-criticism," he declares ; it is on the background of an idealistic phenomenalism that beings, that is to say, phenomena that are
thoughts and thoughts that are phenomena, will stand
out. " I posit ' representations,' nothing but ' representations ' ; I do not posit them as in the self, for that
would actually be positing something else." We shall
find that James holds this very theory, included in his
radical empiricism ; and did not James say : " I am
indebted to Renouvier for all my doctrines on this subject ;
Renouvier, as I understand him, is, or at all events was,

a frank phenomenalist, a denier of forces in the strictest sense " ?

Renouvier accepts from positivism " a fundamental formula," the reduction of knowledge to the laws of phenomena, and from Kantism the idea of categories and forms ; without forms, laws, relations, phenomena are non-existent ; " everywhere," he says in terms closely resembling those of Lotze, " there are but mutual influences, and nowhere separate substances ; those laws, forms, relations alone comprehensible in the world are incapable of being reduced to phenomena, they are only inherent in phenomena." Relation is " the common form wherein categories have their abstract unity." We here come across one of the main ideas of what, later on in the philosophy of James, is to be radical empiricism. " Phenomena appear in representations related to each other ; variously grouped and definite, without the possibility of eliminating their relations in order to define them. Beings no longer appear except as groups and functions of phenomena. We no longer recognise anything as an object of knowledge except phenomena and the laws that connect them, laws which themselves are but species of general phenomena." And here is a sentence perhaps even more significant : " This idealism was not that which loosens and dissolves ideas and would know the elements of composition only as phenomena which it declares itself incapable of synthesising. Nor was it that which regards abstract general terms as fundamental ideas. It was an idealism which does not separate phenomena from the laws whereby synthesis is brought about." Without his clearly perceiving it, it is through ideas indirectly originating in Kant that the empiricism of James becomes deeper and deeper.

" A writer with distinctly clear ideas," as James calls him, Renouvier was as much enamoured of clarity in ideas as Ménard was enamoured of illumination on things. He is the one living author who most insisted on the principle " that unity in the application of things must not submerge clarity." A certain mental reservation prevents him from giving way to the desire which impels the thought of the metaphysician in the direction of unity.

Above all, Renouvier sees differences in phenomena. " The ordinary man," he says, " and the philosopher also, if he trusts his impressions, is keenly struck by the differences of every kind which appear in Nature." The history of the world is a multiplicity of little broken lines pointing in every direction. The neo-critical theory of categories is, from one point of view, only a statement of plurality and discontinuity. And the doctrine of the discontinuity of time still further cuts up and parcels out this multiple world.

Renouvier is for the most part anxious to remain concrete. Superior to James in this respect also, he speaks of " that imaginary region of abstractions where the supposed degree of approach to reality is measured by that of the disappearance of the characters of reality in conceptions."

It was this concrete imagination that led him to create hypotheses on the beginnings of cosmic evolution, on the ideal state. James, who approves in others of this union of strict observation and concrete imagination, appreciated the essay which Renouvier added at the end of the *Principes de la Nature*. Indeed, neo-criticism was favourable to those bold inventions which Renouvier had discovered in Fourier, and Renouvier always appreciated bold scholars who were on the look out, not for a vague unity, but for a plurality of concrete facts.

Men like Prémontval, Robinet, and subsequently Fourier, are to Renouvier what Fechner was to James.

James is fond of insisting on the relation between philosophical doctrines and the temperament of philosophers. A like tendency is found in Renouvier. Philosophical dilemmas, even—nay, especially—those that deal with pure metaphysics, are all the more tragic, seeing that they compel us to choose between two kinds of souls. " The government of the world by divine unity," he says, " is the choice of souls prone to inaction and desirous of seeing everything happen without them, whilst they contemplate and worship. To these must be added the great band of the disabused and the disillusioned," and those who throw the burden of their responsibilities on to others. Not without cause does James speak of the " manliness " of Renouvier. For the theories of Hegel and the doctrines of the unity of being, Renouvier feels the repulsion of the intellectualist opposed to all mysticism, and the impatience of the man of action, of the " pragmatist," who takes vital necessities into account and wills the power to act.

Lequier made him feel the importance of the problem of freedom. " A wonder tremendous : man deliberates and God waits." Our universe makes a blot on the Absolute, said Lequier, and this blot bears its shadow right to God ; it destroys the Absolute. The religious soul of Lequier was brought to a standstill before the mystery. Such was not the case with Renouvier, who appears to have found a solution in Ménard's theories.

In the conversation and writings of the mythologist whose friend he was for forty years, he discovered ever new motives for adopting both the ethics and the metaphysics of individualism. M. Philippe Berthélot affirms that Renouvier " had been so struck " with Ménard's

ideas " that he was a polytheist for some time." Doubts
have been cast on this influence. Indeed, the philosophical and political ideas of Renouvier might well have
led him to his polytheism in its general form without
Ménard's aid. But when Renouvier declares : " beings
are laws "; when he continues : " We know God only
by the existence of that unique law which harmonises the
successive ends of beings " ; when he brings together, in
sentences that might have been written by Ménard, " the
general laws of consciousness and those of the city-state,"
and regards the Greeks as " men who were distinctly
aware of the idea of law " : then these ideas seem to
manifest themselves in the very form that Ménard gave
them. Like Ménard, Renouvier sets himself to make
theological forms and social forms correspond, he combats
the absolute " king of the world," he brands alike
" monastic asceticism and gnostic dualism." Renouvier
pictures the divine world of the Greeks as " a conflict
of rival powers which incarnate in persons and can be
brought to a state of harmony only through agreement
between free wills or by the victory of ordered and
rational beings." Later on he says that he momentarily
adopted " the Greek idea of the universe, the idea of
strife and the balance of forces." Below the divine world,
indeed, he regards forces as struggling and still balancing
themselves in the human world, also free. And Renouvier
would have us judge theologies by the political principles
to which they give rise. He traces back to Hellenism
" as L. Ménard did," he declares " the origin of pure
moral ideas." Finally, regarding more special points
such as the importance attached to the saints of Christianity, divine intercessors, or such as the notion that
religions pass naturally from monotheism to a sort of
polytheism, and even in respect of certain words, such as

the word "living" (the living Gods), Renouvier's thought
and at times his style approach those of Ménard.   Even
more than this, it is possible to determine when Ménard's
influence acts most powerfully on Renouvier : about the
period when the *Essai de Psychologie* appeared.

These various influences, and even more his meditations
on certain philosophical problems (the problem of infinity, the problem of freedom), led Renouvier resolutely
to abandon the Hegelianism from which he started.   "My
thoughts have been thrown into utter confusion, . . ."
he wrote to Secrétan, " I have been an ardent seeker
all my life."   After considerable effort, he succeeded in
shaking off the three monstrous idols of metaphysics,
" infinity *in actu*, the substance of phenomena, and the
absolute solidarity of successive things."

Once this triple illusion of infinity, substance, and
necessity is dispelled, pantheism, the worship of infinite
and necessary substance, is no longer possible.   The
philosophic absolute is a vague idea which serves to veil
with a semblance of logic the mystical aspirations towards
infiniteness, the desires of men eager after glitter and
poetry, the cosmogonic dreams of the Orient, and brings
us right into floods of contradictions, in the direction of
" the inaccessibility of the universal subject " where we
find pure being and pure essence, *i.e.* " the utter void
of being and of essence."

No pantheism can withstand the notion of time, or
that of freedom, the daughter of time ; monism has
determinism as its " invariable companion."   It is
freedom that creates the idea, and the doctrines of the
idea will ever be opposed to the doctrines of the thing,
whether they call themselves pantheism or materialism.
It is freedom that creates the person, the only truly
resisting element in the world.   The negation of all

" essential individuality " leads monism straight to the worst form of that phenomenalism which regards every phenomenon as illusory. All realities " are swallowed up in the Absolute."

This is just why, in the opinion both of Renouvier and of Ménard, this philosophy of the Absolute should please political absolutists, and it is a choice between two political forms that Renouvier offers us when asking us to choose between monism and the theory of freedom. Are we willing to subject " all the beings in the world to one royal authority," to acknowledge a " celestial autocracy," " a theocratic construction " ?

After combating " the philosophical absolute," Renouvier combats " the religious absolute." He speaks of monotheistic races " whose banners bear prescriptive devices : I AM that I AM ; there is no God but God." Like monism, monotheism culminates in " an absorption of being" into nonentity and is based upon contradictions.

Not only do the idea of substance—a category raised to the Absolute—and pantheism fall to pieces, but the very idea of unity is demolished. This idea is barren, it explains " neither number, nor functions, nor the relations between conflicting forces." Any complete synthesis is impossible, both as regards cause and as regards consciousness, for a single consciousness would do away with all distinction between self and not-self, and the subject of a single synthesis of things corresponds to no possible conception. Besides, all individuals are inevitably " absorbed," once an absolute end is granted.

" My consciousness prefers this wretched individual," said Renouvier, " to the entire phantasmagoria of monisms." Let us give back to the individual his rights, " let us distribute," let us share out amongst all beings the notions regarded by monists as belonging exclusively to certain of them.   Each will have its share in causality, each its share in finality.

Individualities, even if we acknowledge them to be created by a single being, are " separate."   Once created, they exist, *qua* units.   Individuals alone are for themselves.

The individual is in time, as also is God, the supreme individual;   everywhere " the order of laws becomes and develops."   There is a Becoming of the All-Being. Indeed, Renouvier thinks that belief in the individual and belief in time are closely connected.   As James observes, he refused to go in search of a deeper reality behind time.   And by the affirmation of the profound reality of time, indeterminate phenomena become possible.   More than this, time is essentially discontinuous. Like James in *Some Problems of Philosophy*, so Renouvier, more particularly in the *Troisième Essai*, pictures to himself pulsations of time, discontinuous thrusts within duration.

By the aid of psychological analyses as well as of the arguments originally formulated by Lequier, neo-criticism proves freedom;   in reality, freedom is implied in the idea of individuality and in the idea of time.   Absolute beginnings may come about.   The absolute beginning, says Renouvier, is the particular mark of difference ;   not only are beings different, but these different beings may be ever new, hence another characteristic common to the philosophy of James and to that of Renouvier.   " To speak of freedom," says James in *The Will to Believe*, " is to carry gold to California."   He cites Renouvier as his true predecessor, his master in indeterminism. Renouvier proved to him the cosmic importance of the principle of activity.

The agreement between James and Renouvier is not simply theoretical. The almost protestant tone of Renouvier and the somewhat puritanic tone of James have a common resonance.

Freedom is an effort, and not an individual effort alone; for Renouvier as for James, in the individual who makes an effort, the world makes an effort. Absolute beginnings are cosmic *points d'attache*; James calls them " turning-points " of the history of the universe. And, like James, while he possesses a very strong sense of creative freedom, he feels the great pressure of external facts all around us; the world may be compared to a vice which yields but occasionally to let the free act pass through. " Nothing is more limited and compassed around on all sides than this power, absolute in one point, and the exercise of which is a question of life or death for the person." He speaks again of " that vast sphere of determinism which on all sides envelops and contains desires, decisions," and which " traces out " above the ends it is desired to follow out " other great and inevitable ends." This conception of freedom so feeble amid the forces of the universe and which yet must be used, under penalty of death, this stern metaphysics culminates in a tragic vision of life, similar to that of James.

The anguish of the philosopher is all the greater seeing that on this freedom depends the final triumph of good. Over against God is Satan; Renouvier agrees with Hugo's Manichæism, nay, with that of Proudhon, and the optimism of Leibniz is " repugnant." Evil exists, " evil for the doer, evil for others, evil at first accidental and then becoming deep-rooted by reproduction and by the natural solidarity of blood and of social relations." With Kant, he believes in radical evil, with

Proudhon in the guiltiness of our species; according to him, the fall is a necessary hypothesis of criticism, the fourth postulate of practical reason. The world is "really moral," as James says, interpreting Renouvier; "it is a world in which there is something that is really evil."

Thus Renouvier is not an optimist, he might have made use of the word James employs; he is in reality a meliorist. Neo-criticism is opposed to all metaphysics of necessary progress. Eagerly does he pursue, right on to these final consequences, the Hegelian philosophy, which he interprets as the cult of fact and the cult of force, which are but one single great depressing cult. On the other hand, he is against all absolute pessimism. Renouvier, as James says, frees himself of pessimism by means of pluralism, "by his belief that it is in the last resort an affair of individual parts of the world and that in the salvation of the person lies the only solution of the problem."

So far we have not examined the question of the existence and conception of God in neo-criticism. Is there one God or are there many Gods? Here we may say that Ménard and Lequier represent two contrary aspects of Renouvier's thought, the former with his love of diversity and polytheism, the latter "in whose eyes the existence of free beings in the universe," says Renouvier, "risked constituting a sort of satanism or diabolical rule, were freedom not the gift of the Creator."

In the *Premier Essai*, Renouvier actually presents the question. He seems—and insists on seeming—to hesitate; this sceptical attitude, in the best sense of the term, being the characteristic of criticism in presence of certain transcendent questions; he does not affirm, neither does he deny; he does not resign himself to doubt, he

6

searches, he looks at the principles and the consequences of doctrines. Renouvier remarks that plurality does not entail contradiction, since in fact " the actual synthesis admits of a plurality of consciousnesses " ; and again, this hypothesis of plurality possesses the advantage of being clear ; and finally, it is in conformity with the laws of logic and the data of experience, adequate to justify the conditions of our experience. We see that he is progressing in the direction of a metaphysical doctrine of plurality.

Is there a plurality of divine consciousnesses ? Here Renouvier readily entertains " the hypothesis of a primitive plurality of distinct consciousnesses in the world." This is the only rational hypothesis and seems implied in the existence of divers actual consciousnesses. He points out the bond between republicanism and polytheism, and creates for himself a social conception of the universe wherein we find the influence of Ménard and the influence of the socialistic theories of a Fourier.

But the argument carries him farther than Fourier—who remained a unitarian—farther than Ménard—who remained a polytheist—towards a sort of atheistical polytheism, as he himself calls it, in which we perceive the influence of Proudhon's ideas. Did he not acquire from Proudhon that " atheistical " method he would apply ? Had not Proudhon previously pointed to this struggle between divine sovereignty and " the morality which goes on unfolding itself from century to century, from crisis to crisis " ? It is Proudhon's revolutionary voice we hear when Renouvier says to us : " We see men set up kings in the times of their primitive ignorance and barbarism, though afterwards they learn to direct their actions more surely by conscience, by necessary ideas, by the phenomena around them." Again and above all else : " Atheism—that act of thought whereby

a free man both overthrows the materialistic or pantheistic idol, and dethrones the Absolute, the king of
Heaven, the final support of the kings of earth—seems
to be the true method, the only one based on reason,
the only one that is positive." And Renouvier, continuing to be here at least dominated by Proudhon, declares
that " true atheism by no means excludes true theism."

Now there remains nothing more for Renouvier than
" a natural, indefinite society of beings," phenomena
set free, a multitude of Gods, a terrestrial Olympus.

So hostile is he to absolute affirmations in these
transcendental questions that he goes so far as to recognise
the great advantage of the idea of plurality in the fact
that it leaves open the door for other solutions. But he
is continually harassed by the thought that his doctrine
of plurality does not solve the problems, that it explains
neither what there is of unity nor of harmony in the
world.

In the *Essai de Psychologie*, the influence of Proudhon
is far less perceptible than before, it is Ménard's influence
that predominates. But the essence of the thought
remains the same; the doctrine of plurality is the
consequence of republican ideas. He believes in Gods
analogous " to the personal beings we know," in " distinct
series of Gods," in "independent societies." The world
is a "republic of beings"; and Renouvier applies to
it the constitution he dreamt of applying to France:
direct government. He speaks of the " government of
beings by themselves."

Who are these divine persons? Are they men who, in
Ménard's words, have scaled the ladder of apotheosis?
It would appear to be so. Renouvier regards the
doctrine of plurality as " the logical consequence of
the immortality of persons." With Ménard, he speaks

of " the apotheosis of souls." In a style wherein we discover hints of Ménard's style, he writes : " The progress of life and virtue peoples the universe with divine persons, and we shall be faithful to an old and spontaneous sense of religion when we call Gods those divine persons whose nature we think we can honour, whose works we think we can bless." With Ménard, he conceives of " laws of the world which enable beings to rise to justice through freedom, to holiness through justice, to divinity through holiness." But he also realises, he says, that the heavens are to be peopled with none but Gods by birthright. Faced with the problem, he adopts the reserve of the neo-criticist. He also maintains reserve on the question of the existence of a hierarchy in these societies of Gods. He hesitates between Ménard's Olympus without hierarchy and " the sacred authority of a single person." The question, he thinks, should be solved by an act of freedom. The reply " depends on ourselves."

At any rate, polytheism is a school of tolerance ; it teaches us to allow free development to reason and imagination ; above all, it is a doctrine of action. Human nature " set free from all absolute sovereignty," exalted personality—these are consequences of polytheism ; and in the distance, as an ideal, the universal republic of " all the inhabitants of the world."

Still, Renouvier was at no time so convinced a poly-theist as Ménard. On questions of primary philosophy he remained agnostic, at least during the period of his philosophy we are studying. From the outset, he says that " the doctrine of plurality is usually agnostic " in so far as it tells us scarcely anything of the number and relations of beings. But is it a very sure doctrine itself ? Both in that of plurality and in that of unity

Renouvier sees two possible and legitimate mental trends. He returns to the agnosticism from which he started.

In a word, he was convinced, as James also was to be, that the way to solve the question depends on temperament and on religious belief. " The motives of self-determination in this order of questions have no longer the same generality." He wished to set up only the " moral probability of a philosophical faith." And this probability depends still more on the history and criticism of religion than on philosophy.

When retracing the phases of his thought in the *Classification*, it would appear as though he scarcely remembered that, in certain passages of his works, he was at the time distinctly a polytheist; he conceives of himself simply as having been an agnostic. " I did not see that the choice between the unity and the original plurality of this principle might be forced by the critical method." He seems to think that the questions stated at the end of the *Premier Essai* and of the *Deuxième Essai* had been left in suspense. Throughout he associates agnosticism with polytheism.

Polytheism was not to be the last phase of Renouvier's philosophy. There may already be found in the first two essays the germs of a new unitarianism. He did not regard the doctrine of unity and that of plurality as mutually exclusive, especially if there were granted the right to people with many other Gods, by means of apotheoses, the celestial abode of the supreme king of the universe.

The limits allotted to knowledge by agnosticism were about to widen out. Renouvier, after considerable hesitation, he said, was about to understand the value, even from the criticist point of view, of the idea of unity. The " idealistic consideration of the unity of the laws of mind," a unity identical with that of the laws of the world and implying the unity of a supreme mind above the two orders of phenomena, then the theme of the first beginning of the universe, and finally the moral idea, all these lead him to a belief in unity.

He wished to reconcile unity and plurality in a new monadology, conceived in a relativistic spirit. The disappearance of the idea of substantial cause, the definition of the monad in terms of its qualities, and of beings in terms of phenomena, lead him to the idea of a pre-established harmony between monads which remain essentially contingent.

But Renouvier did not then adopt this monadism. Secrétan says of him that he drifts, *nolens volens*, towards monotheism; indeed, Renouvier, in the *Essais*, combining belief in a single God with the supposition of a moral order, resolves to found a sort of natural religion. More especially in the *Classification* does Renouvier endeavour to find in a " general representation," in " a single first consciousness," the cause of particular representations, the justification of the harmony of the world and the guarantee of the ideal. Thus he declares that he is taking a decisive step in the direction of religion and " this time " in the direction of Christianity. God is a " morally perfect and very powerful person," distinct from the world as is a subject from its object, finite like his creatures, existing within space and within time.

More precisely, his God is conceived as being in the likeness of man. In his *Premier Essai* he declared that there was nothing extravagant in anthropomorphism, and in the *Essai de Psychologie* he says that practically he is in favour of an " acknowledged anthropomorphism." This " worthy anthropomorphic faith " brings him into agreement with the Christians, with genuine " men of religion."

Renouvier now acknowledges that the idea of creation is not hostile to criticism.

But even though he recognises a creative God, the providence of the universe, he regards him as a " free creator of free beings "; and of the thoughts of these beings God inspires a " certain " number only. Below God there are other personal activities, and if these are not Gods, at all events they are men.

English writers are justified in regarding Renouvier, in the words of Schiller, as " the thinker who gave a powerful impetus to the voluntarism and the personalism of the day "; or, according to Ritchie, as the philosopher who was able to " amend the Kantian doctrine by permeating it with Hume's pluralism and phenomenalism." His doctrine was a thorough-going pluralism, Ritchie continues. The *Nouvelle Monadologie* seemed to Schiller to be an effort, still doubtless too Leibnizian, in the direction of genuine pluralist metaphysics. But above all it was " the ingenious and profound philosopher " of whom Renouvier always spoke in laudatory terms, in whose writings he occasionally discovered conceptions consonant with his deepest thoughts; it was William James who was best able to realise the necessity of meeting the dilemmas formulated by criticism, and of siding with Renouvier in his choice. " Just as Buonaparte," he said, " declared that the Europe of the future would have to be either Republican or Cossack; so, proceeding to the limits of simplification, I feel inclined to say that the philosophy of the future will have to be either that of Renouvier or that of Hegel." And what does James regard as the philosophy of Renouvier ? Above all, it is phenomenalism, the affirmation of absolute novelties, "the acceptance of an irreducible pluralism of data connected by definite laws"; it is the theory of the discontinuity of time, it is a sort of empiricism. Between the Hegelian theory on the one hand, and on the other hand the doctrine which always respects the laws of identity, contradiction, and excluded middle, and arrives at the affirmation of discontinuity and of an irreducible pluralism, we are on the horns of a dilemma; we must take sides for one or the other. James chooses for Renouvier, and determines to continue, in an even more radically empiristic fashion, the tradition of neo-criticism simultaneously with the tradition of men like Lotze and Sigwart. We shall see what new treatment and development it will receive at his hands.

Reading Renouvier proved to be for him a revelation, as we see in a letter of his father. Henry James happened to find the youthful professor of physiology more joyful and confident than usual. "I asked him what he thought was the cause of this change," and the first thing that James mentioned was the reading of Renouvier's works, especially of his "vindication of the freedom of the will."

An American philosopher, Professor Lovejoy, states that James belongs both to the French philosophical tradition and to the American tradition. "Though his personality and his style were singularly American, he none the less truly belongs, as a technical metaphysician, to the apostolic succession of French temporalism." [7]

A deepening and a renewing of his ideas, a genuine revelation, was the impression he received from the work of Renouvier, as was subsequently the case when brought into contact with the work of Bergson.

[7] Lovejoy, *Philosophical Review*, 1912, p. 16.

CHAPTER IV

" BACK to Berkeley," " back to Hume, no more of Kant,"
say the pragmatists. " The true direction of philosophical
progress," writes James, " lies, in short, it seems to me,
not so much *through* Kant as *round* him to the point
where now we stand. Philosophy can perfectly well
outflank him and build herself up into adequate fullness
by prolonging more directly the older English lines."
Hume does not fully satisfy us nowadays ; but if we must
correct him, let us do so while we remain his disciples,
and not have recourse to the " evasions and artifices of
Kant."

Pragmatism has been called Neo-Berkeleianism, Neo-
Humism. To begin with, we may note the pragmatists'
tendency to an "idealistic realism"; this is what Renouvier
means by " the idealism of the English empirical school."
Like Hume and Berkeley, the majority of the English
and American pragmatists of the present day are nomi-
nalists. Matter, cause, vague unities having disappeared
in the mind of Berkeley, there remained nothing more
than a living world of particular realities where his imagination feels itself, as he says " *in particularibus et in con-
cretis, hoc est, in ipsis rebus.*" Hume merely deduced the
consequences of the English doctrine when, with subtle
dialectic, alike empirical and Cartesian, he propounded
the idea that all phenomenon is substance. The doctrine

of Hume and that of Schiller answer this problem in the same way : Are there general things, abstract things ? Ritchie was justified in some measure in speaking of the pluralism of Hume.

John Stuart Mill is the true continuer of the Humes and the Berkeleys. He opposes Hegel, and the more or less Germanised parts of Hamilton's philosophy. That need of clarity which James admires in him and which makes him wish to discover as many laws in Nature as there are distinct qualities and sensations, which compels him to deny the presence of a general element in things, that attempt of pluralist logic, which sees only resemblances and differences in the world, and perceives no identity : all this makes the pluralists regard Mill as a precursor.

But it is mainly his *Essays on Religion* that prepare and proclaim the pragmatism of James and of Schiller. To begin with, his method, even in theology, is still wholly empirical.   " Whatever relates to God, I hold with Sir W. Hamilton to be matter of inference."

These inferences are in reality analogies. Mill, along with Fechner, was the grand master of James in analogies. He weighs probabilities and does not go beyond what the inferences allow.

In order to base belief on simple probabilities, to trust rather in reasons for hope than in motives for despair, one must " take advantage of probabilities as far as possible."   And is not this both being empirical enough to know that there are only probabilities and being daring enough to live on them ? This intellectual courage is faith.

This faith must be acquired especially when the probabilities are apt to " inspire man to effort," when they make human nature and life into " objects of far greater

orth to the heart." Thus John Stuart Mill super-
1poses a kind of pragmatism on to his empiricism.

This method leads him to a personalistic theology;
is in Mill's work that Schiller is to find grounds for
eciding on the conception of a personal and finite God.

For John Stuart Mill, evil exists. He says that we
innot possibly see in the government of Nature anything
:sembling the work of a being both good and omnipotent.
'he power of God is not only finite, it is extremely
mited. Mill gives us the formula of religious empiri-
sm and of a faith which voluntarily limits itself, as it
mits the power of its God. He says the net results of
atural theology on the subject of divine attributes are
ie following: a being of great though limited power,
ithout our being able to tell how and by what it is
mited; of vast, perhaps limitless, intelligence, though
erhaps also confined within narrower limits than his
ower; who desires the happiness of his creatures and does
)mething to ensure it, though he appears to have yet
ther motives of action which he regards as of greater
loment.

The ethics of John Stuart Mill, as expounded in
'ssays on Religion, unquestionably exercised considerable
1fluence on James. Teufelsdröckh taught Mill to see
ie world in all its flow and ebb of good and evil things,
) see the successive defeats and victories, and the con-
:ant efforts of the principles at strife. There exists
principle of evil. Against it man must be endlessly
:ruggling, aware of the freedom within himself, and
nowing all the time that he will win neither a sudden
or a continuous victory. For Mill, as subsequently for
ames, the struggle between the powers of good and those
f evil goes on all the time; it is "a struggle in which
he humblest creature is able to play a part."

The religion of the future will be a belief in the efficacy of every individual effort, however slight, for the improvement of the world.

Mill says that according to this doctrine a virtuous man assumes the character of a fellow-worker with the Most High, a helper of God in the mighty conflict. God offers us his help, but at the same time he needs us and we help him.

Renouvier was fond of quoting these *Essays on Religion*; so opposed to religious and philosophical fanaticism, *i.e.* to absolute pantheism and monotheism, so strongly setting up the worship of a personal God and so full of moral ardour. Mill, in the eyes of James and Schiller, is placed alongside Renouvier and Lotze amongst the defenders of immortality and action. "To the memory of John Stuart Mill, from whom I first learned the pragmatic openness of mind and whom my fancy likes to picture as our leader, were he alive to-day," are the words which form the dedication of *Pragmatism*; James thereby testifying his whole-hearted gratitude to the author of *A System of Logic*, *An Examination of the Philosophy of Sir W. Hamilton*, and *Essays on Religion*.

Bain, who did not consider that there was anything shocking in the elements of experience being, in the final resort, two instead of one, and Shadworth Hodgson, whose analysis of experience did not terminate in a conception of the world as a totality, continued the English empirical tradition. Hodgson affirmed that the universe was inconceivable as an ensemble of the material world and of the spiritual world; to him, it could not be reduced to a single term, as the monist thinks, and could be known only in parts. He returned to empiricism by way of Kant.

While English philosophical thought, in spite of such men as Mill, Bain, and Hodgson, seems either to follow the lead of Germany in recognising an absolute, or else tends towards a monistic materialism, English theology, even when dominated by German ideas, maintains the conception of a religion of the personal God, based on concrete facts. Martineau was the type of these personalist theologians ; one of his followers pictures him as the English Lotze. His personalism is founded on a real pluralism ; the world, he says, is " an aggregate of metaphysical causes which limit and resist our volitional activity," like souls in contact. This is why he rejoiced when war began to be waged upon Hegelianism. Upton, his disciple, upheld pluralism.[8]

The English Protestant Church has produced many empiricists, such as Chalmers and McCosh, who have attempted to reach God by induction.

Spiritism, a very different doctrine, may also be classified as religious empiricism.

Myers is, above all, athirst for immortality ; but he is determined to rely on nothing but facts. Myers' book might well have been entitled : *Varieties of Experiences of Immortality*. To prove immortality, he is resolved to travel the open, frank, and candid pathway of modern science, as he expresses it. He well knew, as James says, that there are compact strata of experiences above one another, and that, however compact, they must be traversed before the Absolute is reached. By this method, as Mazzini, one of his favourite heroes, says, the unknown will be unveiled, showing us nothing but " continuity of life." Is not this idea of an ever-widening field of vision, which helps us to realise and gather up new and high possibilities hitherto impenetrable, endless possibilities—

---

[8] See the works of McCall, especially, *The Elements of Individualism,* 1847. The ideas of Dr Ward and of Denison Maurice in some respects correspond with those of the pluralists. The same may be said of the philosophy of Campbell Fraser and of Mallock.

is it not the same as that which we find, though transformed, in the works of James ?

What are these possibilities ? Moral possibilities in
the first place, and in this connection New Thought and
Christian Science, which James mentions so frequently,
might claim the authority of Myers. Man sees that his
powers are greater than he thinks, that there is a sort of
stratification of successive powers within him, and that we
can make our spiritual life ever more intense.

From the religious and metaphysical point of view,
man feels himself continuous with other souls, as matter is
continuous with matter ; and this spiritual environment
is far deeper and more real than the material environment.
Man feels himself at home in the boundless universe.
His pluralism never causes James to forget this idea
of spiritual continuity as pictured by Myers. In the
depths of consciousness he seeks for those elements that
transcend consciousness. The idea of the transcendental
which he owes to Emerson, and that of the subliminal
which he owes to Myers, blend spontaneously and form
one in his own mind.

Are we to picture this continuity, as Myers conceives
it, after the fashion of a plane surface ? To Myers, as
to Fechner, the surface is not all one ; there is a hierarchy
of spirits. James finds fault with the absolutists for not
graduating the transitions between ourselves and the
Absolute ; Myers considers that there is an infinity of
souls between ourselves and it, an infinity of souls
living in an infinity of environments. Myers readily
inclines towards a kind of polytheism. " It is safer," he
says, " to take refuge in the conception of intelligences
not infinite, yet gifted with a foresight which strangely
transcends our own." Both within and without space
there move immaterial and individual realities.

It is of this spiritual world that we are really the citizens ; it is there we find friends to aid us. Like James, Myers declares that our fight is the fight of the universe itself, that even the purposes of God are brought to pass by the soul's yearnings after the heights. Perhaps, he continues, in this complex of interblending spirits, our own effort is not an individual . . . not a transitory . . . thing. What lies at the root of each one of us lies also at the root of the universe. " Let men realise that their own spirits are co-operative elements in cosmic evolution, are part and parcel of the ultimate vitalising Power."

The Gods hasten to join in this work of co-operation. Incarnate and disincarnate spirits alike strive for the triumph of the good in a universal enthusiasm of " adoring co-operation."

In America, mysticism frequently appears under the form of New Thought, Christian Science, Yogism, Metaphysical Healing. By reason of their " healthy-mindedness " and of the energies they produce, these philosophies would appear to have had considerable attraction for William James.

The panpsychism of Morton Prince and that of Strong may appear as an aspect—though somewhat different— of the same phase of thought. Perhaps these two philosophers contributed to the formation of what may be called the panpsychism of James.

Another philosopher exercised a profound influence over James, one who was for him a sort of older companion. James declares that he owes him more than he can say. Peirce, the logician, points to the necessity of particular and concrete experiences in which ideas may be verified ; he insists on the diversity of " universes of experience," the one a region of ideas, the other of facts, the third of signs or symbols which connect facts with ideas. Peirce, the metaphysician, though believing in the sole absolute reality of the One, agrees on certain points with Renouvier and Delbœuf. He believes in a chance as absolute as the Absolute itself. To his mind, there is in the universe an element of indetermination, of spontaneity, of feeling; for chance is but the outer aspect of feeling.

Chance alone explains the growth, the developing complexity, the endless diversity of the universe, and not only the diversity and irregularity, for the calculation of probabilities teaches us that chance explains regularity itself.

Such is tychism, the name which Peirce gives to his philosophy; and tychism leads to belief in a personal God with whom we hold relationship, in metaphysical collectivism, in agapism, as Peirce says, in the idea of a world in which all co-operate.

Somewhat similar ideas may be found in the work of T. Davidson.

Thus came together such various influences and philosophies insisting on "difference"; from the Hellenic theology of Ménard to the mysticism of Fechner; from the religious theories of Mill to those of Lutoslawski; from the philosophy of Renouvier to that of Myers. But throughout we are conscious of the same striving after empirical precision, the same love of freedom, a demand for diversity which remains the same, one might say, however deeply national and however profoundly personal certain of these doctrines may be.

CHAPTER V

THE ENGLISH SPIRIT: THE AMERICAN SPIRIT

In the eyes of most pluralists, their doctrine is a national philosophy. James would return to the " great English way of investigation and conception." To him, pragmatism is an English way of thinking. The nominalistic criticism of a Berkeley, a Hume, or a Mill must always serve as a model for Anglo-Saxon philosophers.

The importance of particulars and concrete experience is the first characteristic which enables us to recognise pluralism as an English and American philosophy. Indeed, even in the English who adopted from German philosophy the constituent parts of the absolutist doctrine, ideas have an " experimental " character and are as far as possible brought into connection with the particular experience.

Starting from experience in its particularity, English philosophy is led to become a philosophy of the individual. It has been said that the mind of the Englishman desires clarity rather in details than in the whole of a thing, that he wants to understand each thing and not all things, that he is incapable of sacrificing a fact to the harmony of a general theory, and that he prefers a contradiction in the whole of the theory rather than the misunderstanding of one character of the particular fact.

This speculative individualism is a sort of metaphysical representation of a practical individualism, of the need for freedom in action; and belief in the metaphysical worth of the Self may spring from the same necessity which, in practice, found expression in the Habeas Corpus Act.

We also find this individualism in the Englishman's concern about having a religion in which God may be conceived of as a being contrasted with other beings, and appealing to each of them in particular less as a member of a Church than as a personal soul.

The Englishman is anxious to reconcile philosophical thought with religious needs. Pluralism enables him to believe in the existence of a personal God and to understand the existence of evil; to unite finally what appears to him the lasting value of romanticism with his enduring need of an empiricist method.

Finally, if we consider the Stevensonian sense of adventure and peril, the Alcyonian element, as Nietzsche would have said, all that is youthful and venturesome in the soul of Stevenson, the love of risk in Browning, the stern courage of the hero as represented by Henley and Kipling : are not all these so many revelations of that English soul which would attempt to find self-expression in the doctrines of the pluralists ?

All the same, pragmatism and pluralism are even more American than English : Schiller, the main representative of English pragmatism, began his career in America. The American spirit is also largely experimental and is endlessly concerned with the individual's concrete environment.

Above all do the descendants of the men of action and faith who went across to America in the *Mayflower* want truths which are not irreconcilable with their need for action. In church, they want to listen, not to dogmatic expositions, but rather to moral precepts : " practical

Americans," exclaims James, when rallying to his pragmatic banner the lovers of philosophy in the New World.

" Sturdy, staunch, rugged," such is the typical American, hardened to danger and difficulty as is " the stormy petrel." These men of action will live only in an environment of freedom, one in which it is possible to " play the game " and to have experiences, where an individual's efforts depend on his will alone, where they can be effective, where there is continuous and rapid progress, real novelty.

It has often been remarked that the practical character of the Americans is in many of them combined with an idealistic conception of life, with the idea of endless possibilities and indeterminate freedom. The American is rather a practical idealist than a utilitarian. The world should be material for effort. Indeed, while on the one hand it contains endless possibilities of good, on the other it embodies evil elements which must be overcome. The Calvinistic American believes in the existence of sin, of evil, though he also believes that human effort can triumph over them. " With us the need of effort in life is ineradicable," writes James. And these world possibilities must be unfolded by a will that is unfettered. " Our nation was founded on what we may call our American religion, was baptised and brought up in the belief that a man needs no master to take care of him, and that ordinary men may very well by their efforts obtain salvation all together." Pluralism is the idea of a world self-government, the metaphysical expression of the will of " an all-pervading democracy."

Nevertheless these efforts are not all closely co-ordinated. The American conceives the possibility of travelling towards the good along different paths. Hence the large number of sects, hence American tolerance. The desire of independence gives birth not only to a love of practical freedom, but also to this welcome which is accorded the most diverse systems, this democratic catholicity, as Royce calls it. Ménard spoke of the polytheism of the United States. Lutoslawski regards both the North Americans and the Poles as naturally pluralistic. " Reality," says an American philosopher, " comes, from moment to moment, as an infinite *mélange* of systems, never a system in itself."

To say that individuals are free is not to say that they are without bonds ; indeed, their efforts are unco-ordinated, but they nevertheless make for the same goal. The American readily insists on the ideal of fellowship, mutuality. In transcendentalism these ideas held a prominent place, and did not Whitman constitute himself the poet of comradeship ?

Not only is there collaboration and mutuality between men and men, but also between men and God. " It is a great event in a boy's life when he can say, ' I and my father are one.' It is greater when a man finds that he can keep step with God ; that he wants to do and can do the things that God is doing." This is the American's conception of his ideal. For him, even more than for the Englishman, there should take place a sort of exchange of personal services between each individual and the Deity. According to Tausch, whereas for the Continental nations God is a monarch, for the Americans he is the chosen king of the first Germanic societies or the official representative of a modern democracy. To the Americans God is a very powerful person. " God was for my friend," said a psychologist of the religious thought of America, " a very potent element in the trend of events." To man this God is a help ; at times he even seems to be a kind of servant.

This trend towards action, this conception of an ideal he would like to realise in practice by untrammelled fellowship, thereby combining idealism with the need for attainment, do not prevent the American from being conscious that there exist superior and vaster powers by contact with which the life of the soul becomes more intense; and he attempts, frequently by novel and bold experiments, to enter into ultimate relations with these realities. In different ways Emerson, Whitman, the Christian Scientists seek to experience the absolute.

At the time when pluralism was assuming form, the American spirit was on the look out for a new faith, a philosophy wherein there would meet and blend together, as Caldwell expressed it, an idealist conception and the will for practical action, the eagerness after individual effort and the sense of mightier realities in which individual souls are, as it were, immersed. The pluralism of James, after the transcendentalism of Emerson and the cosmic democratism of Whitman, forms a response to these American aspirations. In the mind of James, we find both the need of a world wherein action is possible and the idea of those loftier realities to which his almost Swedenborgian education had perhaps accustomed him. We also find the Calvinistic affirmation of the existence of evil and the transcendental belief in the victory of good, concern for the individual act and the idea of a kind of world fellowship. One of his admirers tells us that he is a friend, a help and comfort to all those nervous, half-educated beings who seek gropingly, to all those who thirst after emotions—a large class in America. But it is not to these only that he appeals; it is also to the man of action, to him who would create a vision of the world in harmony with democratic ideas.

On these points the novels of Winston Churchill

afford interesting testimony. " Philosophy is no longer against religion, it is for it," says one of his characters, " and if you were to ask me to name the greatest masters of present-day religious thought I should mention William James and Royce. . . . Our principal philosophers are in harmony with the quickening social spirit of our times, and this spirit is a religious, a Christian spirit."

He dwells on this love of action and adventure with which philosophers are able to inspire us. " Life itself is an adventure; there is no such thing as absolute safety." Was not this also the meaning of Roosevelt's article: *The Great Adventure*, written in January 1919 ? " Life and death are both part of the same Great Adventure." [9]

Is it not also this same love of adventure which partly constitutes the strange charm of certain poems of Robert Service, just as in a smoother and more classical form, one that is more like the French and inspired with entirely different feelings, we find it in some of the fine poems and rousing letters of Alan Seeger ? The desire for adventure is so strong in both these poets that in spite of their " monism," in spite of their *amor fati*, it shines forth and transfigures everything.

[9] Compare Winston Churchill, *The Inside of the Cup*: " Religion, he began to perceive, was an undertaking." He speaks of the " sense of adventure, the palpitating fear and daring." Winston Churchill: *A Far Country*, p. 449 : " That, too, is an adventure, the greatest adventure of all "; and page 448 : " Democracy is an adventure, the great adventure of mankind. No adventure is safe, life itself is an adventure and neither is that safe. It's a hazard, as you and I have found out. The moment we try to make life safe we lose all there is in it worth while. We have to leave what seem the safe things ; we have to wander and suffer in order to realise that the only true safety lies in development. We have to risk our lives and our souls." It would be interesting to compare such passages with the formula : The world safe for democracy.

CHAPTER VI

PRAGMATISM AND PLURALISM

LIKE positivism, pragmatism forbids the mind to deal with whatever has no concrete results in practice, with what is useless knowledge ; but it differs profoundly from positivism in not being an agnosticism ; according to Schiller there is nothing unknowable ; the mind should confidently venture out in search of the Absolute, and the Sphinx will have no more riddles to propound ; to James, the world at times appears as though transparent, diaphanous.

Moreover, even if there is an unknowable, we can in a way obtain the mastery over it ; by faith we can make our belief true. Through action we are able to know that which would be unknowable to the intellect alone.

There has been a whole outburst of metaphysical systems, many of which, if we are to credit the statements of their followers, claim to be rooted and grounded in pragmatism ; there is a pragmatist right and a pragmatist left. " Systems of philosophy will abound as before," declares Schiller, " and will be as various as ever. But they will probably be more brilliant in their colouring and more attractive in their form." James notes with hopefulness this strange " unrest in the philosophical atmosphere of the time, an interest in new suggestions, however vague."

Out of all the metaphysics offered to him, which

one will the pragmatist choose by preference ? Does
not pragmatism demand certain metaphysical ideas
rather than certain others ? Does it not harmonise
with them, point in their direction ? What will be the
relations between pragmatism and pluralism ? Why are
many of the chief pragmatists also pluralists ?

It must be remarked that the pragmatist frequently
insists on the idea that there is no necessary bond here,
that these two conceptions are relatively independent
of each other. Pragmatism, says James, is essentially a
method, not a cosmology ; it may serve as a starting-
point for the more diverse metaphysics ; and radical
empiricism (a name he gives to one aspect of his pluralist
metaphysics), he declares in the preface of *Pragmatism*,
is independent of the pragmatist method. And Schiller
says : " This question of pluralism has nothing to do
with pragmatism." He even declares that pragmatism
and monism are in a certain way connected ; since, in
pragmatism, truth is at bottom unity and adaptation.
All the same, we shall see that, according to these philosophers themselves, there are precise relations between
pragmatism and pluralism.

Pragmatism is individualistic ; and Dewey, though he
also sees the social side of truth and of reality, considers
that one of the origins of pragmatism is to be found
in the individualistic tendencies of modern life. Schiller
insists on the individualistic character of his philosophy.
The opponents of pragmatism find fault with his tendency
at times to regard truth as a creation of the individual.
To James, individual temperaments are, partially at
least, the creators of their own truths. " Interest shifts
from an intelligence that shaped things once for all,"
writes Dewey, " to the particular intelligences."

But individuals form a society ; the true is that

which is socially useful, says Schiller. This social theory
of truth is expressed in metaphysics by the idea of a
commonalty of assembled personal lives, of a harmony of
persons, by what may be called metaphysical collectivism ; just as the preceding affirmation is expressed by the
affirmation of a metaphysical individualism. We shall
see that these two ideas are capable of completing and
supplementing each other.

Pragmatism and pluralism both claim to be democratic
philosophies. Both speak in the name of those elements
in human nature to which philosophy hitherto has not
given satisfaction, in the name of that " residuum which
has not been converted into thought." It is the need
to reconcile philosophy with the data of common sense
that drives philosophy towards pragmatism first and
afterwards towards realism and pluralism.

As Ward says, the point of view of pluralism is that of
the social and historical study of man. The idea of
conduct, so essential to pragmatism, can, he also says,
apply only to what is individual and unique. Thus
pluralism and pragmatism looked upon the world from
one and the same standpoint, that of " conduct."
Pluralism, we may say, affirms that the whole world
can be explained in pragmatist terms, and pragmatism
affirms that the whole world can be explained in pluralist terms. This is the fundamental difference, Ward
tells us, between pluralism and atomism. The pluralist
regards the individual as mainly defined by his very
activity, his efforts of transformation and adaptation,
his " pragmatism."

Not only does pragmatism affirm that truth is individual
in the sense that it originates in the mind of the individual ;
but it also maintains—and it is this that constitutes the
very essence of pragmatism—that its object is individual ;

our only knowledge is of the individual, and pragmatism is a nominalism. Instead of conceiving truth as a whole, it admits none but particular truths ; it actually parcels out truth. One characteristic of this philosophy is that it requires principles sufficiently numerous to explain the diversity of our facts. The pragmatist philosopher does not attempt by means of abstractions to bring together and to unify the greatest possible number of concrete objects ; the concrete cannot be explained by the abstract.

If we define truth as a whole, we can never possess it ; this was proved by Bradley and Joachim ; their absolutism leads to scepticism. If we would reach such a theory of knowledge as does not falsify all we know, then we must admit the possibility of knowing certain parts of reality without knowing the whole of it ; and if we allow that such knowledge is possible, we must admit likewise that there are parts of reality independent of one another. Pragmatism, says R. B. Perry, affirms that the growth of knowledge is " additive." That this growth may be possible, there must be multiplicity and contingence, independence of terms as regards the relations into which they enter.

Again, by showing that there is no *a priori* necessity which must be assumed by the mind, pragmatistic empiricism makes impossible any *a priori* speculative construction.

Since we must always take into account the concrete given, we shall have to consider the different needs in the human soul and not sacrifice them to the sole need of logic. " The theory of knowledge begins with a pluralistic outlook upon human nature ; our practical nature is distinct from both our æsthetic and our logical nature."

In another way pluralism and pragmatism are connected : both are realisms. For a score of years past the realistic stream has been flowing with ever-increasing volume in the United States. Realism is the fashionable philosophy, we were told in 1909. "Strangest of all . . . in the philosophic atmosphere of the time . . ." wrote James in 1904, "natural realism, so long decently buried, raises its head above the turf and finds glad hands outstretched from the most unlikely quarters to help it to its feet again." The name of the new realisms is legion, says Schiller in 1909. Indeed, there is the simple natural realism, the realism for which consciousness is but a relation between given things, the realism for which consciousness is a transparent environment ; there is the functional realism of the Chicago school ; there is that which insists on the necessity of distinguishing things from our perception of things, as there is that which makes no distinction but affirms the absolute unity of subject and object ; there is an idealistic realism. Thus realism split up into many various philosophies and united with pragmatism until, under the influence of such logicians as Russell, it separated from pragmatism and opposed it.

In fact, realism and pragmatism would appear to be connected, seeing that, if truth is adaptation to things, there must be things distinct from the mind. On the other hand, realism and pluralism naturally unite with one another, and the opponents of the one have usually been the opponents of the other. " It is the duty of a consistent pluralist to be a realist," said Taylor. Royce combats both realism and pluralism, which, to his mind, form " one and the same doctrine." Indeed, the world as conceived by American realists is one in which there are relations of space and time, a stereometric and moving world, as it has been called. " The only reality consists in diversity." To be a realist is to deny absolute unity, to affirm the external character of certain things with reference to certain others.

There are still other bonds between pluralism and pragmatism. For if pragmatism is the cult of the concrete and the mistrust of abstraction, it comes naturally to regard life as "confused and superabundant," as in itself destructive of absolutist ideologies.

Again, the pragmatist's concern for morality and for activity requires centres of indetermination in the world, and makes a pluralist of him. " The world of pragmatism is practical," says one of them, " a world of actions and reactions, and this purely practical world is plural." It is not only a multiple world that the pragmatist requires, it is an incomplete world. " The pragmatist is compelled to believe in the absolute mutability of the universe," writes Bradley. As Lovejoy has seen, there is " a certain metaphysical doctrine which, although not always very explicitly put forward, appears to me to have a rather fundamental place in the characteristic mode of thought of most representatives of pragmatism. This is the doctrine of the real futurity or ' openness ' of the future, and of the determinative or ' creative ' efficacy of each ' present ' moment in the ever transient process of conscious judgment, choice and action." He compares this theory with that of Bergson's real becoming and calls it metaphysical temporalism. To the pragmatist the future is really something non-existent precisely because it exists *qua* future. Dewey's followers insisted on the importance of this idea of change in pragmatism. And indeed if we say that the idea is a plan of action, ought not this plan of action to be conceived in the interests of the future ? The future, then, ought not to be something stereotyped. Inversely, if we believe in the full reality of time, if we locate all facts in time, then truth must leave the non-temporal world of pure ideas ; like everything else, it must be a force, a tendency, an action. According to A. W. Moore, pragmatism leads more directly and immediately to this affirmation of the reality of time than to the affirmation of the plurality of things. " Pragmatism is not directly and from the outset interested in the problem of unity and plurality. . . . It is interested only in the problem of change and development." The dilemma propounded between pragmatism and anti-pragmatism is above all the dilemma which is raised, as he says, between completionism and evolutionism. He affirms that pragmatism is brought over to pluralism solely because it finds in pluralism a conception which makes possible the transition. Woodbridge, too, regards pragmatism as connected with the general idea that experience should not be defined in terms of space but in terms of duration, that it is essentially temporal, essentially directed towards the future.

As a matter of fact, the two ideas of the incomplete and temporal character of the world and of its complex or multiple character seem to most pragmatists to be involved in each other. James considers that the question as to which of these affirmations precedes the other ought not to be asked, seeing that they are conjoint or inseparable. When speaking of pluralism he is referring to a metaphysics which is contrary both to the thought of unity and to that of non-temporality. The world of pluralism is both a diverse world and a moving world, a dual but indissoluble affirmation.

And so pragmatism readily combines with pluralist

metaphysics. " I myself read humanism theistically and pluralistically," says James. And though he might seem, in a certain number of passages, to form independent conceptions of the two theories, there are other passages in which he blends and assimilates them. The very temperament that makes a man a pragmatist generally makes him a pluralist. At times he will regard the two words as synonymous. " The pragmatism or pluralism which I defend," he writes. Pluralism is the metaphysical theory " which agrees with the pragmatic temper best, for it immediately suggests an infinitely larger number of the details of future experience to our mind." Pluralism is based on a pragmatist theory of knowledge, discovered by a pragmatist method and lived, one might say, by a pragmatist temperament. On the other hand, pragmatism may be regarded only as a consequence of a vast pluralist metaphysics ; it is because the world is made up of multiple beings, which develop in time, that truth is conceived as partial, temporal, efficacious.

The opponents of pragmatism clearly saw that it implies such metaphysics. And many pragmatists recognise that this is so.

We see how important is the problem of unity and diversity to the pragmatists. According to Schiller, " to know whether the world is, in the last resort, one or multiple, is the fundamental question of metaphysics." " I myself have come," says James, " by long brooding over this problem, to consider it the most central of all philosophical problems, central because so pregnant. I mean by this that if you know whether a man is a decided monist or a decided pluralist, you know perhaps more about the rest of his opinions than if you gave him any other name ending in *ist*."

Before them, they say, no one had perceived the essential character of this problem ; it had not even been seen that there was a problem at all. James writes : " A final philosophy of religion will have to consider the pluralistic hypothesis more seriously than it has hitherto been willing to consider it." Schiller, too, makes mock of the respect of philosophers for unity ; the unity of things seems more dazzling, more illustrious than their variety. James describes the joy of the youthful philosopher when first he perceives that the whole world forms one great fact and when he casts scornful glances on those who have not reached this sublime conception. " A certain abstract monism, a certain emotional response to the character of oneness as if it were a feature of the world not co-ordinate with its manyness, but vastly more excellent and eminent, is so prevalent in educated circles that we might almost call it a part of philosophic common sense. Of *course* the world is One, we say. How else could it be a world at all ? " " Rational unity of all things " is so inspiring a formula. " Doubtless this is the first time," says James to his audience, " that you have heard this problem raised. I suspect that in but few of you has this problem occasioned sleepless nights, and I should not be astonished if some of you told me it had never vexed you at all." *A fortiori* will the polytheistic hypothesis be generally passed over in silence. The wretched pluralist conception is ever scorned, ever forgotten. At bottom it is scorned because it inspires dread. " A universe with such as *us* contributing to create its truth, a world delivered to *our* opportunisms and *our* private judgments : Home Rule for Ireland would be a millennium in comparison. . . . Such a world would not be *respectable* philosophically." And even though certain philosophers have risked supporting pluralism, they have done it awkwardly. So, the English philosophers—and the American pluralists—often claim to offer the world an entirely new philosophy. Pluralism has not appeared as a gesture of despair, a sort of philosophical suicide; it represents the retaliation of moral and religious instincts against a stationary unity.

Still, we may well inquire whether this is not somewhat exaggerated, since James himself acknowledges that the question of the one and the many has long been discussed, that it is a perfect instance of the puzzles of metaphysics. It may be that pragmatism has stated the problem in terms of new ideas, but the problem existed long before pragmatism appeared on the scene.

The pluralists have seemed to propound this ever-recurring problem in a novel way, they have offered a bold solution and have formulated what they call " a new theory of reality." Hence the success which pluralism has obtained. Pragmatism and pluralism seduce us, as Bakewell says, by their empiricism, their disdain of all *a priori* construction, a certain scientific manner, their democratic and popular aspect, as well as by their individualism, their spirit of revolt against " these old monistic absolutisms," the attraction of risk and the unknown. Do they not offer us " a new world with a large frontier, and, beyond, the enticing unexplored lands where one may still expect the unexpected " ? The pluralists have become increasingly numerous, the result being that we hear mention of the " present-day pluralism," the " new gospel which has not yet made up its mind whether we are to remain monotheistic or polytheistic," the " persistent popularity of pluralism in many circles." " Pluralism is in the air. It is making rapid progress," and while the pragmatists were " revelling among pluralistic ideas to their hearts' content," while James was rejoicing at the " great empirical movement towards a pluralist pan-psychic view of the universe into which our own genera-tion has been drawn " : while " a great number of students were sympathetic towards the new doctrines and wanted more free play for the individual," the monists noted the growing discontent of idealist philosophies ; they com-plained of the lack of any conciliatory spirit in the plural-ists, they saw the pluralist evil spread among the young philosophers. " One of the first symptoms," said one of them, " is an outburst of sharpened intellect and epigram-matic wit." It is even a fact that certain thinkers, not monists strictly speaking, are horrified at the doctrines of those metaphysicians who take up " the most extravagant pluralism."

Indeed, ever since about 1902 the question of pluralism has seemed in both American and English universities the very one on which philosophers were to split. Pluralism is both a subject for lecture courses and for songs. For the 1904–1905 session the syllabus of the department of philosophy at Harvard University announces that " one of the philosophical professors will develop a theory of pluralism on the basis of experience, and in the next term his colleague will develop a speculative theory of the absolute." And in a review played by the students at Oxford in 1907, entitled " The Old Man of Königsberg," Lotze, making a pun on his own name, sings : " I am lots of things " ; while in a song published by *The May Century* we are introduced to " the man who monises " and to " the man who pragmatises " in the following parody of the well-known nursery rhyme :

> " Hickory, dickory, dock !
> The pluralist looked at the clock ;
> The clock struck one,
> And away he run ;
> Hickory, dickory, dock !

> Hickory, dickory, do !
> The monist looked also ;
> The clock struck ten,
> And he looked again,
> And said, ' It is three hours slow ! ' " [10]

[10] Quoted in *The Journal of Philosophy*, 20th June 1907.

On the restoration and rejuvenation of things and problems brought about by pluralism, the change in philosophical perspectives, see Hoffding, *Philos. Contemp.*, p. 192, and *Journal*, 1905, pp. 85–92 ; James, *Mind*, 1907, p 364, *Journal*, 2nd March 1905 ; Perry, *Journal*, 1st August 1907 ; Bradley, *Mind*, 1904, p. 309 ; Bakewell, *Philosophical Review*, 1907, p. 625.

See also A. Seth Pringle-Pattison, 1912–1913, *Gifford Lectures : The Idea of God in the Light of Recent Philosophy*, 1917, p. 387 : "Pluralism in various forms is so current, I had almost said so fashionable, at the present moment."

Ward, *The Realm of Ends*, 1912 : Pluralism now in the ascendant. May Sinclair, *A Defence of Idealism*, 1917, p. vii : "They mean that nineteenth-century monism is a philosophy of the Past and that twentieth-century pluralism is the living philosophy of the Future."

See also the Symposium of the Aristotelian Society, *Proceedings*, 1917–1918, p. 479, and Joad, "Monism in the Light of the Recent Development of Philosophy," *ibid.*, 1916–1917, p. 95 ; also, Aristotelian Society, Supplementary Volume II. : Papers read at the Joint Session, July 1919, pp. 109–158.

In recent works and articles, the word Pluralistic is used with a very extended meaning : "The pluralistic or democratic conception of the State," Leighton, *The Field of Philosophy*, Columbus, 1919, p. 159. "The Pluralistic State," an article by Laski, *Philosophical Review*, 1919, pp. 563–575. "Pluralistic Behaviour," an article by Giddings (here "pluralistic" becomes synonymous with "social") in *The American Journal of Sociology*, 1920, pp. 385–404 ; "The Metaphysical Monist as Sociological Pluralist," communicated by M. W. Calkins, summed up in *The Philosophical Review*, 1920, p. 167 (here "pluralistic" becomes synonymous with "individualist").

BOOK III

WILLIAM JAMES

WILLIAM JAMES is undeniably the most important of the
" pluralistic pragmatists." At the outset we find in his
works on the problem of unity and diversity only ideas
" expressed in passing," as Dickinson Miller says. But
previous to the year 1900, Dickinson Miller was in a
position to declare that the views of James were directed,
in the eyes of a true observer, towards as coherent, radical,
and individual a " vision of the world " as any one of the
philosophies produced by the nineteenth century. This
metaphysics assumed increasing importance in the opinion
both of his contemporaries and of James himself.[11]

How did James come to adopt this theory ? To his
mind, a philosophy is a sort of translation of the way of
seeing things, of reasoning, and of feeling ; finally, it is
an expression of temperament. An analysis of the particular and concrete way in which James likes to see
things, and actually does see them, will enable us partially
to understand his philosophical individuality.

By nature, James is an empiricist. Moreover, his master,
Agassiz, had developed in him, when studying natural
science, the tendency to recognise nothing but facts :

[11] Letter to M. Flournoy, 30th April 1903 : " What I want to get at,
and let no interruption interfere, is at last my *system* of tychistic and
pluralistic philosophy of pure experience."

" Go to nature," said Agassiz, " take facts in your hands."
He was the enemy of all " abstractionists." And James
calls to mind that he frequently cited the lines in which
Goethe contrasts with theory the green and golden-fruited
tree of life. For Agassiz, life consisted in seeing facts.
Chauncey Wright, " the Harvard empiricist of my youth,"
likewise taught James that we must hold fast to facts as
they are and look upon nature as a sequence of quite
simple facts, as an endless construction and destruction.
In the mysticism of Emerson, as in the lessons of Agassiz
and the empiricism of Chauncey Wright, James recognised
this cult of the fact. " The day we have most perceptions,
said Emerson, " should be marked with a white stone."
All these ideas and counsels did but strengthen natural
tendencies. "There was not a single fact," said his
brother, Henry James, " which, *qua* fact, did not give
him a certain amount of pleasure."

The pragmatist indulges in the cult of the particular.
According to Peirce's principle, should not ideas be tested
by being applied to particular realities ? James was
attracted towards pragmatist ideas, mainly, perhaps, by
the nominalist character of the doctrine; "the point lying
rather in the fact," he said before the Philosophical Union
of the University of California, " that the experience must
be particular than in the fact that it must be active ";
the idea must fit into the sequence of immediate experience at a particular point, just when a definite wavelet is
passing, so as to flow along with it. Attachment to the
particular, to percepts in contrast with concepts, is the
distinctive mark of the modern philosopher. The world
is a world of particulars.

Let absolutists indulge in the perverse worship of
abstraction ; James prefers the wretched particular facts
which the absolutist regards as confused, worthless, and

unwholesome. "The knowledge which most deserves adoration," he says in his *Psychology*, "should be the knowledge of the most adorable things; things of worth are all concrete and particular." Assuredly abstract minds have in the universal scheme of things a place of their own, he thinks, just as concrete minds have; but if we would know which of the two types is nearer the divine, there can be no doubt as to the answer.

James draws near to things, and looks at them closely; the monist is he who, placing himself far above things, sees them blend into one another; the pluralist regards each as having a distinct existence.

James likes to feel himself living in the midst of finite human lives, immersed in a finite stream of feeling, in presence of a world of finite experiences. Pragmatism, regarded as the consideration of precise consequences, is but the logical result of that whereof pluralism is the metaphysical result. It is not difficult to understand how valuable James regarded Renouvier's teaching.

Attention to detail and the consideration of things in the plural are expressions of the same tendencies realised both in pragmatism and in pluralism. To James, pragmatism is the struggle against "Truth with a big 'T' and in the singular." What he wants is *things* regarded in their plurality.

As James says in his *Pragmatism*, there exists a strictly empirical temperament, enamoured of facts rather than of principles, of parts rather than of the whole, and one that would see " the very dirt of private fact."

In *Some Problems of Philosophy*, this idea of particularity is even more evident than in the preceding works. James regards as identical the idea of particular and that of parts; to him, empiricism is essentially a philosophy of the fragmentary, of the scattered.

The vision of each of the parts of the universe cannot be evoked by words or images taken from the other parts ; it is what it is, unique in itself.   We cannot define in general terms the qualities of our sensations as breadth or space, nor the qualities of our mind as spontaneity. The sense of the particular is that of the specific.

The world peopled with particular, concrete, definite things, seen in their detail and in all their differences, will be a sort of thicket, a superabundant world.   We must insist on the fact that love of detail in James is always accompanied with respect for the concrete whole.   The concrete is not only fact considered in its particularity, it is also fact regarded as a whole.   Fact is irreducible, because it is both totality and particularity ; finally the two characters imply each other.   Empiricists like Hume on the one hand, and intellectualists on the other, isolate one of these characters ; James, with his concrete vision, prefers to unite them closely.   He deals in masses of durations, spatial densities, irreducible sensations.   That world, said a friend of his, cannot be arranged and connected into as clear a system as it might be were it made up of smaller units.   The sense of concrete totalities is the negation of the idea of an abstract whole.

James regards sensations as something extended in space ; in a certain sense, the human soul itself is corporeal.   James, the psychologist, possesses not only a soul sense but also a body sense.   And not only sensations, but all things, possess density.   Absolutism is content with *thin* ideas.   To classic empiricism, to the empiricism of Hume and Berkeley, concrete though it be, facts have but one side ; you cannot get round them, it is a flat philosophy. Here, with James, we have a philosophy in space, where the facts are solids.   James endeavours above all else to preserve the integrity of perception, as he expresses it.   A true instinct, it has been said, impels him in the direction of the concrete. To fix his eyes on the stream of the concretes, to cling to the concrete character of things, is one of his essential objects. He is ever on the look out for expressions which will more perfectly translate this eagerness for the concrete ; he seeks after plenitude and density. And as pragmatism is the epistemological development of this concrete mode of vision, so pluralism is its metaphysical development.

William James possesses the clear imagination of the savant and the highly coloured imagination of the artist, as well as the sense of reality of both. Did he not think of becoming an artist before he became a physiologist ? He especially possesses what might be called the imagination of the pyschologist. Dickinson Miller has rightly insisted on this fact : according to him, the philosophy of James is the work of one who possesses more than anything else " the sense of our real way of feeling ; he cannot bear that philosophy should not take into account the very sensation we have of life." What James upholds is that consciousness is what it seems to us. Here we have the essential difference between psychology and other sciences. Truth in consciousness is appearance, and appearance truth. In order to know what things or ideas are, the surest way is not to despoil them of all their qualities and try to find out what they are in themselves ; we must rather consider the aspect in which they appear to us ; what things are for us, in so far as they are known by us, that is the essential. Things must be taken for what they appear to us in the knowledge we have of them, for what they are known as, with their finite, their active character, and in this way we shall be brought both to pragmatism and to pluralism. Pragmatism and pluralism are a rehabilitation of appearance. Indeed, such expressions as " to seem," " the appearance " for the most part by no means signify to James illusion, but rather, true reality. " These partial designs seem to unfold themselves after and alongside one another," " the appearance of things is invincibly pluralistic " means to him that this is so in reality. His criticism of ideas, for instance, of the idea of unity, is essentially a psychological criticism. By studying what the idea of unity means to us we finally discover in it many different ideas.

M. Bergson tells us that the ideas of any true philosopher can be traced back to a very simple vision, that they radiate from a single point. To James, this simple vision was no doubt originally psychological in its nature. "On the one hand," says Professor R. B. Perry, "stands the environment, an unbidden presence tolerating only what will conform to it, threatening and hampering every interest and yielding only reluctantly to moral endeavour. On the other hand stands man, who, once he gets on good terms with this environment, finds it an inexhaustible mine of possibilities. . . . ' By slowly cumulative strokes of choice,' he has extracted out of this, like a sculptor, the world he *lives* in."

Consequently James lays stress on the way in which things appear to us, the way in which we feel them. Hence his anxiety that they should retain their own distinctive atmosphere ; hence also his determination that realities should correspond to our ideas : an onto-logical sense, it might be called. He looks upon any theory of the outer world which does away with the idea of externality as of necessity inadequate. A primitive idea is more than an idea : it is simultaneously an idea and an existence.

Hence also the feeling he has of the infinite worth of

each human being. Like Emerson and Whitman, he is conscious how infinitely profound is individuality; he would speak not to the abstract reason which is in man but to the man himself, to the companion, or, as Whitman would say, to the comrade; he approaches him, and, instead of a philosopher speaking to the intellect, we have one comrade speaking to another.

In this world there is no immutable hierarchy; each being is of equal importance. The philosophy of the particular is a democratic philosophy. And is it not the voice of " democratic common sense " to which James wishes to listen, and does he not want to see the world as it appears at first sight ?

Like common sense, the empirical mind will be characterised by a certain reserve in deducing the consequences of an accepted theory, by a certain power of self-restraint, of opposition to the invasion of the field of consciousness by a theory. The empiricist is kept from absolute conclusions by his critical scepticism, he refrains from believing in the ideas that attract him. At the outset, James was attracted by the idea of unity and simplicity, as his father had been. But this idea he resists : he affirms it in one way and denies it in another. Does not sober common sense supply us with lessons in caution ? Does it not see things partly joined and partly disjoined, partly saved and partly lost ?

On the other hand, we must not be too strict in our philosophy, occasionally the links between ideas must be more or less relaxed ; from this point of view the pragmatism of James is a sort of intellectual anarchism, a non-critical philosophy ; as Carus has called it, a relaxed way of philosophising.

Similarly the philosopher may permit himself, apart from and above the present realities, to dream of another world, of other worlds, provided they be the most concrete and definite possible. This idea assumes an increasingly important place in the philosophy of James.

Seeing things in this way, each moment will appear to us like a new universe ; there will be something original, something youthful in nature ; we shall have come back to a candid contemplation of things, to the first appearance of the world.

But were we to content ourselves with noting these characteristics of the philosophy of James, we should not then discover all the profound reasons which impelled him towards pluralism. We must see what, to his mind, constitutes the very basis of the pluralistic temperament. He has said that what divides philosophers into " supporters and opponents of possibility " is difference in belief, what he calls postulates of rationality. " That which makes of us monists or pluralists, determinists or indeterminists, is invariably some sentimental reaction at bottom." From the year 1882 onwards, he sees that two " mental dispositions " oppose each other in philosophy : on the one hand, those content with a passive conception of things, who are, as he says, fair-weather adherents ; and on the other hand, strong and active temperaments. He applies himself to set down with ever greater distinctness the contrast between these two temperaments. He contrasts the strenuous man with the careless, indifferent man ; and, in his *Varieties of Religious Experience*, wholesome philosophical beliefs with unwholesome philosophical beliefs. This idea of mental sanity also reappears from time to time in *Pragmatism*, though here it is between the tough-minded man, and the tender-minded man that the dilemma most frequently arises. As we have said, James delights in violent contrasts ; perhaps it was from Renouvier that he learnt to state these dilemmas. It is, he says, between the tough-minded man, an empiricist, irreligious, a materialist, pessimist, fatalist, pluralist, and sceptic, on the one hand, and the tender-minded man, on the other hand, that the fight is being waged.

Assuredly James does not accept all the beliefs of the hard soul; it often seems as though he would like to reconcile the contending parties. But in most of his works, except perhaps in certain passages of *A Pluralistic Universe*, he feels attracted, if not by all the ideas of the hard soul, at all events by the way in which it is able to accept these ideas. Perhaps, also, the terms of the dilemma which have been set up by James are too simplified. Does not this insurmountable desire that characterises the tough-minded man, this desire to be submerged, to lose himself in the ocean of things, cause us to recognise in him certain aspirations which might equally well characterise what James calls the tender soul, a mystical urge towards martyrdom?

However this may be, James feels within himself a long-standing hardness of heart, which he says is an ultimate characteristic. It is this that explains why he writes a psychology of materialistic tendencies, why he experienced a deep repugnance for the very word—soul —and why he is always, and above all else, an empiricist.

Tough-minded men boldly confront facts. Empiricism is above all a stern and difficult belief. Hume's philosophy "makes events rattle against their neighbours as drily as if they were dice in a box." No fact will have a privileged place. The tough mind is fond of whatever equalises and democratises; it is opposed to aristocracies of every kind. Thus we have, first, a difficult and arduous method which will not rise above facts, which will only deal with them piecemeal, and deal with them just as they are, and, second, the conception of a world solely made up of series of facts : such is the empiricism of the hard soul.   And there are times when William James saw the ultimate philosophy in this conception, for which existence is a crude fact of which the logic must never be examined.

But especially to this hardness of soul does he owe that element which makes of him primarily a pluralist, a feeling of joy when confronted with conflicting forces, the love of effort and adventure, and a certain sombre and stern vision of the world.   It is doubtless under the influence of Calvinism and Puritanism, or perhaps through the tradition of Jonathan Edwards, that he learnt to conceive at times a transcendental deity acting arbitrarily on a world in part radically evil : perhaps Cotton Mather taught him to believe in that " crude supernaturalism " which he made an integral part of his philosophy.

Carlyle, the descendant of a Puritan race, continued this Calvinistic teaching in a renewed form : James learned to " look out on life with its strange scaffolding, where all at once harlequins dance and men are beheaded and quartered ; motley, not unterrific was the aspect, but we looked on it like brave youths." James, as well as Carlyle, admires life as it appears " in red streaks of unspeakable grandeur yet also in the blackness of darkness." He follows him into " those most shadow-hunting and shadow-hunted Pilgrimings." Everywhere around us is necessity, everywhere the din and clash of collisions, everywhere the tumultuous struggle between good and evil.   Such is " the whole pageant of Existence . . . with its wail and jubilee, mad loves and mad hatreds, church bells and gallows ropes, farce-tragedy, beast-god-hood, the Bedlam of Creation ! " " Thus like some wild-flaming, wild-thundering train of Heaven's Artillery, does this mysterious MANKIND thunder and flame, in long-drawn, quick-succeeding grandeur, through the unknown Deep."

Whilst affording James a vision of this motley world, this world of peril and adventure, Carlyle taught him to sense the deep reality of time, the ever moving delusive and dazzling groundwork and foundation of this world, already in itself so dazzling, and so delusion-producing. "Our whole of being is based in Time and built of Time. Time is the author of it." There is no repose in things ; they are in a state of perpetual flux. The vesture of Eternity is being woven unceasingly.

If we work, it may be that, with the help of Time, we shall be able to obliterate some of the black square patches of which at least half the garb of the cosmic harlequin consists ; so let us fight on. "Victory is only possible by battle." "Yes, to men also was given, if not Victory, yet the consciousness of Battle, and the resolve to persevere therein while life and faculty is left." We must make an effort, set ourselves free. "Too-heavy-laden Teufelsdröckh ! Yet surely his bands are loosening ; one day he will hurl the burden far from him and bound forth free and with a second youth." "Our life is compassed round with Necessity ; yet is the meaning of life no other than Freedom, than Voluntary Force." "Canst thou not trample Tophet itself under thy feet while it consumes thee ?"

Carlyle insists on the "large liberty" there is in the world, on the possibility of choice, on what he calls the right to vote of every element in the world.

It is comprehensible that James, mindful of the lessons of *Sartor Resartus*, aware of all that he owed to Carlyle, showed himself at the outset almost as one of his disciples. From him, as was the case with many young men of his generation, he had learnt that activity, conduct, and work —not knowledge alone—are the essential objects and aims of life.

Browning also taught the ever-renewed struggle that enables man to work, combat, and rise higher, the infinite importance of danger.

As we have seen, the Americans have profited by this doctrine of effort. After Carlyle, Emerson, though in a gentler and more mystical way, raises aloft the banner of courage. In Whitman, James saw a vision of the world struggle, the war that is longer and vaster than any war.

Finally, he discovered in Blood, an almost unknown author, a union or blend between mysticism and pluralism similar to that of his dream. Hegelian first, the vortex of thought, which, as James said, was in the soul of Blood, causes him to abandon Hegelianism. Above all he is an irrationalist; whereas reason is an equation, " nature," he says, " is an excess." " Nature is essentially contingent, excessive, and mystical. . . . Things are strange . . . they have cactus forms. . . . The universe is wild, game-flavored as a hawk's wing. The same returns but to introduce the different. The slow circle of the engraver's lathe gains but a hair's-breadth. But the difference is distributed over the entire curve, never exactly adequate." These formulas prove Blood to be both a realist and a mystic: a realist, seeing that he recognises no causes or reasons apart from " the present state and the given fact "; a mystic, for the fact is as he says, a fact supernaturally given, " the whole of nature is but a prodigy." Blood believes in will and reason, though only in so far as they are mystically realised, lived in experience.

Thus finally this philosophy is a voluntarism. " Up from the breast of man, up to his tongue and brain, comes a free and strong determination, and he cries, originally and in spite of his whole nature and environment : ' I will ! ' This is the Jovian fiat, the pure cause. This is reason, this or nothing shall explain the world for him."

Things then should no longer be thought of as parts of a system, but as facts that determine themselves. And these facts are scattered throughout space and time. The universe is one great contingent process.

Hence a sort of scepticism . . . though courageous scepticism. " The fact is that we do not know, but when we say that we do not know, we should not say it softly and feebly, we should say it with confidence and satisfaction . . . knowledge is and should always be a secondary consideration."

James has fully experienced that new ruggedness of which Whitman and Blood sang ; what he asks of reality, perhaps above all else, is " that element which any strong man feels without a sense of repugnance because in it he is conscious of an appeal made to powers within himself : the rough and the hard, the buffeting of the waves, the cold north wind." In his articles of 1882, James was already delighting in this world storm, this " ocean's poem " as Whitman would have expressed it. But at that time this would appear to have been almost a contemplative and æsthetic attitude. Life indeed seemed to him a drama, but the philosopher saw himself rather in the pit than on the stage ; the play " interested " him. " Rather drop the curtain before the final act," he wrote, " to preserve from so amazingly dull a *dénouement* a plot the beginning of which had been so intensely interesting." Even now, however, we note the idea of the existence of powers we must oppose, of a fight in which we must engage ; he speaks of the " crude fact against which we must react." A new feeling is struggling within him, different from that half-materialistic, half-mystical feeling in which the individual wished to be caught up and crushed by forces that were not individual, different too from that pluralist æsthetic feeling just mentioned. The individual must stand firm against the fact itself; the soul must no longer say to the enveloping flood, "Rise, even though thou art to sink us," but rather, "Rise, thou shalt not sink us." James tells us that he would not willingly renounce that element which gives the outer world "all its moral style, expressiveness, and picturesqueness—the element of precipitousness, so to call it, of strength and strenuousness, intensity and danger." "The universe," Blood had said, "is wild—game-flavored as a hawk's wing." William James appreciates this flavour, which adds so much to the value of life. He delights in this "never-ending battle between the powers of light and the powers of darkness"; "here heroism must take its chance, it can rely only on itself"; and yet, here and there "he snatches victory from the jaws of death." "Sweat and effort, human nature strained to its uttermost and on the rack, yet getting through alive"; this it is that fills with joy the man of strenuous heart. He loves "the old heights and depths and romantic chiaroscuro." Smiling and peaceful landscapes possess no attraction for him; in their presence he has the feeling of a tame nature, lacking in spontaneity, the feeling of the "atrocious harmlessness of things." "Let me take my chances again in the big outside worldly wilderness with all its sins and suffering. There are the heights and depths, the precipices and the steep ideals, the gleams of the awful and the infinite."

Deep in the soul of the pluralist is a sort of contradictory desire: the desire on the one hand to feel himself half crushed by the forces against which he struggles, levelling and democratising forces; he wants the sensation of limits he cannot transcend. But along with this desire to feel cramped, so to speak, the pluralist abhors anything that is well arranged, ordered, regular. He wishes to breathe freely, to " take his chance " ; he does not wish to feel that he is living in a prosy, commonplace way, " close to the ground," but rather that he is up aloft, with expanded vision in the midst of aerial perspectives. His philosophy would leave windows and doors wide open. " A radical pragmatist," says James, " is a happy-go-lucky anarchistic sort of creature." Seeing that the essences are scattered about throughout time and space, the man eager for all the fullness of life must grasp them in their strung-along, disseminated, and moving forms.

The paradise of James is the very world itself, with all its crags and cliffs ; what he wants is to live a strenuous life, to " snatch from the game of life its greatest possibilities of excitement." " Son of man," he says as a disciple of Carlyle, " be not afraid of life ; stand firm on thy feet." Accept Nature's offer, risk something in life's battle, risk something, he adds with his master Renouvier, in the search for truth : " There may be observed in men of valiant soul the desire to enjoy some measure of uncertainty in their philosophical beliefs, just as the element of risk acts as a spur in the material order of things."

The world he desires is an ever-changing world ; a motionless spectacle bores him. Hence his love for things in their flux and their becoming, hence his vision of the universe, *sub specie temporis*, in its incessant novelty.

Thus we find complete opposition between the tendencies of this mind and those of a rationalist. " The rationalist mind, radically taken, is of a doctrinaire and authoritative complexion : the phrase ' *must* be ' is ever on its lips, the bellyband of its universe must be tight."

He is on the look out for an *inconcussum aliquid*, a certainty within which he may rest, for *terra firma* ; he loves noble architecture beneath a peaceful sky. He thinks that the world conforms with the postulates of his rationality and morality : "What should exist surely does exist." It is useless to transform things, they are certainly good at bottom. Idle and finally amoral, he casts all responsibility upon the absolute; the absolute sanctions everything, though of course it does nothing.

In presence of the moving world of the pluralist, ever tossed about by clashing waves, the monist experiences a sort of sea-sickness, or rather : " A friend once said to me that the thought of my universe made him sick, as though he were watching a swarming mass of vermin on a carrion heap." " The idea of this ' loose ' universe affects your typical rationalists in much the same way as ' freedom of the press ' might affect a veteran official in the Russian bureau of censorship, or as simplified spelling might affect an elderly school-mistress ; . . . it appears as backboneless and devoid of principle as ' opportunism ' in politics appears to an old-fashioned French legitimist or to a fanatical believer in the divine right of the people."

Still, in spite of his profound sympathy with all who can appreciate the bitterness of pessimism, who can doubt and even blaspheme, who gird themselves with the haircloth of fatalism, as with all who live free in a world that lends itself to their creative activity, with all those hard enough to endure being crushed, as with those minds hard enough to go to the extreme of anarchy, James is unable to follow them right to the end. At first a pragmatist and a " democrat," he recognises that the idea of the absolute may be useful, perhaps necessary, for feeble souls ; seemingly more consistent than Schiller, he admits that different philosophies are needed for different temperaments. More than this, in many passages he offers his philosophy as an attempt at reconciliation or of mediation between the two types of mind. Insistence has been laid on this kind of sentimental eclecticism in the philosophy of James. On this point there is a certain contradiction between pragmatism and pluralism, the pluralism, at all events, of the hard-soul type. And finally there are in him certain tendencies that do not seem to be of the hard-soul type. Did he not attempt to criticise, in many of its details, what he calls the sensationalist doctrine? Is there not in his nature a certain religion, a certain spiritualism, and a certain optimism which, though they are not the religion and spiritualism and optimism of soft-minded men, are also not the characteristic beliefs of men of the hard-soul type? In all his works, from *The Will to Believe* right on to *A Pluralistic Universe*, are we not aware of his need to know that, within the inmost being of the universe, there exist consciousnesses that sympathise with his own? Do we not discover here the belief he first held that realities in the universe answer to the needs of the human soul? It may be that in former days, when conversing with his father, Swedenborg's dreamy speculations had proved attractive to him.

By his very desire, man discovers new things in nature, James tells us in *A. Pluralistic Universe*. Nature responds to our calls and feelings. " Things reveal themselves soonest to those who most passionately want them. . . . To a mind content with little, the much in the universe may always remain hid."

Here James shows himself both sentimental and mystical. No doubt at the back of his mind persisted the transcendentalist and finally Swedenborgian ideas of his father. Nevertheless this mysticism, which in certain passages may seem to go against pluralism, is for the most part deeply allied with pluralism in the mind of James. To begin with, the mystical idea frequently assumes in him the aspect, so apparent in men like Coleridge, Carlyle, and Emerson, of a sense of the infinite profundity of things : every instant has a meaning of its own, everything a boundless significance. And in spite of all the efforts of language and thought, " private sensations " remain incapable of being gauged. Is not this transcendentalist feeling of the ineffability of things also a pluralist feeling ? Each thing seems to be a sort of infinity, all things partake of infinity and are equal. James is able to enjoy the " sense of life which every moment brings," the very fullness of life. This sense, this cult of the present moment, made him conscious of the emptiness of all doctrines that claim to reduce the world to unity and to know its secret. Here, translated in terms of feeling and mysticism, we find the love of the concrete and the particular already mentioned ; under the influence of transcendentalism, nominalistic theories, still so thin when expounded by Mill, for instance, assume form and life. This empiricism of James seems to possess a certain mystical element. The influence of Thomas Davidson and of his " apeirotheistic " doctrine was also to be exercised in the same direction.

In another way too, this feeling made a pluralist of James. If endless suffering exists and we have to realise in ourselves the sufferings of others, then we are conscious that good does not reign alone in the world ; a truly compassionate soul cannot believe in an optimistic monism ; the suicides related in the book of Morrison I. Swift ought to be sufficient to keep a moral person away from absolutism.

As with Emerson and Whitman, so with James, any

man is his neighbour in suffering and his comrade in strife; just as he possesses a sense of the material density of things, so he has a sense of that spiritual density which makes up personality.

No doubt, too, he inherited from his father that idea of "human fellowship," an expression frequently used both in speaking and in writing, said Henry James, the novelist, referring to his father. Thomas Davidson also had taught him the worship of personality, of the soul.

It may be that pluralism is a variety of "philosophic experience." Though he denies that mystical experiences were the origin of his philosophical theories, James seems at times to speak of mystical hours he has spent, where in the silence of speculation he has felt beat the pulse of being and new epochs of his thought spring into birth. Perhaps it was at such times that the pluralist conception appeared and developed in his mind. The very psychology of James is impregnated, one might say, with mysticism; even certainty is for him a sort of feeling, a sense of the idea as in contact with warm reality. Empiricism and mysticism become fused into each other, this deepening of experience, this mystery felt in it, are still experience itself. Thus, even more than in transcendentalism, the mystery that transcends facts is yet in a sense within the facts themselves.

James's empiricism even at times appears as allied to romanticism, as the vision of facts in their strangest characters. The new psychology, he says, is full of "Gothic monsters." He speaks of "romantic facts." Was not Gothic architecture also both naturalism and mysticism? We can understand the discussions that took place between William James and his brother Henry with reference to Delaroche and Delacroix. To William James, Delacroix is "always and everywhere interesting."

In the *Barque du Dante*, he liked that beauty made up of
" queerness " ; everywhere in the works of the romantic
painter is the sense of the ineffable, more especially of
the incalculable.   On several occasions his brother dwells
on the love he had for the " queer or incalculable effects
of things."

Thus, his philosophy is both empiricism and mysticism ;
it is also both empiricism and romanticism.

However it may be, it is not the mystical soul, but
rather the strong, tough soul which most clearly shows
itself in the philosophy of James.   The philosopher must
have a vision of his own, he says in *A Pluralistic Universe*.
What was present in the mind of James, previous to all
theory about mental sanity or mental hardness, was a
great fresco : shadows and dazzling lights, crags and
precipices, and the strivings of men.

THE CRITICISM OF MONISM AND RADICAL EMPIRICISM

Pluralism sets itself over against monism.   The pluralist theory begins with a refutation of monism.

It may be that James did not oppose monism at the
outset ; when he began to philosophise he would have
wished that " any separate phenomenon should be regarded as fundamentally identical with any other phenomenon."   He wanted to experience the existence of a
sort of fundamental homogeneity of the universe ; he
sought a kind of philosophical opium, a world method
both sentimental and mystical whereby we might satisfy
our moral and intellectual needs and the full expectation
of the human soul.   He did not then think that some
day he would actually endeavour to embrace a philosophy
inacceptable at first sight (on certain points, at least) for
our sentimental needs, and understand that the essence

of the moral life is not to " feel oneself in conformity
with what the great All demands." He was not insensible to the Hegelian influence which really always
remained more or less pronounced in his mind.

But he soon sees that there may come about an un-
healthy hypertrophy of the sense of unity; he knows
how to confine his aspirations towards unity within
right bounds by leaving intact " the incommensurable
sensations" and the principles, monads, or atoms which
at the time he looked upon as necessary for deducing
the concrete world.

Only by degrees did monistic doctrines appear to him
dangerous and to be condemned. In the *Dilemma of
Determinism*, published in 1884, James demonstrates the
incompatibilities between action and the idea of unity;
in the *Berkeley Speech* he applies his logical method to
the problem of unity. We find, scattered about most of
his works, criticisms directed against monism.

He did not feel the scorn for absolutism that Schiller
did; for he knew that it was a salutary reaction against
the arid atheism of certain representatives of the associa-
tionist school, that it was bent on enveloping facts in
wider harmonies. More and more, however, he sees in
it a philosophy too ultra-simple : " a simple conception," he says, " is the equivalent of the world only to
the extent in which the world is simple "; life and
nature are superabundant, naturally frittered away and
squandered.

For James, pluralism is the most noticeable, the
choicest example which enables us most effectively to
see the nature of a method that takes the idea of unity
as it appears in our consciousness and endeavours to find
out what definite results it may have in our experience ;
in the *Berkeley Speech* and in *Pragmatism* he resumes,

almost in the same terms, his criticism of the idea of unity, and offers this criticism as the clearest example of the way in which concepts must be determined pragmatically.

The method which James uses for dissociating the idea of unity—and dissociation of this idea is its destruction —is a positive, psychological, particular, and practical method. We ought to study the appearances both of unities and of diversities in the world as it is " known as." The world will have just as many unities, just as many diversities as it appears to have. Therefore the method will be essentially one of experience and of restriction.

Only in this way can we make our ideas clear, the essential aim of the pragmatic method, as Peirce said ; we must not be satisfied with repeating number one or number two or any other number, we must see the different ways in which these numbers act in experience, in personal life. We shall inquire which theory suggests most details, which sets working the greatest number of definite activities. We shall wish to know not only whether the world consists of one or more elements but where these elements are to be found, from what exact point of view diversity appears and from what point of view unity appears. It is not a question of origin that we shall ask ourselves, we shall simply try to determine present and, even more, future relations.

By this method the definitions of the ideas themselves will be transformed ; for instance the unity of an object will be practically defined by the possibility of passing continuously from one point of it to another.

Thus we shall be led to see, not unity in its unity, but rather, if we may so express it, in its diversity, and so to realise intellectually each particular unity in a particular way.

Here pragmatism is a " purely intellectual " way of

dealing with the problem of the one and the many. James denounces the sentimentality of the monist who seeks for unity at all costs; no doubt the word unity possesses emotional value and that is an important value from the point of view of pragmatism; but here James wishes first to determine its purely intellectual value, to see how we can form a clear mental picture of unity. Here then we find ourselves confronted not with a mystical James, nor even with a James holding an ethical conception of pragmatism, but with an almost intellectualistic James.

Nevertheless, the moral consequences of the idea should have a part to play, and then pragmatism comes before us with all its characteristics. We must not have our eyes ever fixed on principles, but directed to their consequences and the resulting activities. Philosophy should be, in the expression frequently used by Dewey and his followers, essentially " prospective." " These ultimate questions turn, as it were, upon their hinges," as James says. Consequently he trusts to moral postulates; in this connection it is possible to speak of the moral character of his method. Above all, the world of will, of individual action, of moral realities, must not be an illusive world.

Thus indeed, taking into account the realities of nature and the realities of morals, we shall return to the data of common sense. Common sense tries to find the most economical solutions as well as those that afford most play to freedom of action.

Whenever a problem has to be solved, James endeavours to observe the facts, to distinguish and divide the terms, to see the consequences in concrete life, to feel the concrete needs of the human will. His method is at once that of a psychologist for whom reality and appearance are one, that of a practical person who insists on discovering in the world of facts the consequences of ideas, and that of a thinker resolved on criticising ideas as they are in themselves. Empiristic, intellectualist and pragmatist, psychological and scientific, bent on the converging studies of psychological experience, clear ideas, practical plans of action, distinct facts and profound inner necessities, this method would lead us again towards the original data of common sense.

Behind or below experience there is nothing but experience itself; experience stands out upon itself, is based upon itself, is self-contained and self-supporting. It is by starting with this conception that we are able to understand the criticism of unity as formulated by James. We must then study what radical empiricism is, what is that philosophy he conceived as a philosophy of identity under a pluralist form.

Let us just consider the real, that original flux which has not yet been conceptualised by our reflection. This real world, the world of solid objects, is also the world of our ideas; at bottom, extreme realism is identical with extreme idealism, and the realism of James has rightly been called an empirical idealism. And it is not only the critics of James who have used the word monism with reference to this conception wherein thought and being are blended in pure experience, it is James himself: " It is a monism if you will, though an altogether rudimentary one."

An irreducible multiplicity underlies this unity, and radical empiricism, which at first appears as the affirmation of identity between thought and being, also appears as the affirmation of an essential multiplicity. The world is so diverse that we cannot even say that it is wholly diverse, that it is solely multiple, discontinuous, and heterogeneous ; here and there are to be found continuous currents, homogeneous masses, unities.

This, according to James, is an empiristic philosophy, because in it the parts are more important than the whole, because the whole is but the sum of the parts, because it is " a philosophy of mosaics, of facts in the plural," of facts without support or substance other than themselves ; whereas rationalism tends to explain parts by the whole, empiricism sees the universe distributively, not collectively. James adds that this is a *radical* empiricism because it takes into account not only facts but also the relations between facts. This empiricism does not set up the dilemma between absolute unity and absolute diversity. There is a certain unity and also a certain diversity, and they are not incompatible, but rather complementary. And so his idea of the existence of relations makes this empiricism quite different from that of Hume, for instance. The various experiences rest upon nothing, but they rest upon one another. This is the reason why pluralist philosophy conceives the possibility of a compromise between unity and multiplicity. Those whom James calls the royalists of philosophy dub all their opponents with the general title of anarchists. To pluralism, however, the world is not a mass of incoherences as is the world of appearances to certain disciples of Bradley. It is by making itself " varied," as flexible, as rich, " as malleable as mother Nature," by accepting the whole of the real—democratically—that empiricism can be genuinely radical. It must therefore not be thought that, in order to be a pluralist, we must affirm multiplicity without any unity. The pluralism of James is as far from absolute pluralism as from absolute monism, but James likewise knows that pluralism is, in a sense, absolute in itself. The slightest thrill of independence,

the least separation between things, is enough to over-
throw the monist edifice. And so he can insist without
peril on the continuity and homogeneity of certain masses
of experiences, he can take the unity of things and their
variety as they offer themselves to us without being a
monist. Thus also he avoids the necessity of having
recourse to abstractions and substances, and in a general
way he avoids the criticism levelled against empiricism
by Green and his school. The relations between experiences are also themselves experiences. It is not only the
criticism of these monists that lose their value, it is their
theory itself on its positive side ; for it is based on the
affirmation that relations have an existence superior to
that of the terms they connect, that relations are universals ; in radical empiricism, relations are not less real
but they are also not less temporary, less contingent or
less particular than facts.

These relations are themselves essentially diverse ; they
vary from simple simultaneity, simple " withness," to
resemblance, to relations of activity, and finally to relations
between continuous states of consciousness, to the absolute
continuity of the stream of consciousness.

These relations are so independent of one another that
we may imagine a world in which there would be only
" withnesses " and nothing else, or one in which there
would be only correspondences in space and no resemblance whatsoever, or resemblances without activity, or
activities without design. And would not each of these
universes have its own particular degree of unity, and
may not our own universe be divided into certain parts,
some of which possess one kind of unity and the rest
another ?

The reason, then, that James admits relations into his
universe is by no means a determination to make it more

orderly, it is simply to make it more conformable to reality, and reality is rugged and chaotic. And so the universe of James is more rugged and chaotic than that of the empiricists of old. These relations and connections become involved, ravelled, knotted, and then unknotted. "You would have to compare," James tells us, "the empiricist universe to something more like one of those dried human heads with which the Dyaks of Borneo deck their lodges. The skull forms a solid nucleus, but innumerable feathers, leaves, strings, beads, and loose appendices of every description float and dangle from it, and, save that they terminate in it, seem to have nothing to do with one another."

Relations mostly seem to have nothing in common with one another except the fact that they happen to be together. Of course there are those immense general receptacles, time and space, and also the Ego. But does not space divide as well as unite? Besides, each mind, according to James, brings with it its own edition of space. Unity and continuity within self appear to be perfect, but is there not a gulf between each consciousness, and have we not here the most irreducible pluralism, the most utter insulation we can imagine? Everywhere the path to unity is obstructed with specific ideas or things. "The parts of the universe are, as it were, fired point-blank; each stands out as a simple fact which the other facts have in no way summoned, and which, so far as we can see, would form a much better system without them." Arbitrary, jolting, discontinuous, swarming, tangled, muddy, painful, fragmentary—such are some of the adjectives with which James attempts to qualify his universe. There is something crude, something jostling about the world. Everywhere we see the barriers breaking down which would make of the stream a continuous current; everywhere, in the Fechnerian metaphor, waves are forming which tumultuously dash against each other.

And yet amid this multiplicity, a certain unity is always perceived, a unity which, indeed, will finally not appear as less confused than this multiplicity itself; for it consists in the fact that we cannot attempt to isolate a phenomenon without this phenomenon resisting and proving itself as one with the rest of the universe. We see this readily when studying the self, but it is the same everywhere; each part is united with its neighbours by a sort of " inextricable interblending." We have just said that any fragment of the universe asserts itself as independent of all the rest; at the same time, each asserts itself as inextricably one with the rest.

What are these relations themselves and what is the nature of the bond they set up between the terms ? Sufficient attention has not been paid, James thinks, to certain kinds of relations, very common in our experience, similar to those of the adornments of the Dyak's skull to the skull itself; the bond between these adornments consists in the fact that they are all connected with the skull. Thus in the world there are numerous relations of " coterminousness," of confluence. When we find minds that know one and the same thing, we are dealing with experiences of confluence. Hence it can be understood how our consciousness fits itself into the outer world from time to time, at disconnected moments, how there exist interactions between it and the other consciousnesses at definite instants, also disconnected. There may be all sorts of floating, varied, free relations between things—contiguity, resemblance, simultaneity, proximity, superposition, intention, concomitance, and addition; in this way we see that there is a great amount or rate of disconnectedness in the world, that its unity is frequently a kind of concatenation, a relation between independent variables, a partial confluence of things.

If we believe in this independence, this fluidity of relations, we are thereby in possession of a new argument against Bradley's theories : why then believe that one thing in relation with another is in relation with it eternally ? There may be external determinations being made and unmade, momentary relations. James consequently arrives at a doctrine which may be compared with that of Moore and Russell. But it must be noted that, in his mind, the idea of external relations essentially implies the idea of the existence of time, and change of relations he regards less as mechanical displacement of universals in a wholly intellectual domain after the manner of the Cambridge logicians, than as movements to and fro in fluid duration.

Since relations are external to terms, these latter may have at the same time many relations : " this very desk which I strike with my hand strikes in turn your eyes ": a given thing is surrounded by numerous relations ; everywhere sameness is found at the heart of difference, and difference in the midst of sameness. The reason why radical empiricism tends towards pluralism is precisely because these superficial, momentary, and extrinsic relations are so numerous throughout the world.

The pluralist world is a world wherein certain phenomena may disappear, says James in *Some Problems of Philosophy*, without others being in any way affected by this disappearance ; it is a world in which the idea of absence corresponds to a reality ; " the monistic principle implies that nothing that is can in any way whatever be absent from anything else that is." That certain things have no relation whatever with certain others is the principle which might be called the principle of absence.

It is this principle, one might say, that makes possibility possible. Where there is totality, James would readily affirm, there cannot be possibility.

We see that the theory of external relations is nothing else than the affirmation of realism and pluralism, identical in their principle. " Pragmatically interpreted," says William James, " pluralism . . . means only that the sundry parts of reality *may be externally related.* Everything you can think of, however vast or inclusive, has on the pluralist view a genuinely ' external ' environment of some sort. Things are ' with ' one another in many ways, but nothing includes everything, or dominates over everything. Something always escapes. ' Ever not quite ' has to be said of the best efforts made anywhere in the universe at attaining all-inclusiveness."

Pluralism, realism, the pragmatist theory of knowledge, the theory of possibility, the theory of time, all these different conceptions of William James are aspects of this affirmation of the externality of relations, and it is this very affirmation that enables static realism—which is content to say that relations are external—to be transformed into a realism of the moving and changing world.

Will science succeed in unifying this world which appears to us so multiple ? But even in the domain of science itself, with its atomic and kinetic theories, we have the reappearance of primitive discontinuity. Besides, no scientific theory will permit us, in the concrete world, to pass from one quality *qua* quality to another quality.

Let us go now from the observation of reality and the observation of science to philosophical ideas and, no longer starting with facts in order to reach ideas, study in themselves these very ideas. To analyse them and to see their direction, we shall have to use the pragmatist-intellectualist method already defined. We now enter upon the criticism, strictly so called, of the idea of unity ; in what connections and from what points of view are we to affirm that the world is one ?

Do we mean by this that the world is one because it is named the world ? Do we mean a " unity of speech " ? Well then, the world is one ; but a chaos, once named, possesses quite as much of this verbal unity as does a cosmos. We stop the pluralist as soon as he begins to speak : " the universe," someone murmurs, " he mentioned the universe." Assuredly, but that is a simple question of words. And does even this unity, properly speaking, apply to the world ? Certainly not, it applies to the idea of the world ; or, to be even more precise, to the idea of the world in so far as this idea is mentally contrasted with that of other possible worlds.

Do we mean, in more substantial fashion, what might be called a unity of continuity ? Certainly there are continuities ; one might even not illegitimately say that there exists nothing else than one great continuity ; whatever things one chooses, by however long distances they may be separated, are finally united by several influences. Still, though physically there might appear to be continuity between the parts of the universe, such is not the case psychologically ; in order to go from one mind to the external world or to other minds, it is necessary, says the radical empiricist, to begin over again several times ; and to go over sorts of chasms ; minds are separate worlds, durations perceived by each of them are essentially different, and, moreover, pragmatism does not altogether fill up the gap between subject and object.

Shall we speak of unity of influence ? No doubt it

will be possible to follow many of these lines of influence in the world of radical empiricism ; here things overflow into one another, and these confluences are influences ; James, in spite of the idea of the externality of relations and the principle of absence, maintains in this connection that there is a sort of universal " participation " of things in one another.

Among these lines of confluence James places " the fact of getting to know things." The act of knowing is a kind of meeting-place between knower and known. Knowing is participation, though not a Platonic participation, but one in which the idea is on a level with the subject.

As there are systems of knowing, so there are systems of feeling.

So also are there instrumental systems formed by the agent and that wherewith he acts. In a hundred ways we unify the world, " by colonial and postal systems, by consulates and commerce." If only we choose aptly the intervening points, we can go from one point to another of the world continuously. But however slightly we miss our way, we find ourselves stopped, and the large amount of discontinuity which obtains in the world stands revealed.

After unity of influence, shall we speak of causal unity ? Shall we expect to find, in a single fiat, the origin wherefrom the multiple appearances diverge, like the many-coloured branches of a fan ? But why not conceive of an irreducible diversity at the beginning of the world ?

Are we to be told of generic unity, the unity of homogeneity ? This would perhaps be the unity most pregnant with consequences, the most interesting for a pragmatist, for we should then be authorised, thinks James, to use one and the same method for all parts of the universe and should always obtain the same results. But we cannot unify the world in this way; we can form certain groups of like phenomena, but the groups remain different from one another. And if we remind the radical empiricist of this elementary monism, this realism-idealism from which he started, he replies that that unity is but a unity of confluence, of participation, or perhaps only, though James does not say this expressly, the unity of background with respect to the multiplicity of figures on a picture.

If the philosopher dwells not on the past but on the future and on the meaning of the world, he may conceive of a unity of plan. But acts carried through consciously and voluntarily are rare in our experience, improbable in the universe. Besides, we are ever witnessing a struggle of wills and opposing plans. Then, too, the very appearance of evil in the universe causes us to reject the hypothesis of a providence controlling it in a certain and determined fashion.

And lastly, no longer following the chain of events in the past nor continuing it into the future, if we would embrace the world in one glance, we are able to conceive of two kinds of unity: the one æsthetic, the other logical.

The desire for " æsthetic " unity does not meet with entire satisfaction; things do not relate one story but several stories, which either intermingle or follow one another.

The desire for logical noetic unity, for unity of the world within the consciousness that knows it, the last and most subtle trick of monistic metaphysics which, in order to unify the world, asks simply for the look of this " one knower," leads us only to contradictions, and we are unable to arrive at complete noetic unity; we know only partial " knowers " on the one hand, and on the other particular objects, the concrete details of which would disappear once they were apprehended in a universal consciousness.

This critical analysis which destroys monism by splitting up the idea of unity, and by bringing the fragments of the idea into contact with the experiences against which what remains of it is broken, is several times met with in the works of James ; at first he had not conceived of the most spiritual and refined kinds of unity (unity of plan, æsthetic unity), and noetic unity had appeared in a less general form in the *Berkeley Speech* than in *Pragmatism*. In *Problems* the discussion assumes a somewhat different aspect and starts with a distinction between the various kinds of monism. But as a whole these critical analyses offer the same characteristics, they are connected with the same empiristic tendency which is also found in *Problems*, but here and in *A Pluralistic Universe* there is a change in one very important point. Whereas previously James sometimes opposed monism almost as an intellectualist, and with rationalistic weapons, in *A Pluralistic Universe*, he uses those given to him by anti-intellectualism and seems even to be an opponent of monism, not so much because it is a doctrine of unity as because it then appears to him a doctrine of the intellect.

James criticises the idea of allness as he does that of unity. The idea of *all* may be held either in a material or in a spiritual sense. If held in a material sense, it really corresponds to nothing, for in the physical world there is no such thing as allness ; there are but elements, such as our sense data ; it is the mind alone that constitutes wholes. On the other hand, if the idea of allness is held in a spiritual sense, then the whole appears as different from the parts, as produced by the reaction of a higher witness on elements. Thus on the one side we are confronted with empiricism, on the other with theism, but nowhere is a pantheistic and absolutist conception implied.

Let us admit for a moment the idea of the absolutists. Will it be said that our truths and our errors, our evil and good actions, exist and find their reconciliation, transmuted, in the absolute ? But it is no less true that there is one point of view, our own particular one, where error is contrasted with truth, good with evil. Consequently, it would be necessary to say that each error, each evil action on the one hand is in the absolute and is there as a certain degree of good or of truth, and that on the other hand each of them is within ourselves and appears here as evil and error. But then, if it is the absolute that considers me, I appear along with all the rest of the universe within the field of its perfect knowledge ; if it is I who consider myself, I appear separate, I appear with all my needs and all my faults within the field of my relative ignorance. This ignorance and this knowledge are not devoid of consequences in practice, because for me ignorance produces defect, curiosity, misfortune, pain. Consequently there are things which are true of the world considered in its finite aspects and not true of the world considered in its infinite capacity. Consequently there is for absolutism a sort of radical discrepancy in the world. This applies specially to such a philosophy as that of Royce, where the absolute is regarded as a sort of passive spectator. Thus we find a contradiction in idealism, since on the one hand it tends to admit that being and appearance are one, and on the other hand it admits of an essential distinction between them.

The philosophy of Royce cannot evade pluralism. It admits of a sort of hierarchy in points of view on phenomena, but these different points of view, these different witnesses can only be persons, and so pluralism is introduced. And the fact of the existence of persons, continues James, is not a defect in the universe, for there is a sort of excess of ourselves over the absolute. "Our ignorances bring curiosities and doubts . . . our impotence entails pains ; our imperfection, sins."

These are phenomena that exist in and for ourselves. They are not ideas floating about in the infinite, they refer to us, they form part of individuals.

This absolute to which we have recourse is finally but the transposition—by no means the solution—of the problems propounded by immediate experience. We discover in the absolute the very contradictions that characterise the finite, and that in an aggravated form, for monism, assured that by means of the absolute it could find unity, has broken immediate experience into discontinuous fragments. Reality thus is first broken up, then dissipated. The invaluable particles of experiences that we possessed have dissolved away.

It is in its intellectualism that we find the radical defect of monism. The monist imagines that by calling the world a unity he can thereby make things comprehensible ; he imagines that a change of name changes the essence of things. He imagines that to name a thing is thereby to exclude from it that which the word by which it is named does not contain. He also imagines that there is no middle course between complete unity and absolute separation ; that when we admit separation, however small, between things, we can no longer understand their union.

How is monism to be proved ? Will it be proved by the aid of mystical experience ? But this, says James, is no philosophical proof. Or else, in order to prove it, shall we start with a definition of the idea of substance ?

The pragmatistic criticism, however, of such philosophers as Berkeley and Hume has shown that there is nothing positive in the metaphysical interpretation of the idea of substance.

In the end, the absolutist philosophy gives us the feeling of a world mirage; and the criticisms of James are on the whole identical on this point with those formulated by Schiller from the time he wrote *Riddles of the Sphinx* onwards.

The absolute is the great " de-realiser "; it gives to Nature a far-away aspect of "foreignness." Not only does it take away from our world its reality, but it tells us nothing of the world it promises us.

Moreover, if the absolute exists, wherefore our universe rather than any other possible universe? From the absolute we cannot again descend to the concrete. Hence the great number of problems raised by absolutism.

And these problems appear only because the absolutist desires to enjoy the contemplation of a mystical unity, to concentrate his mind in a sort of monistic mono-ideism.

The world of the Hegelian appears to us as a world devoid of possibility, deprived, as James expresses it, of the oxygen of possibility. The result of such a doctrine of unity is a repose similar to that of the mystic absorbed in divine vision, or of the determinist who delights in seeing phenomena follow one another, or of the pessimist, pessimism, according to James, being linked with determinism just as determinism is linked with a certain monism; in a word, it is quietism, indifferentism in all its forms. Here culminates the sacrilegious violence of Hegel, " that Philip II, that Bonaparte of philosophy," who respects neither time nor space and succeeds only in proving " his own mental deformity."

James opposes all those systems that seek unity above all else, not only the monism of Bradley but also, on this point at least, the transcendentalism of Emerson—though so concrete at times—and the metaphysics of Royce, which, while allowing the individual a share in divinity, is yet tame and hesitating. On the other hand, he opposes the monism of matter and force, the ideas of Lewes and Spencer, Grant Allen and Clifford.

No doubt monotheism retains the divine personality denied by monism. All the same, its God often dwells on heights as inaccessible to the true believer as is the absolute. God then appears as " the Louis XIV of heaven."

After having expelled this absolute unity both from metaphysical and from religious philosophy, James would also like to see it expelled from scientific philosophy. Why believe that Nature is not lavish of her time and efforts, that she always proceeds towards her ends by the shortest way and the most economical paths ? Let us cultivate a less miserly imagination. Again, one physical formula cannot explain everything, neither does any physical formula account for the qualities of physical phenomena, the qualities of sensations.

What James repudiates with all his might are all the philosophical pseudo-principles which " nauseate " anyone possessed of a healthy philosophical appetite.

If the result of these analyses and criticisms is accepted, then, according to James, there disappear the problems raised by all monism : the problems of evil and of free-will, for instance ; agnosticism disappears at the same time, and the idea of an absolute seems useless now that experiences adhere and unite together. Finite consciousness, perception in all its wealth, free-will, and possibility are now recognised as capable of existing.

" The world is neither a universe pure and simple nor a multiverse pure and simple, neither is it a universe and a multiverse at the same time, as the Hegelians say, but simply a great fact wherein manyness and oneness are set alongside and succeed each other. The world cannot be formulated in a single proposition."

Pluralism will assume various forms, according as it opposes such or such particular form of monism. Thus there is a noetic pluralism, a finalistic pluralism.

Shall we say that the vision of a multiple world springs mainly from our need to make up separate wholes so as to be able to act more freely upon them, and that it possesses a practical interest rather than a theoretical one ? But is it certain, replies James, that we may not be more interested, for our practical aims, in setting up continuities than discontinuities ? Whereas, according to Bergson, practical needs have led us to conceive of discontinuities, certain practical needs, according to James, compel us to discover or to create an ever greater unity. Both these philosophers in their metaphysics, partially at all events, react against a certain natural pragmatism, a certain natural utilitarianism, by showing us : the one, a profound continuity ; the other, discontinuities in the universe.

Radical empiricism would thus clearly appear to point in the direction of pluralism. It is a philosophy of *experiences*.

Pluralism may even appear to us only as a new name given to empiricism, since empiricism is above all a philosophy of the parts in contrast with a philosophy of the whole.

This radical empiricism is to have certain definite consequences on different points of the philosophical system of James. Even in his *Psychology*, James insists on the existence of certain discontinuities, certain " interruptions," which seem to happen in the course of a consciousness.   There are breaks in the quality and the content of thought, or at least there appear to be. Perhaps the tendency in James is more and more to discover that this appearance is a reality.

Besides, the more James developed his metaphysical theories, the more do his psychological ideas seem to have evolved.   Perhaps at the end of his life, James would have conceived a psychology different from the one he wrote, a pluralist psychology showing everywhere discontinuous blocks of continuities as he actually did conceive in his Psychology blocks of duration, bales and skeins of consciousness, bundles of ideas, bits of experiences.   We find confirmation of this idea in some phases of *A Pluralistic Universe* : " all our sensible experiences, as we get them immediately, do thus change by discrete pulses of perception "   and " Fechner's term of the threshold . . . is only one way of naming the quantitative discreteness in the change of all our sensible experiences.   They come to us in drops.   Time itself comes in drops."   This idea is to find its clearest expression in *Some Problems of Philosophy.*

Realism is connected with radical empiricism.   " If we go from parts to wholes, we believe that beings may first exist and feed, so to speak, on their own existences and then secondarily become known to one another.   We believe that existence is prior to knowledge, that the fact of a thing being known does not change it in itself, since the relations between beings may change without the beings changing."   On this point the theory of James is identical with that of Russell.

Radical empiricism has also certain consequences for the theory of truth.   Truth resumes its place among particular things, is entirely made up itself of particular things; it consists of all the intervening links between idea and reality.

No doubt James is enough of a radical empiricist to admit in some passages that this chain whereby idea is linked with reality has interruptions, that there is a gap between idea and reality, that these are two entities distinct from each other, that here too we have pluralism. But whether truth be conceived of as a continuity of particular experiences or as a duality, it is always conceived of in a definite and finally a pluralist manner.

But instead of speaking of truth in the singular we must speak of *truths*, and radical empiricism here leads on the one hand to the affirmation of a multiplicity of subjects and systems created by these subjects, and on the other hand to the affirmation of a multiplicity of bodies of reality.

There is a multiplicity of " knowers." There is no omniscient mind, the world is known but partially, by particular subjects, and we are led to what James calls a " noetic pluralism," which indeed will be completed by what we might call a " noetic collectivism," by the idea of a union, a harmony, between the different knowers.

These different subjects will be able to take multitudes of different views of one and the same thing. "The universe is a more many-sided affair than any sect allows for." There is a logical way, a religious way, a geometrical way, nay, there are logical ways, geometrical ways, religious ways of conceiving things. One mind, though baptised the absolute, cannot have a complete view of reality; " the facts and worths of life need many cognizers to take them in. There is no point of view absolutely public and universal." No single individual can construct reality in all the ways in which it is capable of being constructed. Hence the idea that we must study all experiences in all their varieties. And there are as many varieties as there are individuals ; each has his own way of seeing the world. If we are to give a name to these affirmations, we might call it the polysystematism of James.

To these ideas might be traced back some of James's moral conceptions. While exacting from the individual moral earnestness, faith in an ideal, he does not intend that any particular ideal should be imposed, there is no one single ideal. Hence his moral pluralism.

And so the world may be manipulated according to different systems and every time the world reacts profitably. The polysystematism just mentioned is completed and explained by what might be called a polyrealism ; the multiplicity of systems is explained by the multiplicity of realities, by the mutual independence of the departments of nature. These more or less independent realities may be attacked by employing different conceptions in turn, by assuming different attitudes. To each attitude there corresponds a reality with which it naturally fits in ; to each truth there corresponds a reality which exemplifies it. There are different universes of speech ; there are even an infinity of them, and these different universes should not be confused. Among the spheres of experiences, James specially notes those " bodies of truths " which are the sciences, and those universes of speech which consist of the worlds of poetry, those of mythology. Each of these universes admits of ideas which it exemplifies ; in each, the conditions of truth, the practical effects of the idea, differ profoundly.

And so the affirmation of a plurality of systems and a plurality of reals is a consequence of radical empiricism. But radical empiricism is also capable of showing us that these different systems of realities mutually interpenetrate in a certain way and that they are all included in the moving reality of psychological life. According to the point of view we adopt, we shall see the different realities become distinct from and superimposed on to one another, or else blend into one another.

THE ANTI-INTELLECTUALISM OF JAMES

Gradually James gives away the idea that the real is conformable to principles. The principles and concepts of reason cannot be imposed upon reality. If empiricism is radical, it can no longer be intellectualistic. Reality is essentially alien to rationality, to what we conceive as rationality. The flux of percepts cannot be translated into the language of concepts, this is what James calls in *Some Problems of Philosophy* the affirmation of " the insuperability of sensation." The anti-intellectualism of James is asserted more and more clearly in proportion as, partly influenced by the ideas of Bergson, he sees all the consequences, all the logical difficulties, that follow in the wake of intellectualism. From neo-criticism he advances in the direction of Bergsonism.

The intellectualism which James combats, especially in his latter works, is the " Platonic " theory that we find in the definition of a thing what that thing really is, that the essences of things are known when we know their definitions, and that reality consists of essences. Hence intellectualism is led not only to draw conclusions from the definition to that which is in reality, but also to exclude from reality that which is not in the definition. This is why he comes to say that things which are independent or simply distinct from one another can bear no relation whatsoever to one another, that there is no unity between things that are multiple, that a given thing remains what it is and cannot change. Intellectualism is a theory of separation, and separation as he conceives it makes things into motionless essence. By isolating things, he makes them stationary, all the more so because he regards fixity as nobler than change. And when he afterwards reverts to the real world, the intellectualist no longer understands it ; intellectualism finally renders the world unintelligible. Anti-intellectualism, one might say, makes it intelligible.

The anti-intellectualism of James is one aspect of his empiricism. In the beginning is the fact, and our conceptual thought is never the full equivalent of the fact. This anti-intellectualism is based on the distinction between percepts and concepts. Percepts are singulars always different from one another and each different from itself, in a way. To know them is to cling to particular, individual, momentarily variable characters, to remain inside the stream of life in a constant attitude of expectation. Thus we have James's empiricism here as something that closely approaches the theories of Bergson. Concepts should enable us simply to return with fuller assurance into the stream of that temporal experience which is the only valid reality. At times they may serve to enrich experience, but what they cannot do—of themselves alone and apart from percepts—is to express experience, to cause it to be understood.

James had always sought the fullness of reality. More and more he insists on this fullness given in the perceptual flux. Each moment, he says, appears to us as a paradise from which the rationalists will in vain attempt to drive us, now that we have criticised their state of mind.

"Ever not quite," he writes in his article on Blood, "is fit to be pluralism's heraldic device. There is no complete generalisation, no total point of view, no all-pervasive unity, but everywhere some residual resistance to verbalisation, formulation, and discursification, some genius of reality that escapes from the pressure of the logical finger." Between all things there is a multitude of relations which seem contradictory from the point of view of rationality. Life is a continual negation of our logical axioms ; two notes similar to a third may not be similar to each other ; the same is blended with the different. Anti-intellectualism is a theory of composition ; experiences encroach upon one another. But it is at the same time a theory of separation altogether distinct from the intellectualistic theories of separation, there is no whole except if we think by means of concepts, there are no parts except if we see by means of percepts.

Such a conception differs alike from classical empiricism and from absolutistic rationalism. It is in the name of the same intellectualistic logic and of the same principle of contradiction that some deny the reality of the sensible world and others deny the existence of the absolute. And neither of the two sides succeeds in being in agreement with itself, for the absolutists when speaking of the absolute and the empiricists when speaking of experience do not accept the rules of that ordinary logic which they use to destroy the doctrine of their opponents but which proves incapable of helping them to build up their own.

This criticism of intellectualism shows us what must be our mode of cognition. We shall have to come into contact, says James in *A Pluralistic Universe*, with things through a living sympathy, a sympathetic imagination. We must employ the deepest powers of the soul in becoming acquainted with realities. We must place ourselves within the living and moving thickness of the real, in that reality which is pure incessant novelty. What we apprehend of it, however little, is absolute.

In affirming the superficial character of intellectual knowledge and insisting on the continuity of things, as well as in the part allotted to intuition, these theories of James can be intimately linked up with those of Bergson.

There is one problem that presents itself : How are we to harmonise this anti-intellectualist theory with the idea that a realm of conceptual reality exists ? In re-editing one of his old articles in *The Meaning of Truth*, James himself mentioned that he no longer regarded percepts as the only real things. " I now treat concepts," he says, " as a co-ordinate realm." There is a universe of truths which comprises the universe of the possible and of the past ; here we meet dead truths and un-discovered ones ; here are found melodies which the musicians of the future will discover, geometrical rela-tions not yet known. In his latter works, *A Pluralistic Universe, The Meaning of Truth*, James insists on this conception.

According to the way in which James examines the problem of the existence of general ideas he gives to it different solutions. James is a nominalist, a concep-tualist, and a realist in turn. He is a nominalist in the sense that the " particular concrete " alone possesses profound truth and real worth for him. He is a con-ceptualist in the sense that, in his mind, there exists around our particular ideas a fringe of general meaning, and, on the other hand, that there is a certain element of generality in things ; the sameness of the colour white is a postulate which acts and serves our purposes ; " so the nominalist doctrine is false of things of that conceptual sort and true only of things in the perceptual flux." And this affirmation even proves to us that James super-imposes a realism upon his conceptualism: "what I am affirming here is the Platonic doctrine that concepts are singulars, that concept-stuff is inalterable, and that physical realities are constituted by the various concept-stuffs of which they partake." Thus would James combine logical realism with an empirical way of thinking; he recognises the paradoxical nature of his enterprise.[12]

His empiricism leads him to make these various realms, which at first he had kept apart, coincide in the end. He regards concept-stuff as identical with percept-stuff. Concepts are like mists rising from perception itself wherein they condense afresh whenever this is necessary in practice. "Concepts and percepts are wrapt and rolled together as a gunshot in the mountains is wrapt and rolled in fold and fold of echo and reverberative clamor." Thus on the one hand we have a distinction between these different realms of reality, and, on the other, mutual implication. In the last resort, concept-stuff is identical with percept-stuff.

To some extent, then, it is comprehensible that, in *Some Problems of Philosophy*, James should find himself holding ideas which are at times akin to those of Russell and sometimes to those of Bergson. Concepts are in a Platonic realm altogether apart from perceptual reality while at the same time they are inseparable from this reality. According to the point of view, they can either loose themselves from perceptual reality, or else they can not. In the same way, James agrees with Bergson

[12] It must be noted that his realism is somewhat different from that of Russell: the existence of concepts is a lower existence; they come from experience and return to experience. Their very eternity is probably a defect, if we compare it with the fullness of temporal existence.

regarding the idea of the internality of relations, and with Russell regarding the idea of the externality of relations. Things are seen as either discontinuous or continuous, according as they are regarded from the logical or the psychological point of view.

"TEMPORALISM" AND ITS RELATION TO RADICAL EMPIRICISM

Continuity and Discontinuity

The reason why there are different points of view about the universe, the explanation of what we have called polysystematism, is to be found in the fact that there are different designs or purposes—this is what James calls teleological pluralism or the pluralism of finality. The world does not proceed in one single direction, " it is full of partial purposes, of particular stories . . . they *seem* simply to run alongside of each other." These particular meanings and ends can be realised only in time. We shall see how the affirmation of the profound reality of time is in several ways connected with radical empiricism.

To the radical empiricist, reality is plasticity, indifference. This plasticity, this indifference, is a possibility of change. " Change that takes place " is one of our first felt experiences ; we have the feeling of genuine experiences succeeding one another. Time sets going the world of radical empiricism which we had hitherto regarded as static, and makes a really multiple world of it.

Radical empiricism, pluralism, and " temporalism " are closely linked together. First, time has to be accepted, because we must take facts as they offer themselves, for if all was determined beforehand and contained within the Platonic essences, time would be nothing but an illusion. Then it is because relations are external to terms, because relations between things may change, because at a given moment things may enter into fresh relations and abandon their former ones, that time is capable of existing. Finally, it is series of experiences in the plural that time modifies. " The flux is that of the conjoint and separated things, of the things in groups, of the things continuous, and of the things separate."

In *A Pluralistic Universe*, James insists on that continuous dialectical movement of things which constitutes time. Things appear in a state of constant unbalance. Experience does quite naturally what Hegel would have his absolute do ; on the one hand, it works by constant contradiction ; on the other hand, it works by constant combination. Everything contains within itself its neighbour, as the absolute, it is said, encompasses facts. The parts of experience blend ; we cannot say that this is here and that farther away : " They run into one another continuously and seem to interpenetrate." There is interpenetration of all the concrete pulses of feeling. Contradiction and combination, such then is experience. Dialectic appears as an abstract statement of the concrete continuity of life. The absolute of the absolutists is not richer in contradictions, not more inexhaustible in our thought, than is the fleeting moment for the empiricist ; always closely linked with a given thing is another thing which cannot be separated from it. Every idea, says James, in language very similar to that of Royce, means something different from itself and yet identical with it, signifies an absence, an ideal presence which is an absence. Things are not themselves only. Both the Hegelian philosophy and the Bergsonian philosophy force us to conceive them as " their own others in the fullest sense of the term." " Every smallest state of consciousness, concretely taken, overflows its own definition." No doubt, James remarks, how easily such a conception might lead to monism, and so he would have us observe that interpenetration between things is not complete and does not exist between all things but only between those that come after one another. Moreover, strictly speaking, they do not comprise one another; it is a succession, a succession of " specious presents," each of which, it is true, comprises a little of the past and a little of the future, but which, nevertheless, follow one another in time.

This affirmation of time is essentially the affirmation that the world is not all made, that it is ever making itself. If the world were complete, why should time exist ? " The thing of deepest—comparatively—significance in life," says James, " does seem to be its character of *progress*, or that strange sense of reality with ideal novelty which it continues from one moment to another to offer." " Ever the edition of the world—or rather editions—are being completed or amended, they are never ' eternal.' " Whether James conceives that this novelty appears more particularly when man acts and gives form to matter, or that it endures, so to speak, throughout all the continuous stream of our life, it remains an essential characteristic of the world of the pluralist. The logical theory of external relations made it possible, the observations of psychology—the most concrete and most real of all sciences—bring it before our eyes. It is enough, says James in *Some Problems of Philosophy*, to consider what he calls our perceptual life, to feel the continual gushing up, the incessant germination, efflorescence, and proliferation of all life, the " perfect effervescence " of novelty. And this novelty, which thus

appears before us, is a reality, for, in consciousness, truth
is appearance and appearance truth. Because we experience it within ourselves, novelty exists. A second
reason for which it cannot but be real is that if, placing
ourselves above this stream, we try to see what is thus
mirrored in it, we do indeed see ever-changing novelties:
" New men and new women, accidents, events, inventions,
and enterprises ever break out and pour upon our world."
Under the influence of the Bergsonian philosophy, James
emphasises more and more this character of radical
novelty he had already shown strongly in his *Psychology*.
" There will be news in heaven," he would frequently
remark.

This character of novelty is essential to the idea James
forms of freedom ; because, to begin with, freedom is
nothing else than novelty, originality.

But pluralism and temporalism are connected in yet
another way. Perhaps this is the central fact in the metaphysics of James, and the essential link between all his
philosophic conceptions. Instead of the universe of the
monist where all is in all, the parts of the pluralist universe
hold together only by their ends ; experience grows by
its borders ; the world is a sort of multitude of continuing
editions, but they do not continue regularly ; it is distributively, in places, one letter appearing here and another
there, that the editions are completed. The world exists
as an " each-form " distributed in space and time. The
pluralist form of the universe is, he says, " the each-form,"
it is " strung-along." Thus does experience increase in
scattered fashion ; here the ideas of time and multiplicity
join one another.

They are going to be joined even more closely ; the
pluralist world, we read in *Some Problems of Philosophy*, is
a world wherein the present is added on to the past, and

the expression "added on" must be taken literally; there is actually addition of the present on to the past; it is an "additive world" in which the total is never made up.

All philosophy is forced to postulate that there exists something to postulate being, but it may postulate either much or little of it. Parmenides and Spinoza need the whole of being at once and postulate it all at the beginning of their philosophy. James needs only being by degrees and postulates a little of it and then another little part, and so on; and even does not think that the whole of being should ever be given. Being gives itself by degrees, it never gives itself as a whole. Regarded from this standpoint, pluralism is but a fresh name given to empiricism, since empiricism is above all a philosophy of the parts in contrast with a philosophy of the whole. Moreover, this theory of the reality of time is connected with anti-intellectualism as it is connected with empiricism, since "the parts are percepts, built out into wholes by our conceptual additions." The paradox of Zeno is, to James, an argument in favour of anti-intellectualism, just because, according to him, it is an argument in favour of discontinuity.

In *Some Problems of Philosophy*, more than in all his other works, appears his definition of empiricism, and we see how he solves the problem of the infinite. "The reader," he says, "will note how emphatically in all this discussion I am insisting on the distributive or piecemeal point of view. The distributive is identical with the pluralistic, as the collective is with the monistic conception. We shall, I think, perceive more and more clearly . . . that piecemeal existence is independent of complete collectibility, and that some facts, at any rate, exist only distributively, or in the form of a set of eaches which (even if in infinite numbers) need not in any intelligible sense either experience themselves or get experienced by any one else as members of an All." Empiricism and the theory of time are connected in a new way ; empiricism requires us to take things one by one, each in its turn ; it implies time.

But the time that it implies cannot be a continuous time. In order not to be confined in the labyrinth of the continuous, we must deal with the real processes of change " as taking place by finite not infinitesimal steps, like the successive drops by which a cask of water is filled when whole drops fall into it at once or nothing. This is the radical pluralist, empiricist, or perceptual position which I characterised in speaking of Renouvier." " It will be necessary," continues James, " to adapt it perhaps more closely to experience, but it must finally be adopted. Change takes place by finite and perceptible units of approach, by drops, by buds, by successive steps, all these units coming wholly when they do come, or coming not at all." There is no middle course between complete production and non-production. Consequently that which is given us is drops, waves, pulses of movement. The succession of the stages of change is not infinitely divisible. If a bottle could be emptied only by an infinite number of successive diminutions, it would never be emptied. If we take things as they appear to us, says James in *Some Problems of Philosophy*, we have to reject the idea of continuity ; continuity here is but a fiction of the mind.[13] Accordingly, although James makes use of comparisons somewhat like those of Bergson, they yet mask a somewhat different conception, for whereas he regards duration as indivisible, this indivisibility is rather, it seems, in some even of his later works, that of a

[13] Even when James expounds the ideas of Bergson, we may note certain shades of meaning peculiar to himself.

compact instant, and of notes each held for a long time, though in sudden succession, than that of a melody which is fleeting and of continuous duration.

Such is this empiricism of James which conceives an absolute obtained by addition, an additive absolute. The anti-intellectualism which James expounds in *Some Problems of Philosophy*, in a form closely resembling that given to it by Bergson, brings him back to a conception which seems opposed to that of Bergson, to the conception of Renouvier. It is the infinite and the continuous that constitute intellectual illusions. Our dividing and sub-dividing intellect, repeating the same acts indefinitely, creates the idea of infinity, an idea that is finally incomprehensible and absurd. It is the finite, the addition of being to being, immediately and in finite quantity, that is the truth present in the perceptual flux, a truth perhaps incomprehensible to an understanding that examines it externally, though not absurd *per se*. "Better accept, as Renouvier says, the opaquely given data of perception than concepts inwardly absurd."

We may ask ourselves if there is not a contradiction between this idea of discontinuity and the psychology of James, where the continuity of the stream of consciousness is emphasised. James appears to give a hint, in *Some Problems of Philosophy*, of the solution he would perhaps adopt. There would indeed be contradiction should continuity be defined mathematically, but if, remaining closer to perception, we say that there is continuity when we regard the parts of a quantity as immediately next to one another and not separate, we may then believe in a continuity consisting of discontinuous parts.[14]

[14] And yet James says in *Some Problems of Philosophy* that the whole of the perceptual flux is continuous. There is discontinuity only between parts of the flux at some distance from one another.

Only if one accepts anti-intellectualism and the theory of the discontinuous as here stated can one really be a pluralist and believe in " absolute novelties, sudden beginnings, gifts, chance, freedom, and acts of faith."

In many ways, then, the idea of time and that of plurality are connected in the mind of James ; while to believe in eternity is to affirm the existence of a universe made all of a piece ; to believe in time is to affirm the existence of a real plurality. Admit a plurality, he says, and time will be its form. We might equally say for him : Admit a time, and plurality will necessarily be its content. These two words designate two views of one and the same thing : the world, dispersed and parcelled out, multiple in space and time, ever incomplete though ever in process of completion. The very centre of pluralism is just where these two ideas meet in the idea of a world completing itself here and there.[15]

FREEDOM

It is these two characters of movement and multiplicity that explain the existence of freedom. In the first place, for a radical empiricist there are everywhere only indeterminate variables. No doubt things are partially coherent, but apart from the points in which they are connected with one another, they have other elements, free elements. And chance does not mean anything else. In a thing of chance there is an element peculiar to this

---

[15] Perry makes a similar observation when he writes : " In the first place, indeterminism may be regarded simply as an aspect of pluralism. This latter doctrine emphasises both manyness and irrelevance ; indeterminism singles out and emphasises irrelevance " (*Tendencies*, p. 249). In the temporalism of James, Perry attempts to separate two elements which he regards as quite distinct : the affirmation of the existence of time and the dynamic and deterministic conception of time.

thing that is not the unconditional property of the All. Chance, as James also says, signifies pluralism and nothing more. Novelty and chance are two names for one and the same element of reality. Pluralism is essentially indeterministic.

Freedom, for the very reason that it is novelty, chance, is the choice between simple possibilities. There are real alternatives, relations which at a given time may or may not take place, there are "future contingents." The theory of possibility is one of the theories that mark out the road between radical empiricism and the pluralism of James : temporalism, the theory of an incomplete world, the theory of novelty, indeterminism, the theory of possibility. Here we come to one of the most important dilemmas of the philosophy according to James. There are men in favour of possibility and men against possibility, "possibility-men and anti-possibility-men." The latter, who are rationalists, live in peace in a world ruled by necessity ; they believe in a final issue of things ; the former are empiricists and believe in a "reserve of possibilities alien to our present experience." They affirm the existence of simple possibilities. To the pluralist indeterminist, "realities seem to float in a vaster sea of possibilities from which they are drawn and chosen." First there are quite intellectual possibilities. "The philosophy which begins in wonder," said Plato and Aristotle, "can image to itself each thing as different from what it is, its spirit is full of air, and this spirit plays around each object." But there are also practical possibilities which may rise and threaten our action ; the tough-minded man can imagine threatening possibilities in front of him, by his side, everywhere. To believe in real possibilities, to consent to live on a scheme of possibilities, is to be a true pragmatist, a true pluralist, and a strong affinity is seen to exist between the two doctrines, seeing that the temperaments that live them must be the same. The empiricist is able to formulate the universe in hypothetical propositions; the pluralist is able to live in a dangerous universe. On the other hand, the rationalist believes only in necessities on the one side and impossibilities on the other: he formulates the universe into categorical propositions and inclines to an optimism which leaves no room for action.

But then, it will be asked, is not this existence of possibilities itself purely and simply a possibility? This objection is present, though somewhat vaguely, in the mind of James. Let us accept this possibility, he replies; it is a hypothesis in which we can believe; more than that, since we are pluralists and pragmatists, philosophers of action, we ought to believe in it.

"Possibility as distinguished from necessity on the one hand," James tells us, "and from impossibility on the other, is an essential category of human thinking."

This idea of the possible is closely bound up with the idea of time, since the profound reality of time comes from the fact that each moment is a choice between possibles, and since it is owing to the very continuity of time that the possibles are to become real. Indeed, when James in *Some Problems of Philosophy* asks himself the question as to how the possible is realised, he says the reason why this problem seems obscure to us is that we cut up by means of language the perceptual flux, each moment of which in reality implies the other moments. He attempts to solve by experience the contradiction which would appear to exist between the fact that action born of freedom seems to stand out distinct from the previous life and contrasted with it, and, on the other hand, continues it. And it may be that, in our personal experience, we apprehend the essential process of creation.

So pluralism is here not only the affirmation of the externality of relations, it is the affirmation that there are creative relations, and that, just because there are external relations, there are also internal relations ; the existence of external relations makes creation possible, but creation—the continual transition from the possible to the real—is an internal relation. Freedom is both absolute beginning and continuity of evolution.

MORALISM AND MELIORISM

This philosophy of the incomplete, the possible, and the new, brings us to the moralist conception—to pluralist moralism, as James calls it.

The world, a great thing ever incomplete and endlessly continuing, goes in a certain direction, but its course, though determined up to a certain point, is not completely determined. Hence possible successes and defeats, falling and rising values. Owing to the union of these two ideas, —a certain direction of the world, though a wavering direction, so to speak, and an uncertain one—we have the " moralistic view " of the universe. The world possesses a dramatic temperament which philosophy should not destroy. He who holds this conception considers that there is evil, evil to overcome and suppress. " Evil is emphatically irrational, and *not* to be pinned in or preserved or consecrated in any final system of truth . . . it is an alien *un*reality, a waste element." The problem of evil cannot be solved from a metaphysical point of view, it constitutes only a practical problem, we ought not to understand but to suppress it. Evil is not essential to good, as monism thinks; it does not constitute a necessary part an eternal element of reality.

Only if we accept all these ideas : radical empiricism, the vision of a world that is incomplete and as it were full of possibles, the existence of evil, which is the fourth postulate of practical reason, to borrow Renouvier's expression, can we have a moral view of the world; what, from the pragmatist point of view, constitutes the essential worth of pluralism, is that it is the necessary postulate for the adoption of this moralist theory of the world. " Our moral nature, taken seriously along with all its exigencies," says Flournoy, " is the first and the last word of the philosophy of James."

In this world of the incomplete, the fortuitous, the possible, where novelties come about piecemeal, as it were, in spots, in patches, by separate blots, by distinct strokes, individuals can really act. There are, he says, many human imaginations that live in such a moralist world, in this world which can be saved if we wish it strongly, which grows here and there, owing to the scattered contributions of its various parts; of people content with what they can do, with the poor and yet so rich results disseminated all about space and strung-along in time. Man, each single man, can carry through a work of redemption, of salvation. Each man can help to save the world by saving his own soul. The world can be saved piecemeal—pluralistically.

No doubt it is necessary that all should co-operate. And though certain people have predominant influence (the heroes who create categories, those who found ideals that are new), each depends on all the rest; the world of the pluralist is one in which all the parts affect one another mutually. " Even though we do *our* best, the other factors also will have a voice in the result. If they refuse to conspire, our goodwill and labour may be thrown away. No insurance company can here cover us or save us from the risks we run in being part of such a world." Certain parts may really go astray and do harm, they may really cause injury to the other parts of the world.

And so life claims from us a strenuous nature, for the salvation of the world depends on the energy supplied by its different parts.

Hence that feeling of insecurity which the world of the pluralist gives. It lacks both stability and serenity. For the intellectualist, the human mind is confronted with a ready-made world, unable to determine its character afresh. It refuses to attach any value to arguments that proceed from " must be " to being. For the pluralist, the world is made by our beliefs. Its character depends on our faith, being depends on " must be." For, even if the details of the world are independent of our thought, it is not affirmed that the whole character of the world cannot be determined thereby. " A philosophy may indeed be a most momentous reaction of the universe upon itself." Only in an incomplete and multiple universe can individual faith find room, only there can the whole character be expressed in hypothetical propositions as we have seen.

Then we feel that our life is a real combat, that our victories are really victories for the world and our failures cosmic defeats. Why should not our actions, the turning-points of our lives, be the real turning-points of the world, the stages at which the world grows ? The world does grow and change, in and by ourselves.

The pluralist must have this element of insecurity in the world, this Gothic element, as James calls it. " What interest, what savour, what excitement can be found in following the good path if we do not feel that evil is also possible and natural, nay, threatening and imminent ? " In this uncertain world, tough-minded men will be able to feel " the exultations and the anguishes, the invincible love for man." They will give " opposition, poverty, martyrdom if need be, as solemn festivals to their interior faith." " For my part," says James, " I do not know what sweat and blood, what the tragedy of this life mean, except just this : if life is not a struggle in which, by success, there is something eternally gained on behalf of the universe, then it is no more than idle amusement. . . . Life indeed gives us the sensation of a real combat, as though there were something truly disorderly in the world that we, with all our ideals and fidelities, are called upon to redeem. It is to this universe, half lost and half saved, that our nature is adapted." He who has a moralistic conception of the world desires not to be certain of success, he wants to take his chance. One single chance of salvation is enough for him ; what matters all else, what matters it if he himself be lost so long as his cause may some day triumph.

Pragmatism and pluralism, both theories are here one in the unity of the temperament that lives them. They should always be based on a certain hardihood, a certain inclination to live without insurance or guarantee. To minds willing thus to live on possibilities which are not certainties, there is around all quietistic religion that is certain of salvation a " faint odour of fatty degeneration."

James cannot accept complete pessimism, which only an extremely hard-souled nature, the Nietzschean superman, at certain moments could fully bear ; nor can he accept " the white-robed harp-playing heaven of our sabbath schools and the ladylike tea-table elysium." The world cannot be defined by a superlative ; we should take it as it goes, and define the various stages with reference to one another by the help of a comparative. Consequently moralism is completed by meliorism. The man who has a moralistic view of the world, though he may not have " moral holidays " like the absolutist, long periods of rest, can at all events enjoy the comforting thought of meliorism. Meliorism is " the salt that keeps the world from corrupting, the air that fills the lungs." In it the world has a chance, a real chance, of becoming good. And even if we regard this chance as illusory, at all events the world can be continually improving. Perhaps we must even give up all hope of final reconciliation, adopt " the most moralistic " view. The ideal for the hard-souled man is not absence of vices, but vice—and virtue clutching it by the throat. Amelioration is not the suppression of evil, but rather perhaps an ever re-won victory over still resisting and still existing evil.

.We can see what pluralist idealism will be. Pragmatism is by no means the negation of all distinction between the ideal and the real. This conception of meliorism, indeed, takes for granted an idealism, a faith in a pure ideal reality, isolated from all its environments, cleansed of all the dross of the material world, a pluralist and exclusive idealism, as Perry expresses it.

We also understand that belief of James which may be assimilated with the ideas of yogism and mental healing : man is capable of transcending himself. Within each of us are infinite reserves and levels of power, and James dwells on these innumerable possibilities, these mines of influence, these unknown riches.

What are we going to do with these forces ? Are we going to apply them to the whole world ? No, for our freedom is limited and we must think only of partial reforms. " What," says James, " really is this philosophy of objective conduct which seems so neglected and antiquated, though so pure and strong and healthy when compared with its romantic rival ? It is a recognition of limits ; the will to feel at peace after successfully performing some task." If the universe belongs to semi-independent forces, how indeed can they help coming into conflict at times ? And this idea that our responsibilities are limited like our powers does not weaken, it rather intensifies, our moral consciousness. And lastly, does not the essentially pluralistic process, by which we form an ideal, teach us that reality may be partly good and partly bad ? We must join forces with certain parts of nature that may be utilised by us, and we must turn against others. Here is something capable of endowing us with courage : the causes of evil appear finite when we no longer believe in the one Spirit and the one Substance, and to each of the causes of evil we can say in turn, the fight is now between you and me. These ever succeeding struggles, instead of crushing our courage, will fortify it ; they will form stages on the way, and by successive victories we shall map out our road to victory. Thus we must take all things in detail ; all our ideals should be realised and our difficulties overcome piecemeal, not only, as we have already seen, because the world is saved by and in individuals, but also because these very individuals can act only on certain determinate realities. The pluralist, though feeling within himself endless reserves and levels of possibilities, knows that " disseminated and strung-along successes " alone are permitted to him ; he contents himself with them.

James speaks of our salvation, of the salvation of the world. He is always deeply religious. This idea of salvation, it must be noted, is not to be regarded as meaning a universal ideal, the same for all. Human nature cannot be reduced to a sort of single model or copy. What may be affirmed, nevertheless, is that this ideal should be tolerance, it should be the society of individuals.

By means of all these struggles, the individual grows and the sacredness of his character is more and more evident. The final aim of our creation, says James, would appear to consist in the greater enrichment of our ethical consciousness amid the more intense play of contrasts and the greater diversity of characters. The pluralist therefore will naturally be " tolerant towards all that is not itself intolerant " ; other individualities will draw out his own individuality. He is naturally a democrat ; is not the democratic idea, as occasionally conceived by Whitman, an essentially individualistic idea ?

Still, democracy is not a general levelling process. External social distinctions which might appear superficial will be regarded by the pluralist statesman as deeply significant. Nor should democracy end in the destruction of individual initiative ; as the world is saved in and by individuals, so " the strength of the British Empire lies in the strength of character of the individual Englishman taken all alone by himself."

Such is the religion of democracy spoken of by William James, a religion full of admiration for free creators, for the energies of individuals.

It might even be possible to find, scattered about the writings of James, what might hint at a programme of external politics ; thus he affirms that " religiously and philosophically our ancient national doctrine of ' live and let live ' may prove to have a far deeper meaning than our people now seem to imagine it to possess." James is led to stress the idea that all forces should develop freely, provided they do not interfere with one another. And his remarks seem very definite and significant.

THEISM AND POLYTHEISM

If we inquire into the consequences of pluralism in the realm of religion, we must at the outset insist on the fact that here, as elsewhere, the pluralist is an empiricist : he starts with facts, with religious experiences. These experiences he has to study in all their diversity. For James, the method of religious philosophy is to be an individualistic empiricism. Indeed, religious experiences are not only documents, they are revelations. As Royce states, James thought that the individual, the " unconventional in religious experience is the means whereby the truth of a superhuman world may become more manifest." It is individual experience in its most deeply individual aspect that will enable us to fathom that deeper and vaster consciousness which, it may be, constitutes the universal consciousness. Thus we have union between empiricism and religion, between individualism and religion.

Starting with facts, the pluralist can imagine analogies after the great example of men like Fechner and Mill, and run the risk of believing in these analogies. Why should we not be surrounded by higher consciousnesses, by lower consciousnesses ? Why should plants have no soul at all, as Fechner believed ?

Theism is revived by James owing to pluralist hypotheses and hypotheses which he takes from spiritism, for, to his mind, spiritist facts are most fertile in analogies serviceable to the religious man.

James is both a pluralist and a dualist ; over against the chaos of beings stands out a divine personality. The idea of God will give more breadth to the expanded vision of the world, a deeper resonance to metaphysics ; it will also make the world less alien and more intimate. God is not a name, an abstract being; he is a finite mental personality existing in time, a divine I, or rather a Thou—The object God and the subject I ever remain two distinct personalities. Being a finite personality, God cannot know everything; it is possible that certain consciousnesses may know facts that he does not know. "The vastest subject in existence may all the same be ignorant of many things that other subjects know."

God at times seems to be for James synonymous with "the ideal tendency in things," and if God is but the ideal part of things, how could he be the whole of them? He is only the part of things whose life is most intense, whose consciousness is most concentrated, embracing most facts at one and the same indivisible moment.

God does not create things from outside. In one sense, it may be said that things form part of him in their ideal capacity, but they are not created by him like things external to him. He does not create everything, nor is his creation a sort of mechanical arrangement.

Hence we understand that the existence of evil can in no way prove the non-existence of God. Evil exists, and God—along with ourselves—fights against it. God co-operates with us. He is quite genuinely a Providence, though not a Providence that traces a perfectly straight line of facts. Bifurcation is continually taking place in the universe; deity is continually arriving at fresh decisions.

These determinations made at the points of bifurcation in the universe may appear as miracles. James thus reaches what he calls "crass supernaturalism, piecemeal supernaturalism," whereby God intervenes, by fits and starts, as it were, in the history of the world. By sudden dashes, the ideal world inserts itself into the real world. If the nature of an idea lies in its particular, practical consequences, does not the existence of God really lie in the miracles he performs from time to time, at definite moments ? Is not this also a way of explaining the acts of freedom in the world, those absolute beginnings of which James speaks, following on Renouvier ? From this point of view, it is when the ideal world and the real world intermingle or clash that real novelties spring forth.

But while God is helping and co-operating with us, we are contributing to make God ; he then himself appears as the fruit of our efforts. James says that he does not see why the existence of an invisible world might not partly depend on the personal reactions of any one of us to the promptings of the religious idea. He claims that God himself might borrow from our fidelity to him the power and greatness of his being. We are dimly conscious that, through our belief, we are doing God the greatest and most eternal service. The loyalty of each individual to his God assumes a worth that is infinite.

What meaning is to be attributed to this conception of deity ? Is it for man a help and a servant which man seems to create in order to serve God ? Are we to witness a return to primitive religious traditions, renewed by the democratic spirit which will not tolerate idle superiors and expects effective service from the one to whom it renders service, and also by the practical spirit ? The God of the pragmatists, it has been said, is a faithful old servant, intended to help us, to bear our cross and drag along our impedimenta amid the sweat and dust of daily trials—Or are we to regard this as an ideal conception of deity ? The God of William James—like the God of Renan—would then be the " category of the ideal," and by this hypothesis also we should understand the creation of God, of the ideal by man, and the powerful help given by God to men. These two ways of considering deity, the one making it so familiar, the other so subtle, blend together in the mind of James.

This however would not be sufficient to explain completely the God of James : he is a help, a friend, a servant, we said. But, we must add, a help, a friend, a servant singularly exacting, ever laying on us fresh duties and tasks, creating around us an atmosphere of storm and peril in order that our highest possibilities may be revealed.

So far we have spoken of the ideal part of things, of God in the singular. But God might well be many; wherefore should God be solitary ? Since deity is of finite essence, why should it not be multiple ? A profound personalism, as we have seen in the case of Renouvier, leads naturally enough to polytheism. Long before he wrote *The Varieties of Religious Experience*, James speaks in the plural of the powers that govern the universe, of the Gods. More particularly in this work of his do we witness a sort of multiple apotheosis. Or rather James, previous to *A Pluralistic Universe*, did not like to affirm the multiplicity of the Gods any more than did Renouvier ; we feel that he believes in this multiplicity, but he offers this belief almost as an hypothesis ; he wishes but to show that it has as many claims on our thought as the monotheistic hypothesis has. " Primitive thought," he says, " with its belief in individualised personal forms, seems at any rate as far as ever from being driven by science from the field to-day." According to this view these different Gods are not on the same plane of deity. " The universe might conceivably be a collection of such selves, of different degrees of inclusiveness, with no absolute unity realised in it at all. Thus would a sort of polytheism return upon us—a polytheism which I do not on this occasion defend."

In *Pragmatism* the same idea returns, though mostly perhaps in another form. James here insists, as he had done at first, on the political or social aspect of his polytheism. Wherefore should God be an " exalted omnipotent monarch " ? In truth, God is but one of our auxiliaries, *primus inter pares*, " in the midst of all the shapers of the great world's fate."

Will not the tough-minded man thereby lose his toughness of mind, feel himself blend more or less into those spheres of activity that transcend himself ? " No indeed," James has already replied, in a passage of *The Varieties of Religious Experience* which anticipates the objection. For there are parts of the world that are not protected by the Gods, there are heroes whom Athena's shield does not cover, there are also things evil, irremediably lost, that God leaves aside. Both theism and polytheism again bring us, more strongly than ever, the pluralist sense of insecurity.

No longer do we feel ourselves subjects of a monarchical universe, but rather free citizens of a world republic. The world becomes " a sort of republican banquet, where all the qualities of being respect one another's personal sacredness, yet sit at the common table of space and time." He writes : " The universe of the meliorist, according to social analogy, is conceived as a pluralism of independent powers." Here, with other influences, we find that of T. Davidson, who, believing in a " republic of minds," had had considerable effect on James.

Indeed James, in *A Pluralistic Universe*, offers us a different aspect of his polytheism, a less harsh polytheism. His polytheism—his theory of the multiplicity of consciousnesses—cannot be traced back in his book to that of Renouvier, but rather to that of Fechner. He wishes to

feel in the world, around and above him, other consciousnesses than his own.

Only on this hypothesis does the world become "sympathetic," rich, and full : " Isn't this brave universe made
on a richer pattern, with room in it for a long hierarchy
of beings ? "

And so James conceives a " social organisation of co-
operative work, a sharing and partaking business " ; he
mentally pictures the world as " a joint stock company,
whose shareholders have both limited responsibilities and
limited powers." The pluralistic philosophy, says James,
is above all a social philosophy. To it the world is a
multiplicity of lives which may be of every possible
degree of complexity, infrahuman, superhuman as well
as human, " evolving and changing largely in their
efforts and attempts, and making up the universe by their
accumulated interactions and successes."

REAPPEARANCES OF THE IDEA OF UNITY

Will these interactions some day be able to make the
universe perfect ? No, the tough-minded man would
perhaps say, and James frequently prevents us from enter-
taining this hope. He will not, can not promise that the
world shall attain to perfection. And if men can be set
in two categories : " those who believe that the world
must and shall be saved and those contented with believing
that the world *may be* saved," James may generally be
classed in the latter category.

Generally, we say. As a matter of fact, James does not
always retain the attitude of the tough-minded man.
We have seen that evil was mostly regarded by him as
essential, as not having to disappear. And yet, in other
places, James pictures evolution as a necessary diminution

of evil, perhaps finally as leading to a disappearance of evil. The problem of evil is not considered in pluralism, we have said ; for evil is a fact. But in certain passages he tells us that if evil were eternal, there would then be a problem of evil, for in that case God would be responsible for it.

Again, we may inquire whether evil is not finally conceived by him as just a privation of being and nothing more. Then it would appear to be no more than a shadow, and this shadow vanishes at the end of evolution. We shall simply be delivered from evil "at the end"; it will be blotted out. Perhaps the universe, says James, has in evil one chance only to be wholly good, but that is sufficient. However, from its very existence it prevents pluralism from being ultimate, of a lasting nature.

Owing to it, indeed, the world may be one, the world will at last be saved, wholly saved. If, as James says, in spite of all its bifurcations and hesitations, the world is advancing towards a definite goal, then the sweat and blood of the world no longer have any meaning.

And the element of danger in which James delights sometimes disappears. God was but playing an idle game of chess with us. He parried our moves, seemed interested in the game, but his final victory was assured.

What is worse for the pluralist is that this victory will be the reign of unity. It is seldom that James shows us creation going in the direction of ever more intense contrasts, more diverse characters. The tendency of the world is towards unity. God, like the great men of whom James speaks, conceives " unifying ends," though in vaster proportions. In those common receptacles, time and space, why should not certain of our experiences also some day become common ? Do we not see the world continually becoming one through the ever increasing relations between its constituent parts ? Why not imagine complete union in the future ? Thus radical empiricism finally welcomes monism, as a hypothesis.

It might be said that beliefs opposed to pluralism have often exercised their influence upon James. "The transcendental system has a charm of its own," says James in *The Will to Believe*. A true transcendentalist, he delighted in discovering the unity of spirit behind the veil of appearances. In *Human Immortality* he, inspired both by Fechner and by Myers, propounds a transcendentalist theory of the soul, in accordance with which particular souls proceed from a single immense reservoir, an infinite thought, a mother consciousness. This has rightly been regarded as a theory but slightly pluralist in its character. It would not be pluralist at all, did not James tell us that there may be more than one spirit behind the veil of appearances. At all events, we scarcely see how, with his theory of common immortality, James can acquiesce in our desire to survive in the whole of our individuality. And yet it is this doctrine that he expounds again in an article of the *Psychological Review*, in which he builds up a transcendentalist theory of psychology. Is it not also because he is more or less influenced by this transcendental monism that he proves the continuity of things and the unity of experience ? For experience, in spite of its variety, is one at bottom, and finally the different realities distinguished by "polyrealism" blend in a single reality ; perceptual reality contains all the ideal systems ; percepts and concepts are made up of the same stuff ; percepts fade away into concepts ; concepts condense into percepts, thus forming incessant changes and exchanges in the valley of life.

The religion of democracy, the religion of Whitman, is also transcendental in its essence. The gospel of

Whitman and that of Emerson resemble each other. It is as a transcendentalist democrat that James speaks when, in his *Talks to Teachers*, he would see behind individuals the common substratum of mankind.

More recent philosophies attract James frequently towards a sort of monism. First, for a long period, the philosophy of Royce, then the idea of vaster consciousnesses enveloping our own. The idea of Myers, which indeed may be taken in a pluralistic sense, is often on the point of becoming a monistic idea in *The Varieties of Religious Experience*. In *Pragmatism*, in *A Pluralistic Universe*, he endeavours to find a solution that will at once satisfy certain requirements both of the pluralist and of the monist.

Royce emphasised the necessity, in the case of a universal " knower," to base on logic or rationality the existence of known beings. James declares that the pragmatists cannot dispense with this being if they would prove the reality of particular beings. Does not James in *The Will to Believe* actually show himself favourable to the hypothesis of a divine thinker who would think everything? Nor is the Bradleyan idea of transmutation absent from the book.

Again, James hesitates long in presence of a difficulty essential to his own psychology quite as much as to the metaphysic of the absolute as conceived by Royce; he asks himself how, within one consciousness, there can be other consciousnesses.

If we follow the line of his thought in this direction, we shall see a new monism emerge from pluralism.

In 1905 he interests himself in what he calls the problem of the domination of far-reaching consciousnesses over those of lesser scope, and declares that he does not understand these speculations very well. But he already speaks of experience pure and simple as being an absolute.

In *A Pluralistic Universe* he discusses the hypothesis of the absolute as formulated by Royce, and shows us some of the variations of his ideas on the problem. In a word, we may say that *A Pluralistic Universe* is the least pluralist of all his works, the one in which he endeavours to approach nearest to that monistic philosophy which always, *nolens volens*, attracted him. Royce, in conceiving his absolute, started from a comparison with psychic phenomena ; selves are compounded in the absolute, just as ideas, feelings, sensations—which are smaller " selves "—are compounded in our normal self ; it is here that James sees the formation of the central knot in the metaphysical problem. Such a compound of thoughts long seemed impossible to him. And while this compound seemed untenable to him in psychology, it also seemed quite as untenable in metaphysics.

He then sees that it is less the " absolute " idea in itself that he criticises than the whole class of suppositions, of which it offers simply the most remarkable example, the idea of " collective experiences claiming identity with their constituent parts, and yet experiencing things quite different from these latter."

But, he says to himself, " if *any* such collective experience can be, then, of course, . . . the absolute may be " ; the thing to do, above all else, is to find out if these experiences exist. The question becomes more definite ; it is once more, as it had been in the first instance, a psychological question. Are we to say, as James had said in his *Psychology*, that every complex psychic fact is a separate psychic entity, coming above the crowd of other psychic entities which are erroneously called its parts, and taking their place and function, though without having them, strictly speaking, as elements or constituent parts ? In that case we should have to deny the absolute and, along with the absolute, Fechner's Earth-soul which comprises within itself other souls. We should have to affirm nothing but the God of theism; for the logic of identity tells us that a thing cannot be different from itself.

But is such a position acceptable ? In the name of the logic of identity we break up the universe, we make it essentially discontinuous or discrete. It seems incomprehensible that the fields of consciousness which so regularly replace one another, each acquainted with the same matter though integrating it into an ever wider concept, should have nothing in common *qua* existences though they are identical *qua* functions. Are we to say that it is their object, their matter, that makes them identical ? But then this object, this matter, is at all events known differently, and we are still confronted with diversity.

Happy are the pantheists, James seems to be saying, if they alone are privileged to believe in the compounding of consciousnesses. But such cannot be the case ; our intellect cannot immure itself alive. Indeed, Fechner, Royce, Hegel seem to be pursuing the better path. To Fechner, the veto of logic is a thing of which he has never heard mention. Royce hears this voice, though he takes good care to pay no heed to its justifications ; Hegel is acquainted with these prohibitions, but he only despises them ; and all three proceed joyfully along their way. Shall we be alone in admitting this right of veto ?

And so the empiricists seemed to be the intellectualists ; rationalists, like Royce and Hegel, despised logic.

" I faced the problem with all the sincerity and patience I could bring to bear upon it ; I struggled for years,

filling hundreds of sheets of paper with notes and memo-
randa, discussing with myself this difficulty: How can
several consciousnesses be a single consciousness?" It was
necessary to abandon soulless psychology, or else either to
accept the idea that the logic of identity is not the only logic
and adopt a higher (or lower) form of rationality, or else
to admit that life is wholly and fundamentally irrational.

Why then not give up this soulless psychology, it will
be asked? Why not recognise spiritual agents, souls, a
deity? James, however, could not accept the idea of a
soul; this would mean the abandoning of his nominalism.
The soul is but a name. And so we have but to consider
the two things that remain: either invent a logic, as
Hegel tried to do, or completely and absolutely give up
logic.

James adopted the latter alternative. The problem
ceases to be a problem to him, because the conceptual
terms in which it is propounded make a solution impossible. And it is Bergson, he tells us, who encouraged
him in thus abandoning both logic and intellectualism,
that very logic in whose name he had first attacked
Hegel's philosophy, and which then, in agreement with
Hegel on this point, he condemned as inadequate.

If we give up intellectualistic logic, we should recognise
that psychical phenomena are compounded with one
another, and, more generally, we may admit that in the
absolute all phenomena blend together. As in experience
itself, they are their " own others." The absolute ceases
to be an impossibility.

In these abnormal or supranormal facts which always
seemed so pregnant to him, and in religious experiences,
James finds the strongest suggestions in favour of a sort
of confluence of our consciousnesses into vaster consciousnesses. He speaks of experiences of an unexpected life

that follows death, of experiences of joy that follow despair. This is the Lutheran idea, he says, of humbling ourselves in order to rise; it is the theory of Mind Cure, we give ourselves up to unknown forces, and fresh reserves of life reveal themselves to us; these experiences are in no way connected with our ordinary experiences, they reverse the ordinary values; at the same time, they seem to enlarge the world into vast unthinkable reaches. This cannot be explained by the understanding, in the sense generally attributed to the word. To grasp these experiences, we must admit ideas similar to those of Fechner: in the universe there is a soul that sympathises with that of the believer; there is continuity between our soul and this vaster soul, which by reason of this very continuity is capable of saving us. And so, in this view, there is a superhuman life which we can share; and James, to enable us to grasp this experimental monism, again employs the metaphor of the great psychic reservoir of which he made use in *Human Immortality*.

And yet at the last moment he once more embraces pluralism: the only way to escape the mystery of the fall is to be a pluralist, and recognise that, however vast, " the superhuman consciousness is not all-embracing." It is not absolutely true that " all things interpenetrate and telescope together in the great total conflux"; although, indeed, every given thing comprises a multiplicity, although between a given thing and its neighbours there is what James calls inextricable interfusion.

Thus we seem to see the outlines of a new doctrine forming themselves, whereof hints are given us by this realistic absolutism, this empirical philosophy of identity; if particular things are their "own others"; if everywhere there is that multiplicity in unity of which the monists speak; if in all our ideas there is, as it were, the presence of an absence; if the present moment comprises in itself that infinite complexity which the idealists presuppose in the absolute; if our self cannot be wholly distinguished from its causes, its environment, its objects, its past, its future, our own body; if the present overflows on to the past and the self on to the not-self; if our self is always a part of a self; if, lastly, the totality of our self is not something which can be conceived but only something which can be felt: then a new absolutism becomes possible. Why not say that we ourselves form the margin of a more truly central self? " May not you and I be confluent in a higher consciousness, and confluently active there, though we now know it not ? "

This monism, however, can scarcely be expressed in words, it is an act; to reflect this act, as it were, we must think in non-conceptualised terms. Why does life not respond to the questions asked of it by intellectualism ? Because intellectualism asks it questions which do not concern it and which it has not to understand.

Hence the absolute ceases to be a thing impossible. But to attain to it, it is preferable to follow the concrete and hypothetical method of Fechner than the ever more or less abstract and deductive method of Hegel, Royce, and Bradley. Then we shall reach " a pluralistic panpsychic view of the universe " somewhat approaching theirs in its essence.

And so James endeavours to find an answer to the problem set by Royce in a metaphysic which may be compared to the metaphysics of Strong and of Bergson and to the speculations of Morton Prince. He puts in the forefront that which was the monistic background of his philosophy: the idea of pure experience. Is it not essentially non-dualistic, as he says ? He claims to have reached " a new philosophy of identity." The pluralist philosophy, like that of the absolute, regards human substance as the divine substance itself; radical empiricism, he says, is a pantheistic philosophy and a panpsychism, but within identity itself it enables us to distinguish—as Fechner and Lotze had suggested and Bergson had actually done—rhythms of qualities, and according to it there is no complete and finished totality containing as data all the details of experience.

Thus James is not one of those tough-minded men of whom he speaks in *Pragmatism*. Pure pluralism would be pure anarchy to him. He is not contented with this jungle of facts. He would like to be conscious of a certain intimacy and sympathy in the Universe. He even goes so far as to say that the reason why he adopts pluralism is because it offers him a friendly universe. James regards God as a fellow-being; pluralism, he says in *A Pluralistic Universe*, especially panpsychic pluralism, satisfies him because it produces a consciousness of friendly souls in the universe. He must needs have a religion. Religion, James has told us, is that which makes the world dramatic and dangerous; it is religion that amplifies the echoes and reverberations of the world; it opens out unknown depths to the mind, making it dimly aware of terrible dangers. But he likewise tells us: religion makes the world calm and peaceful; it constitutes the certainty that the world will be saved. Comparing pluralism with monism in *Some Problems of Philosophy*, he says that the one is more moral, the other more religious. The very religion that brings war also brings peace. James did not see both aspects of religion at the same time, he saw them successively, and he tells us: pluralism is religious because it regards evil as real; pluralism is not religious because it regards evil as real; and, finally, he seems to regret that evil has so deep a reality for pluralism.

In his opinion, the idea of God is necessary in order that there may be guaranteed to him " a permanently present moral order." " A world with a God in it to say the last word, may indeed burn up or freeze, but . . . where He is, tragedy is only provisional and partial."

Of course James will never accept complete monism. He rallies to the idea of a " monistic pluralism." In *A Pluralistic Universe* he appears to wish to keep himself half-way between pluralism and monism. He wants the pluralist to grant him a certain unity and the monist a certain plurality. He reproaches the monists for being intransigent. The monist cannot accept the idea of something that is partly this and partly that. The monistic spirit is " violent." " It cannot suffer the notion of more or less." " It flies to violent extremes." It denies the legitimacy of the category of " some " ; it accepts only the categories of " all " and of " none." " On the other hand, compromise and mediation are inseparable from the pluralist philosophy." In this sense, James remains a pluralist.

Even when he is trying to be a monist, his metaphysics does not altogether reach this position.

" Ever not quite," might be said, borrowing Blood's phrase, quoted in *The Will to Believe*. " It is fit to be pluralism's heraldic device."

We may add that the empiristic, pragmatistic, and pluralistic way in which James deals with the problem of unity ultimately tends to lessen its importance. The only thing now left is to see how much unity and how much diversity there is in the Universe. " The world is ' one ' in some respects and ' many ' in others. . . . Once we are committed to this more sober view, the question of the One or the Many may well cease to appear important."

Thus a kind of immanent dialectic would seem to drive James from pluralism in the direction of a monism within which he attempts to integrate pluralism. *E pluribus unum* is finally his motto, as it was his father's ; in what way can unity be conceived for this to become possible ? Must one even " conceive " unity ? How is monism to relax, or rather to deepen, in order to make room for pluralism ? Perhaps thus, in the last resort, should these problems be stated if we are thoroughly to understand how they appeared to James.

Whilst he is more and more bent on solving the problem of the One and the Many, both the reader and James himself wonder if this problem is not losing its importance and even its meaning, since we can recognise a " monistic pluralism," and, in particular, since we are dealing with mental acts which transcend the intellect and may be expressed either in terms of monism or in terms of pluralism, as one wishes.

What we have stated may enable us to account for the fact that, strictly speaking, there are no disciples of William James. Those who at first might have been regarded as his followers have gradually drifted away from some of his teachings, or else have fused them with different doctrines, as R. B. Perry did.[16]

But we must consider the great influence he exercised over philosophers like Schiller, and, in a general way, over the personalists of Oxford, and over such personalists

[16] In his articles in *The Monist* of 1902 and in *An Approach to Philosophy*, he shows us reality everywhere evading the logic of the intellectualists. Pluralism alone can give a faithful idea of it. Mainly by the help of the idea of different realms of reality, he affirms the indetermination of things, their radical variety. But ever, even when he came nearest to personalism, he insisted on the " realistic " element of pluralism. We must study more and more precisely the world given to us. The criticisms of Royce by no means prove the inadequacy of a realist and pluralist philosophy, provided that the pluralism is not an absolute pluralism.

as Bakewell and his companions of the school of California. On the other hand, we shall see that the formation of neo-realism cannot be explained without taking into account the ideas of James.

The few thinkers we have now briefly to study are not disciples of James, but rather philosophers in whom there is frequently found the distinguishing characteristic of James, love of the concrete and the diverse, of life with its perils and struggles.

Dickinson Miller sees in nature discontinuities, absolute isolations, disjoined experiences ; like James, he completes his radical empiricism by a dynamic pluralism, by a theory of " ethical chance."

Lowes Dickinson, a brilliant and interesting writer, appears to have seen in these ideas more particularly what might be a source of moral inspiration. " As I read Man," he says, " he is a creature not finished, even approximately. . . . He is a being in process of creating himself, full of possibilities and potentialities." And these human possibilities are indeed, as James has said, the possibilities of the universe. We must, says Lowes Dickinson, bring man to see that the universe intends to advance towards the objects we set up ; we must fight, and on the issue of the fight the issue of the world will depend to some extent. " In fighting for Good we are assisting something real that is divine ; in fighting against Evil we are resisting something real that is diabolic." The mythology of the future, setting forth the world as a mighty battlefield, will, according to Lowes Dickinson, be dualistic, or rather, pluralistic.

Dresser, while remaining a determined monist, also has recourse to the works of James for lessons in energy ; he exalts man as the builder and possessor of his own destiny ; man has but to listen to the " voices of freedom " to see before him endless possibilities which evolutionism opens up for him, and to set forth, worshipping chance as a God.

In the articles and works of H. M. Kallen and of Goddard we are also confronted with an heroic conception of life. The world is at every moment of time full of new perils, says Goddard; philosopher and poet are to reveal to us a varied and dangerous world. H. B. Alexander expounds a "new Manichæism." Evil is real and God has to struggle against it.

Perhaps these thoughts are symptoms of a profound state of American mentality, ever on the look out for a religion of democracy and action; this mentality has endeavoured to find in the philosophy of James a belief destined, it may be, to succeed that of Emerson and that of Whitman.

Do we not also find the same tendencies in quite different philosophers, who differ from one another as well as from James, and who yet all unite, we might say, in this affirmation both of the world struggle and of the world alliance?

In the books of Santayana we occasionally catch a glimpse of a confused and chaotic world similar to that of James; we have the idea of an essential irrationality throughout existence. "What the rationalist calls nonentity is the substrate and locus of all ideas having the obstinate reality of matter, the crushing irrationality of Existence itself." The platonism of Santayana is superimposed on to a profound irrationalism.

William James mentioned how interesting were Fawcett's books: *The Riddle of the Universe* and *The Individual*. In these works, previous to his philosophy of Imagining, Fawcett desires to unite the "anti-Hegelian thought of Schelling and Schopenhauer and the literatures of the British-American empirist school."

He is an anti-intellectualist, an irrationalist. The intelligence that forms part of the world of appearance cannot enable us to comprehend truth in its fullness. Fact is fact only by virtue of its own right and might. The groundwork of nature is alogical, and the alogical expresses itself by force. The universe is a struggle of many forces. "Plurality withal is as basic as Unity." The world is incessant change.

The War must necessarily have had an influence on these tendencies. While, then, American thought rejects certain of the ideas just considered, a certain conception of force for instance, on the other hand it is led more and more to conceive of a finite God who protects finite individuals, and this theological trend towards a God ever more personal and near to us and responsive to our call has been frequently expressed in the *Hibbert Journal* during the past few years. A God who is our comrade, who struggles by our side, and who, through war, leads us on to peace and the free society of individuals and peoples : such appears the God of the philosophers of America.

Hence the reception accorded to the later works of Wells, both in America and in England : *The Soul of a Bishop* and *God the Invisible King.* A finite God surrounded by Nature and Necessity ; a God who is our ally in the struggle. The God of Wells is akin to the God of Renouvier and the God of James. Indeed, even more than in these two works, where behind the finite God we see the veiled and omnipresent God, do we find ourselves face to face with the finite God and with him alone in *Mr Britling Sees It Through.* " They (the theologians) have been extravagant about God. They have had silly absolute ideas—that he is all powerful, that he is omni-everything. But the common sense of men knows better. . . . After all, the real God of the Christians is Christ, not God Almighty. . . . Some day he will triumph. . . . But it is not fair to say that he causes all things now. It is not fair to make out a case against him : it is a theologian's folly. God is not absolute, He is finite. . . . A finite God, who struggles in his great and comprehensive way as we struggle in our weak and silly way, who is with us, that is the essence of real religion. Why, if I thought there was an omnipotent God who looked down on battles and deaths and all the waste and horror of this war, able to prevent these things, doing them to amuse himself, I would spit in his empty face." Soon God will appear to Mr Britling, God the master, the captain of mankind, God who fights against might and darkness, "God the Invisible King," a young and audacious king.

And in the features of the old experimenter in *Joan and Peter*, who delights in introducing novelties into the world, who creates freedom and watches over his experiments from afar, we recognise once again the young and audacious king.

And yet, is Wells to stop here ? There is the God who rules the world, but there is also the God whom we feel and who lives in the human heart, towards whom our efforts are directed, a God who is free necessity. And here as in the case of James, though in a different way, we again transcend pluralism. The Veiled Being is every-where present.

Is not also this conception—found in Chesterton—of an ever new life, full of miracles, of adventure and romance, and yet where one feels at one's ease, this " military fidelity," neither optimistic nor pessimistic, which binds us to life and to our " divine captain," in spite of all the differences which separate from the heterodoxy of James and Wells the thought of Chesterton, that profound orthodoxy to which profound paradox leads . . . is not this a conception akin to that of these authors ?   God transcendent and personal is essentially free, and not only miracles but also laws, not only the supernatural but also nature, are manifestations of his free, irrational choice.   Moreover, is not nature supernatural ?   Like Blood and James, Chesterton insists on this element — however faint — of irrationality, which causes nature never to be wholly reasonable and makes it always slightly supernatural.

Without being a pluralist, strictly speaking, he emphasises the division and separation of things, the reality of persons.   " It is the instinct of Christianity to be glad that God has broken the universe into little pieces, because they are living pieces. . . . Christianity is a sword that separates and sets free.   No other philosophy makes God actually rejoice in the separation of the universe into living souls."   Hence the possibility of love when we are confronted with persons, and of wonder when we are confronted with things ; hence, too, the possibility of action.

And is not God himself a society, quite different from that Oriental deity, the God of Omar and of Mahomet ? " There is a sort of liberty and variety existing even in the inmost chamber of the world."

And the idea of adventure persistently recurs both in *Orthodoxy* and in Chesterton's tales and novels : the idea of incessant peril, of the precipice close by, of possible perdition.   " To the Christian, existence is a *story*, which may end up in any way."   An immortal crisis, a crossroads which ever presents itself anew, a cross-roads in the middle of the valley: such is life for Christianity. "Christianity alone has felt that God, to be wholly God, must have been a rebel as well as a king."

So in the orthodoxy of Chesterton, as in the heterodoxy of Wells and James, fairly similar ideas recur, in spite of the essential differences which separate Chesterton both from James and from Wells, and even distinguish him from them.

BOOK IV

FROM PERSONAL IDEALISM TO NEO-REALISM

CHAPTER I

THE OXFORD SCHOOL AND SCHILLER

ABOUT the year 1898 a group of friends was in the habit of meeting frequently for the purpose of discussing philosophy. They attacked both naturalism and absolutism, setting up against these doctrines a philosophy of individuality, which, moreover, by reason of its idealism, claimed to have remained faithful to the Oxford tradition.

They expounded their principles in a volume entitled *Personal Idealism*. A volume which had appeared the previous year and also bore the same title was destined to prove the beginning of the Californian school, just as the latter volume began the Oxford school. In both of them the ideas of *Personal Idealism* and of *The Limits of Evolution* are fundamental. Sturt indeed declares that the expression came quite naturally into his mind and that of his friends before they had made acquaintance with Howison's work entitled *The Limits of Evolution*.

What pluralist elements are to be found in this new Oxonian metaphysics? We do not think it possible to call most of the members of this group pluralists, as Howison does. They simply show tendencies towards a certain pluralism, counteracted by certain other philosophical or religious ideas.

Sturt studies objects in their concrete totality, their personality : the supremely good thing, he says, is personality. He sees things moving and active ; the " idol " of absolutism is the idol of passivity. Mystical and pessimistic, the absolutist sinks to sleep within the bosom of the absolute. The personal idealist, on the other hand, builds up for himself a philosophy of effort ; the whole universe exerts itself and is free ; even within the universe all things are free and possess qualities of their own ; there is no absolute dependence, only a relative dependence and independence and a free God.

We see that here there is no pluralism, strictly speaking, and yet, by reason of the importance attributed to personal wills and individual efforts, Sturt belongs to the same class of thinkers.

It is the same with Bussell, who would gladly free the individual from the tyranny of the One ; the same with Underhill, who insists on the holes and the saltus that are in the universe ; the same with Boyce Gibson, who momentarily joins with those he calls " pluralists or voluntarists," though but provisionally, as he himself specifies. Indeed, he superimposes monism on to his pluralism. He claims that we cannot insist on the pluralist postulate as being the ultimate postulate, and considers that the true function of present-day pluralism is to prepare the way for a rational and fruitful monism.

The final essay in the volume is by Rashdall ; it seems to be a kind of statement of the general ideas of the group.

Rashdall must have been profoundly influenced by Lotze and the theologians—especially Ritschl—whose theories have their root in the teaching of Lotze. He deplores the fact that most English philosophers are acquainted with Hegel only, and with him but superficially, instead of studying H. Lotze, who, he says, was the only original modern thinker of the first rank, of profound Christian ideas. Rashdall's theology is the continuation of the theology of Martineau and Lotze.

He regards the problem of personality, in his own words, as " the apex of the whole philosophical pyramid." And though he does not recoil from the word absolute, nor from the idea of unity nor the conception of an extra-temporal substance, he yet criticises monism severely. One consciousness cannot be included in another consciousness. The very fact that there are consciousnesses in the universe constitutes the negation of pantheism.

The only thing to be said is that above the imperfect human personality, scarcely remembering one year what it was the other year, rises the personality of God, a good, eternal being (though within time like all things), having with men relations similar to the relations of men with one another, having feelings like our own, experiencing pleasure and even, at times, something akin to pain. Will it be alleged that all these determinations make God finite ? Be it so. Everything real is in a sense finite, and God is limited by us who are created by him. Although it seems to Rashdall that God must be omniscient, he does not think that God must feel everything, understanding being far wider and more extensive in him than sensibility. " God does not experience my hunger," says Rashdall. And yet, God has enough feeling, enough humanity to compassionate the troubles and misfortunes here below.

Indeed, everything is not good in this world ; according to both Rashdall and James, the distinction between good and evil exists in the nature of things. Here, as in the case of James and Renouvier, evil, the fourth postulate of practical reason, is made possible by a personalist theology.

And so the world appears, not as one great consciousness, but as a great ensemble of consciousnesses one of which deserves to be called God, as a city-state of intellects, a community of persons where the latter have nothing to give up of their own distinctive qualities. In this way, Rashdall claims to reconcile pluralism and monism.

The theory of Rashdall strongly resembles in certain aspects that of McTaggart, as Rashdall recognises. In both there is the same mental image of God as one consciousness in the midst of other consciousnesses; the same conception of the limited power of God; the same affirmation that persons are the only reality. The differences between them seem mainly due to the fact that Rashdall is less individualist, less " pluralist " than McTaggart, whom he blames for not introducing sufficient unity into the world, for representing it as independent of all consciousness. Had he been more profoundly idealistic, McTaggart would have more firmly established the unity of the universe, a unity different from that of an abstract system.

In more particular details Rashdall and McTaggart do not agree. Rashdall does not believe in the pre-existence of souls, one of the dogmas of McTaggart. The latter denies that God is perfect, seeing that his perfection would destroy the equilibrium of the world city-state. But is it right, answers Rashdall, to transfer an argument valid for the world of humanity to the totality of things ? Is not that again being too little of an idealist ? All these contrasts which Rashdall finds between his theory and that of McTaggart can be traced back to one and the same problem: Has God a very pronounced pre-eminence over other consciousnesses, or do we simply look upon him as a fellow-citizen? Rashdall calls his idealism "theistic idealism" in contrast with the "social idealism" of McTaggart and his more radical individualism.

Thus Rashdall parts company with the absolutist McTaggart because he is more "religious," because he believes in a more powerful deity. He parts company with him by reason of an idealism which he regards as more consistent, by reason of the conception—arising from this idealism—of a world more completely organised. What then are exactly his relations with the pluralists, and how can we class him with them? In his essay in *Personal Idealism*, he attempts, as we have seen, to justify a certain pluralism. Consciousnesses, he says, are separate and distinct. "The real is that which is for itself, and every spirit and consciousness (in its measure and degree) is for itself." The world, he distinctly states, though in quasi-Hegelian tones, is not a single spirit. Consequently we had to study Rashdall's works along with those of the pluralists. And yet he claims that he is not a pluralist if we use pluralism in the restricted way he does, as the affirmation of the co-eternity of souls and God. Certainly he has no *a priori* objection to pluralism, but neither has he any reason for believing in it. How, in particular, can pluralism account for this general unity and for the different unities found in experience? Indeed, the God of Rashdall occupies "more room" in the world than does the God of James or of Schiller: he is the cause of all our feelings and wills. Rashdall believes in a sort of "will in God": he is omnipresent, continually present, at least, in the consciousness of man. Is this indeed the personal finite God that Rashdall first offered us?

Or is not some theory of divine thought here felt to be necessary ?

Thus Rashdall might seem less of a pluralist than McTaggart the absolutist; and yet, if we apply to him the criterion adopted, whether consciously or not by the pluralistic pragmatists, a criterion which enables them to distinguish their partisans from their opponents, he then appears more akin to them. McTaggart goes farther away from pluralism, because he denies time; Rashdall draws nearer to it, because he believes in time.

The school of Personal Idealism, the Oxford school, if not completely pluralistic, at all events, in the case of Sturt, Bussell, Boyce Gibson, Underhill, and Rashdall, shows several of the characteristics of pluralism. From this group came one of the protagonists of pluralism, Schiller, whose *Riddles of the Sphinx* is one of the most brilliant, and at times profound, expositions of a philosophy of becoming, of individuality and of spirit.

Schiller was led to pluralism mainly by the needs of his own nature; by his moral aspirations (since for him, as for Lotze, metaphysics must be quasi-ethical); by the desire for effortless and untrammelled action, for easy movement, far different from the more tense volition of James; by the æsthetic love of diversity; by a certain romanticism; by the sense of individuality in its unique, as it were impermeable, character; and, at the same time, by the sense of the social and the collective; and, finally, by appreciation of concrete facts, though this was less pronounced in him than in James. The influence of Lotze in a certain measure, of Mill's last essays, and of James, did but strengthen these deep-lying tendencies.

James started first with realism; Schiller, like his companions in personal idealism, continued the idealist tradition of Oxford. Schiller's philosophy, says Dewey, is "a translation, in effect, of monistic intellectualistic idealism into a pluralistic voluntaristic idealism." In *Riddles of the Sphinx*, his first work, does he not contrast the transcendental self with the phenomenal self ? Does he not speak of the history of the world as of the history of the interplay between God and the self ? Later on, he finds room in his philosophy for realistic ideas. All the time, however, we discover a certain idealism behind his realism.

And yet Schiller is far more violent than James in his criticism of the absolute. The fight between monism and pluralism is keener in England than in America.

Schiller's pluralism is first, as he says himself, a criticism : " It is simply a negation of monism."

Even admitting the existence of the absolute, it would be useless to know it : more than this, such knowledge would be harmful. From a practical standpoint, pantheism is but simple atheism. Can one love—revere— the absolute ? In the absolute there is everything, good and bad alike. The idea of the absolute destroys all action and all love ; to the absolutist, all is good. Whatsoever action we perform, our action neither enriches nor impoverishes the All, which continues as rich as before— if indeed there is a before and after in the absolute. The actualities are destroyed in their germs, which are the possibilities. The possibilities of good, true, and beautiful things are annihilated. In the dialogue, " Protagoras the Humanist," Schiller points out the consequences of monism: "*Antimorus.* Then you are probably ignorant, too, of his son, Sophomorus ? *Philonous.* Entirely. What prevented him from becoming famous ? *Antimorus.* He said *it was all one*, and did not care." All action founders in the absolute. Science disappears, as well as religion and morality ; not only does pantheism, precisely because it seems to explain everything, explain nothing, but it reduces the world to an illusion devoid of meaning; it prevents us from applying to concrete and particular things—which it annihilates—concrete and particular methods; it repudiates all idea of evolution. On the other hand, to how many insoluble problems does it not give rise? How has the world been able to detach itself from the absolute? How can the absolute appear in the form of consciousness? How is change possible? How can absolutism ever account for the opulence of the finite individuality? No wonder that hitherto it has been impossible to set up a consistent monism.

The very concept—that of infinite totality—on which absolutism is based, is equivocal. A whole cannot be infinite—the word, infinity, simply meaning the impossibility of forming a whole; besides, we can come to such a whole as the universe only by an ideal summation of the parts; such a whole will never be real, at least never so real as its parts. The absolutists also say: given a reality, it must be put into totality. Is this necessary? All beings may be regarded more or less as independent of a totality. Then we can build up the whole in different ways that are alike legitimate; how are we to distinguish the one that is valid? It is possible to conceive a spiritualistic monism, even a materialistic monism, more acceptable, claims Schiller, than spiritualistic monism. Nor are these the only objections that Schiller brings against monism; he shows, still remembering Kantism, that the idea of cause cannot be applied to the noumenal world; he maintains, before James insisted on the idea in *A Pluralistic Universe*, that Bradley's " sophistic " is based on language and that language is inadequate for reality. He asks why it is more difficult to assume

14

several ultimate existences than to assume one only, and states that really there is nothing in monism to recommend it.

In order to posit the One, do we not see that we must destroy the world ? Absolutism leads its adepts to conceive man as the dream of a sleeping God. To experience the dangerous charm, the *vertigo* of this unity, we in our turn must dream and adopt the methods of the Indian Gymnosophists and of the modern Mind-Curers.

Leaving aside all these mystics of unity, as Schiller calls them, let us follow him in the contest with a philosopher whom he admired, with Lotze when the latter claims that he is compelled to conceive of unity in order to explain the pluralism he had so clearly formulated. It is a strange combat, for Schiller's very way of discussing and arguing seems to be borrowed from Lotze.

Is Lotze's problem a real one ? asks Schiller. Must we seek an explanation of the universal interaction of things ? Interaction is essential to the existence of the world, and that in a more fundamental manner than Lotze himself suggests. To say that things interact in the world is to state a proposition obtained analytically, to state what is implicitly affirmed when we say that there is a world.

Hence must an explanation be given to the fact that there is a world ? Did not Lotze himself say that such questions should not be asked, seeing that the existence of the world is the ground and the presupposition of all our reasoning ? And so there is no need to conceive a unity in things other than that consisting in their real interactions. Unity is but the possibility of their mutual interactions, and this unity of things is no more deserving of respect than is their plurality. Lotze's argument, far from being a royal road leading towards monism, is simply the common road along which both monism and pluralism alike pass.

After attacking a problem which he had no need to tackle, Lotze solves it by a method he had previously precluded himself from using. Had he not pointed out the defects of the conception of substance?

Indeed, the consequences of his theory are anything but satisfactory. Why should immanent causality be more intelligible than transcendent causality? Why should it alone be intelligible? Does Lotze not confess that this apparently perfect intelligibility is due solely to our familiarity with that idea of an immanent cause which we imagine we experience in our own activity? But is this any reason for exalting into the absolute this sort of causality? The reason we have this sense of inner change is that we are conscious beings. Can we argue from our consciousness to that of the absolute M, admitting it possesses consciousness? The reason why we change is either because things outside ourselves impel us to the change, or else because we are in a state of unstable equilibrium. And so in both cases we must refrain from attributing change to the absolute.

Lotze's theory explains neither causality nor change; it reduces the ordered succession of events to an empty *chassé-croisé* of letters within the alphabet of the world. Whatever the change may be, it will be arbitrary and inexplicable, seeing that the root equation $M=M$ can continually be expressed in endless ways. There is no world more indeterminate than that of the absolutist, in which phenomena succeed one another by chance. The huge, shapeless bulk rolls on, as destitute of meaning as a world of eternal returning.

Lotze himself confesses that his philosophy may naturally enough end in pessimism. The God of Lotze may be the origin of all possible worlds, of the worst as of the best ; he has no real moral attributes.

Against monistic and absolutistic theories Schiller sets up a pluralism. In his theory of knowledge, in his pragmatism, he shows himself to be a pluralist. Whereas, to the absolutist, he tells us, all truth is in itself unity and absolute coherence, and also forms with other truths a great coherent whole ; to the pluralist, truth is above all a concrete and individual thing, and it becomes more and more precise and particular and experimental, even at the cost of its internal and its external coherency. Here, as with James, we find the two theories of polysystematism and polyrealism. To begin with, truth, being multiple, can adapt itself to the sight and the standpoint of each individual.

> " There are nine-and-sixty ways
>   Of composing tribal lays,
>   And every single one of them is right,"

quotes Schiller. If we admit the efficacy of human activities in building up truth, instead of an absolute truth we reach a truth which is not a unity ; by our changing activities, truth may be built up in different ways, and pragmatism is a pluralism.

Not only are there different systems by which we can make truth and build up reality, but—and here is the explanation of this first idea—there are different realities ; first, two radically opposed to each other, the everyday world and the world of science ; then, within the world of science itself, there are different bodies of truths that are independent and sometimes mutually contradictory. We are constantly passing from one world to another, as in passing from dream to reality. From the point of view of an idealistic experimentalism " we may conceive ourselves," says Schiller, " as passing through any number of worlds separated from each other by (partial) discontinuities in our experience."

The criticism of the monism of Lotze in *Humanism* and the pragmatistic theory of Schiller enable us to glimpse certain characteristics of his pluralism. It has its direct origin in the pluralist conception as expounded by Lotze in the first stage of his philosophy : unity is but the appearance of diversity. Phenomena need no substratum ; as the physical world does not need an Atlas to sustain it, so the moral world does not need an absolute to confer reality upon it. Monism is a possibility, it is " in potency," whereas plurality is in act. The One has not the same kind of existence as the Many ; it has the existence of the possible only ; that is why insoluble problems are raised when it is " hypostasised." Schiller's vision of the world is more chaotic, more confused and diversified than is the vision of Lotze. The reason is that in this matter Schiller is dominated by James. He regards the world as a perpetual ebb and flow, " a rough-and-tumble tussle."

He likes to show that the bonds of the pluralistic world are loose, that things possess various qualities, are " coloured, fluctuant, evanescent, troublesome."

If there were no fundamental plurality, could there be an evolution of the cosmic drama ?

To him, the world is indeterminate matter, an ever-ambiguous possibility of contraries. Each time we act, we choose between two divergent universes. In our experience, says Schiller, dwell endless possibilities of " alternative " universes.

He is brought by these two ideas, a plurality of elements in the world and indeterminate matter, to a metaphysic of evolution, or as Schiller expresses it, a metaphysic of the time process.

The four basic dogmas of this metaphysic are : that the becoming of the world is a process, that it is a real process, not simply thought out, or a derivative of thought, that it has a definite beginning and a definite end in time, that it is irreversible.

The world is incessantly incomplete ; in it something new is continually appearing, first because it contains inexhaustible possibilities of developments, then because it may find itself in contact with other unknown worlds. It may be that its development is mainly continuous, but why not also believe in discontinuities, the effects and signs of a universal exuberance ?

Schiller's individualism is all the time linked with his theory of an incomplete world. The worth of the individual dwells in its flexibility. Individualities are infinitely varied, from that of a drop of water to that of a human being. Individuality may continually increase. It is an ideal as well as a reality, the loftiest of ideals, the profoundest of realities.

To reach this ideal—and here again the influence of James is perceptible—we must struggle, struggle intensely, be willing to risk something; otherwise, life loses all its charm and allurement.

The struggle is one between the good and the corrupt parts of the universe. To Schiller as to James, there is evil, deep-rooted evil in the world. Moreover, nothing but the deep realisation of evil can free us from pessimistic and from optimistic quietism alike, both being monistic beliefs we are to reject.

Schiller arrives at a monadology, the conception of a world consisting of free and active spirits which have been and cannot cease to be, the idea of a cosmic society, a collectivism of personal lives. In this ideal society he finds the complementary notion of an ideal individuality.

The individuality of which the whole of nature dreams is the life of perfect individuals in a perfect society, capable of existing only in society, as society is incapable of existing except through them.   Man is a social being ; is it not natural that Schiller's humanism should conceive of the world as a great society ?

God himself is part of this society ; the God of Schiller, of James, and of Rashdall is a personal and finite God. Otherwise, how are we to explain freedom, change, evil ? And yet it is he who created the world and continues it in being.

This God appears to be a one God, seeing that for fellow-citizens he seems to have—not other Gods—but eternal spirits, immortal souls, living in pre-existences and metempsychoses.   Immortality, Schiller tells us in *Riddles of the Sphinx*, is a natural consequence derived from the pluralist hypothesis.   He is less affirmative, however, regarding immortality in his other works ; but, whereas James sometimes says that personally the question has no deep interest for him, immortality remains for Schiller one of the main philosophical questions, one, moreover, that religion alone can answer.   Thus Schiller's philosophy, like that of Rashdall and many personal idealists, ends in religion.   His God is not the heterodox God of James, but rather the one personal God of the believer, towards whom we may be led by this philosophy wherein the ideas of Lotze, Renouvier, and James appear transmuted by the Aristotelian tradition of Oxford.

As we have seen, the pluralism of James is not wholly free from certain monistic tendencies.   It is the same with that of Schiller, in whom, perhaps, these tendencies are more manifest than in James.

Monism, says Schiller, is both the condition and the goal of pluralism.

It is comprehensible that, in a certain sense, it is the condition of pluralism. The unity of things, he says, adopting the ideas of Lotze, springs from and dwells within their plurality, unity being, as we have said, no more than another name given to the " possibility of interaction." Pluralism therefore implies a certain unity. But this One which we take for granted is, as Schiller says, the most insignificant thing in the world ; it is a unity " which goes without saying." Here monism is by no means a principle of explanation, neither does it call for explanation itself, it is simply the statement of the fact of the interaction of things ; hence it is along this line that we must accept the affirmation of the pluralist philosopher in his *Riddles of the Sphinx* : the universe is a one, a totality.

And yet does it not sometimes appear to readers of Schiller that the idea of unity assumes more real consistence, that it becomes the idea of an " intrinsic coherency " of experience, and that instead of being a simple possibility of pluralism, it seems to become a possibility of monism ? He regards unity as being at the origin, but also at the end, of the cosmic process. It is " the potential harmony of the whole of experience." Is not that the language of the other Oxford school, the school of monism ? This harmony should be complete, continues Schiller, and is he not using an idealistic argument when he says that " if it be not harmonious throughout we can feel no confidence that it is harmonious in any part " ? In truth, we do not know if Schiller in these passages is thinking of the present or of the future world. As a rule, doubtless, he applies his monism to the future.

In considering reality, if we start by observing the man who desires, wills, acts, *i.e.* if we follow an essentially humanistic method, on the one hand we see the agent retaining his unity in the midst of his efforts, and on the other hand we see him expressing his unity by his will to conceive the world as a cosmos. We must suspect that progress towards unity corresponds in nature with this human desire for unity. And, indeed, just as for Schiller the absolutist theory of truth is true *qua* ideal, so the world which Schiller suspects to be at the end of evolution is a harmonious world. Schiller approves of the idea that philosophy is a unification of the universe ; monism is a theory that is valid for the world, once the cosmic process is at an end. It is then the last moment of dialectic which, after passing from abstract unity to concrete diversity, reaches the final synthesis : concrete unity ; such seems to be the thought of Schiller expressed in Hegelian terms. And so Schiller here seems to be " allured " by the very mysticism of unity for which he reproaches the Hegelians ; he takes pleasure in " the fleeting vision, more or less clear, more or less obscure, the beatific vision of that perfect harmony of total experience." Thus he conceives of a total truth, superior to all partial truths, because it satisfies all the needs of man ; it is to seek this truth that man should ever go forward, eager alike for goodness, for happiness and for beauty, " offering the world his requirements in their entirety, their inseparable union."

This is rather a " harmonism " than a monism, Schiller would say. Does he not recognise that there may be differences of opinion, that men may " agree to differ " ? This harmony, however, in which men will be brought to renounce all truths capable of clashing with the truths of other men, in which all friction has disappeared and no irruption of any kind can disturb our security, is no longer pluralism.

Schiller himself was aware of these monistic tendencies of his. In a debate before the Aristotelian Society in 1908 he regrets that "Professor James should sometimes write as though the logical sins of absolutism entailed the utter condemnation of every metaphysical belief in the unity of the universe." He repeats that monism may become true; he goes farther and says that he can "propound no absolutely cogent proof of metaphysical Pluralism." He insists on the monistic tendencies found in *Studies in Humanism*. He repudiates the over-bold assertions of the first edition of *Riddles of the Sphinx*. But even in the *Riddles*, do we not already find him—though at other times he insisted so strongly on the temporal, the incomplete character of things—saying that time, whose origin is in eternity, will end in eternity, sheltering his world of monads from all danger, setting it above the sphere of change, foreseeing a final conclusion to the cosmic process, anticipating the end of time itself?

The fact is that his pluralism is not pure and un-adulterated pluralism; in particular, he is not the tough-minded man of whom James speaks; at times reality appears to him of a feverish, barbarous, hideous nature, and an endless fight seems to him a futile one. From 1906 onwards he tends to cut himself clearly apart from certain partisans of irrationalism, while maintaining his objections to absolutist philosophies.

Several critics have noticed this final monism of Schiller. Moore criticises the "inconsistencies" of this philosophy, McGilvary speaks of this "solipsistic absolute into which we are all and each of us finally rolled up," and does not James, in his section on Common Sense in *Pragmatism*, assail the idea of the ultimate as well as that of the absolute, *i.e.* in essence, perhaps, the metaphysic of Schiller as well as that of Bradley? Here we may find, after all, not contradictions, but the expression of the free activity of a mind which is conscious of the attraction of diverse ideas.

Certain disciples of Schiller would seem to have cut themselves aloof from monism in more radical fashion.

Frank C. Doan borrows from Schiller the idea of an incomplete and diverse world: " The more a sense of unity develops in an experience, the more that experience withdraws from life." Reality appears as a multiplicity of fluid atoms, so to speak, a stream which carries away things that resist and things that yield, concepts and feelings, continuities and discontinuities.

This reality, adds Doan, perhaps remembering the theories of the school of Chicago, is ever bringing us face to face with new problems ; and man is ever acting upon it.

Within ourselves, corresponding to this flow of atoms, we are conscious of " a plural array of feeling tones " ; from them stream our many plans, our diverse undertakings, partial harmonies in process of growth. Doan asks us to be phenomenists in ethics, to endeavour to concentrate on particular tasks, to refrain from speaking of happiness or perfection in the singular. He says that the moral life is pre-eminently " pluralistic." Both heroic and pessimistic, aware that all pleasure is fleeting and all joy " elusive," we must be content with these non-unified experiences, with these partialities, the acuteness of these contrasts, these tragic insecurities. We have to drain to the dregs the tragic cup of finitude. Thus shall we create a pragmatism that is militant, active, affirmative ; thus shall we experience the dramatic feeling of our fugitive and evanescent joys.

Influenced by the Bergsonian philosophy, Doan is able to see the world in its continuity ; he also sees it in its discontinuity, like James ; he contemplates problematic and interrogative reality like Dewey, he sets up against it the youthful audacity of man, just as does the school of Leonardo ; and he has learnt from M. Rauh, the author of *L'Expérience Morale*, to apply his mind to special problems, to content himself with daily tasks, transforming them by a tested ideal ; out of all these elements he has created for himself a vision of reality.

His answers, however, to metaphysical problems seem uncertain ; at times he appears to be advancing in the direction of that " collectivism " of which we have often spoken. " The relationship between this finite self and any other higher self, human or divine, could be only social and not ontological."

At times he conceives, as the basis of reality, a kind of self-contradictory absolute, shattered by itself, and whose contradictions are an ever reviving excitant. Nothing but a reality of this sort can explain " these incertitudes, these tragedies, these sicknesses of the soul."

Occasionally his philosophy seems as though it must rather terminate in a vague cosmic humanism that is essentially monistic. It is this latter attitude that he has seemed to adopt more recently ; hence we wonder what he is able to retain of his earlier pluralism. Doan seemed to be one of those pluralists to whom pluralism was—to employ Schiller's expression—the alpha and the omega of philosophy, one of those to whom individuality, contrast, finitude were not simply facts but inestimable values, and yet he abandons this pluralism in favour of monism. All the same, he remains faithful to his metaphysical pragmatism, to what he calls his mysticism of the will.

Brett, also sensitive to English and American influences, in a brilliantly written book shows us Gassendi as one of the ancestors of pluralism, perhaps of pragmatist pluralism. If the idea of unity—he puts the saying into the mouth of Gassendi—gives no valid result, if the monistic doctrine is indeed one of inertia, if also we are delicate souls enamoured of the golden mean and of nice distinctions, then let us declare ourselves pluralists.

The naïve—as he expresses it—and yet fully graded pluralism at which Brett arrives is mainly a respect and a relish for qualities; it is in the realm of qualities that are to be found the really irreducible factors of the universe. And so we may conceive the world as one whole from the standpoint of quantity, but at the same time as real multiplicity from the standpoint of quality. It is only because of the existence of differences between things, of nuances or gradations, that we are able to understand their interactions.

Moreover, Brett, along with Schiller, regards unity as both the foundation and the end of cosmic evolution.

It is an interesting work to study, one after the other, these two pluralists, both dominated by the same ideas, which each transposes according to his own distinctive temperament, one rather influenced by practical, the other by æsthetic, conceptions.

CHAPTER II

As we have stated, pragmatism and pluralism are, in a way, connected. All the same, we have just seen that there is an idealist pluralism, that of the Oxford school. We may add that there is also a pluralist idealism, that of Howison and his school, which may be called the Californian school.

Howison's book, *The Limits of Evolution*, is the result of twenty years of meditation, he tells us. Some of the essays in the volume are dated 1882 and 1883.

In the course of these twenty years, Howison proceeded from Hegelianism to pluralism; by studying the notes in the earliest of the essays and comparing the more recent with the older ones, we are able to follow the evolution of his thought. At first he seems to have been Hegelian pure and simple. The *Journal of Speculative Theology* printed his works; he took part in the *Symposia* of the absolutists; he was a member of the Concord School of Philosophy. About 1883 he wishes to reconcile the affirmation of the existence of the individual with Hegelianism; he imagines he has found the principles necessary for a rational theism in a tradition beginning with Plato, continuing with Aristotle, Spinoza, and Fichte, and ending with Hegel. Then he weans himself from belief in impersonal ideas; he believes in objective causes analogous to our will. More and more does he consider that Hegelianism and the affirmation of the individual are contradictory terms. He reads the works of James and Schiller, who have already partially expounded their pluralism; he also reads the works of Royce.

He does not seem to have studied the philosophy of Lotze nor that of Renouvier; the only predecessors of his pluralism that he quotes are Aristotle, Leibniz, and Kant. It is in Kant that he first finds the conception of the ideal domain, the kingdom of ends, that is essential to his philosophy.

Howison's intellectual temperament differs profoundly from those of James and of Schiller. In particular he lacks the sternness of James, that will to live in the midst of contending forces. His fundamental preoccupation, the problem that dominates his entire work, is that of immortality. Besides, Howison conceives the individual only as related to the general; he sees the world only *sub specie infinitatis*; to him, limitation is decadence, the universal is the divine. We are far from that cult of the finite and the particular which at times the pluralism of James showed itself to be.

True, Howison—and in this he is very similar to James—would not at any price have a world monotonous and devoid of variety, even though its monotony were the monotony of perfection.

But perhaps this is one of the very few characteristics that bring him into sympathy with empirical pluralism; through his vision of an orderly and peaceable world, of the infinite and the general, he represents a special variety of pluralism, pluralist idealism, of which we find no more than hints in Schiller and the Oxford group.

Howison's method then seems in its origin very different from that of the other pluralists : he sets up as an enemy of pragmatism and all irrationalism.   He embraces the entire *a priori* theory of Kantism.

And yet, can we not find in Howison the same way of arguing as that adopted by his pluralist colleagues ?

He says that we have to inquire persistently what our conceptions are really making of mankind, of its vocation and destiny.   Indeed, Howison stops there and declares that his critics are mistaken in regarding him as a utilitarian in metaphysics.   He declares he has no desire whatsoever to set up conscience simply as a categorical imperative out of harmony with theoretical consciousness. But shall we be compelled in spite of all to accept this ill-omened truth of which he tells us ?   Before embracing it, must not greater circumspection be shown in our survey of this truth than in that of any other ?   We must accept it only when it is no longer possible to do otherwise.   As a genuine pragmatist in spite of himself, did he not give up his monism because it went against the postulates of the moral nature ?   Howison dedicated his principal book : " To all who feel a deep concern for the dignity of the soul."

Howison is now to apply this method, as thus defined, to what he calls the great problem of philosophy, the problem of unity.   On the one hand, he attacks the philosophy of evolution, so destructive of the reality of the human person, of moral good, of truth, of absolute beauty, of personal immortality, of divine personality ; on the other hand, he attacks the monism which " absorbs" and annihilates everything, the monism which is at war with the interests that characterise human nature and which leads to determinism.   Will science be postulated ? Science, the pantheistic evolutionists of America tell us, leads to pantheism; this Howison denies. Does it not rather prove the part played by inventions, the supremacy of the personal mind? Besides, there is an immanent logic by which monism is necessarily self-destructive; the philosophy of Hartmann, pseudo-idealism, on the one hand, the intellectualistic materialism of Dühring, on the other hand, are the two *reductiones ad absurdum* into which monism is condemned to fall. "Monism moving towards pluralism, through agnosticism and its self-dissolution," is the title of one of Howison's essays. His arguments are not only directed against neo-Hegelian monism, and against the monism of Hartmann, but also against the milder form of monism advocated by Royce. There can be no possible alliance between monism and pluralism. Our pluralism must allow of no compromise.

Hence nature appears to consist of individual and spontaneous persons who have a noumenal reality, of indeterminate centres of consciousness of Leibnizian monads, defining themselves, with reference to their final cause, in terms of the ideal. Is not the spirit, every spirit, individual, in spite of the Hegelian philosophy? Is not the system of free spirits animated by an intense variety which is the very principle of its existence? And so it is a monadism, a spiritualistic pluralism, a spiritualistic idealism, as he calls it, that Howison advocates, similar in certain respects to that of James Ward; or, from another point of view, if we contrast not the philosophy of the One and that of the Many, not the philosophy of spirit and that of matter, but the philosophy of humanity on the one hand, and that of non-humanity, of superhumanity, of impersonality on the other, then Howison's metaphysic is a personal idealism, according to the name he himself gives to it, or else a humanism. Is not human personality the "active nexus" of nature?

15

Also Howison's philosophy seems to be a sort of apotheosis of mankind. But we must only call it humanism on condition we do not set over against man other principles of nature; that which constitutes the worth of man, his spirituality, also constitutes the worth of nature. At bottom, man and nature are identical.

For Howison, as at times for James, God is the category of the ideal. He is the ideal, the " unpersonated " ideal of every spirit, *i.e.* of every real thing; he is the fulfilled ideal. And in this pluralist system he remains a part only, the central part of divine society, a definite though infinite being, amid other beings also definite and infinite and whose soul is similar to our soul. To Howison, as to the other principal pluralists, God is but a *primus inter pares.*

Thus in the city of God the basis of the individuality of each is the recognition of other individualities, each admits the existence of other individuals because himself is an individual. "*Ego per alteros*" is the motto of all in this kingdom of ends, this universal republic wherein all are equal, this " co-operative " of rationality. God knows that all spirits have a reality as absolute as his own, and as sacred.

Seen from these heights, the world assumes a new aspect; efficient compulsive causes disappear and final causes alone are active; everything is considered in terms of final causes. The kingdom of nature is but the mirror of the kingdom of grace.

As it is difficult to believe that final causes can really produce anything, the elements of the universe should be eternally given. Here the God of Howison is no more a creator than is the God of McTaggart. Souls exist before the body and live after it. They are not born. For a personalist, what would the transcendentalism of

Human Immortality mean ? According to James, there are supposed to be spirits that make us move. But these spirits, says Howison, are none other than our real selves, they are our spirits. Useless to seek for mysterious entities ; each of our selves is a principle of the universe. If, as James says in *Human Immortality*, they were but the fleeting result of the insertion of a part of the universal soul into a brain, we should be but a simple—and that a fleeting—thoroughfare for the one spiritual activity. Nothing could be less pluralist, as Howison has well shown, than this idea of James. Personal immortality is essential to a personalistic pluralism, such as that of Howison, while, according to James, it is not a fundamental philosophic idea.

Shall we thus be led to polytheism ? Here the positions are changed ; Howison shows himself far less of a radical pluralist than James.

But when on the point of accepting the idea of the perfect and thereby static character of the world, Howison shows a feature of his mind, *i.e.* that impatience of monotony which we have already mentioned. Perhaps it is in this respect that he is most profoundly pluralistic. To him, evil is real.

Hence certain moral and theological consequences already found in other pluralists ; in morals, the conception of a certain risk inherent in our actions, the idea of infinite possibilities, although " the most gloomy possibilities of James," to use Schiller's expression, are not envisaged by Howison, but only the divine possibilities of souls, aspiring after the beautiful and the good.

That these possibilities may be realised and that evil may be overcome, we must have the help of God. Here the objection may be made : is not God omniscient, and do not possibilities disappear once there is omniscience

in the universe ?   To this objection Howison replies as
did James : God, in order to live in the pluralist world,
should satisfy himself with this knowledge of possibilities
as possibilities.   It is by providing for these possibilities
that he can come to the help of man.

Howison claims that he rejoins the Christian religion
through pluralism.   Does not the Christian regard God
as his friend, as well as his father ?   The God of Christianity, says Howison, continuing the American tradition,
did not indeed come to be served but to serve, to be an
active member in an active society.   Let us then break
away from all belief in a monarchical God, and accord to
God the right of citizenship in this republic of the world.

And so we have noted in Howison not only the existence
of a monadical metaphysics, but also what distinguishes
pluralism from monadology : the affirmation of the evil
and the possible in the world, the conception of a world
neither morally nor physically complete and perfect.

Nevertheless, it soon appears that Howison does not
believe in time, notwithstanding a few passages that
might at first compel one to think that he did ; and we
shall see that, from the very fact that he rejects time, his
pluralism vanishes.

Time and space are but logical creations of spirits ;
the whole of the spirits form an ideal world, apart from
time.   The act of creation itself becomes an extra-
temporal act, an eternal fulguration whose meaning is
that " God is a complete moral agent."   The whole of
evolution is expressed in terms of extra-temporal logic.

After saying that the ideal world, the force behind all
things, is itself immovable, is it possible for Howison to
regard it as a " pluralistic " world ?   The negation of
any temporalist doctrine is in the case of Howison, as in
that of James and Schiller, manifestation of a profound

monism, more profound in Howison than we found it
in those other philosophers.

To start with, Howison denies time because all things
are souls, one might almost say, concepts. His metaphysic terminates in a sort of conceptual world, though
in a very different sense from that of the Cambridge
logicians. As he says, there is a very real bond of relationship between the things of this world : the fact that all
of them are souls and notions. And this bond is all the
more real in this metaphysic so strongly tinged with
Leibnizianism because souls exist in so far as they are
perceived in one and the same glance by God, by the
all-embracing Idea ; they can all be deduced from one
another as concepts proceeding serially from one and
the same intelligent nature. God is the unifier of this
society of concepts ; he is universal coherence in so far as
it is conscious of itself. He is unity in variety as well
as variety in unity. Things exist only in and through
God, *i.e.* diversity exists only by reason of a deeper
unity. An individuality can be defined only through
its relation with God, *i.e.* with the totality of spiritual
things, in a word, with the whole universe.

Howison goes farther than this logical and conceptual
monism ; he declares that consciousness and the material
universe are two names for " one and the same indissoluble Fact, here seen from without, there seen from
within." Whatever be the centres of consciousness, the
same All is ever present.

Without unity, then, the world would not exist, and,
to quote Schiller once more, if unity is the first word, it
is also the last word of this philosophy. The one ideal
of beauty, good, and truth, contemplated by all men
alike, tends to make of the world one whole. The realm
of ends, while it is above us is also before us at the goal

of universal evolution ; some day the world will be unified. If, as Howison says, everything that distinguishes us from the deity is a defect, if by right each individual is all, if his individuality is decadence, " pure passivity," then, is not pantheism at the end of evolution ?

As Schiller wished, we have separated the idea of unity as a condition of the various phenomena from the idea of unity as the end of these phenomena. But Howison's monism does not permit of this severance as does that of Schiller. When time no longer exists, the kingdom of ends is within us as well as above and before us.

As we see, Howison's idealism, so similar to the personal idealism of Oxford in certain respects, in the end closely resembles the quasi-Hegelian metaphysics of McTaggart.

Does not Howison include McTaggart among the idealistic pluralists ? Is he not at one with him as to the importance and reality of immortality, and the perfection of spirits in the ideal order of things ? Schiller rightly placed them side by side in the preface of *Humanism*.

And yet it is not without reason that we include Howison—and that he includes himself—among the pluralists, whilst we have classed McTaggart—and he has classed himself—among the absolutists. In spite of all, his world is more shifting and therefore more truly diverse than that of McTaggart. Opposed alike to absolutism and evolutionist naturalism, the limit of which he endeavours to trace, as do Sturt and Underhill, his ideas are not very different from those of the Oxford school of personal idealism.

Howison scarcely expected to find disciples ; he had them, all the same. Quite a number of names appear at the head of the essay dedicated to him, on the occasion of an anniversary, by the University of Yale.

Let us observe, however, that the pluralism of almost all these philosophers seems at last to disappear and fade away, or end in a kind of monism.

Bakewell wrote in the year 1898 an article on Pluralism, mainly inspired no doubt by James, whose influence is seen in certain of the expressions he uses, such as : "the block-theory of the universe," "the block-world idol which is the modern Juggernaut"; inspired also by Peirce, who teaches him to see "breaks in the uniformity of nature," and lastly by Lutoslawski, a recent article from whose pen in the *Philosophical Review* supplied Bakewell with a subject of discussion.

He is convinced of the supreme importance of the problem of the one and the many; he seeks throughout the world for an element of picturesque diversity; he is a metaphysician imbued with the pluralistic feeling of the absolute, infinite, and divine element in the individual, a moralist aware of the necessities of action, of the exigencies of the ideal, of all our emotional and religious values; he speaks in the name of those "who have felt most strongly the pulse-beat of practical life," of all who do not and will not express philosophical opinions, of all the "doers of deeds," and perhaps more especially, he seems to say, of business men.

His method is as near akin to the pragmatist method as is that of Howison. While the consequences of a doctrine do not make the doctrine true, at all events they may predispose us to want it to be true, and, once verified, to accept it joyously and "with open arms."

Examining the question in this way, we at once see that monism, the idea of a world all of a piece, is anything but calculated to satisfy men of action. "Such a view would rather make it one big Punch and Judy show, in which we were mere puppets, bandied about by the play of hidden forces and dancing to the music of the almighty bassoon."

He completes this moral objection by one based on a theory of knowledge. What is wanted is not the conception of an absolute unity, but such a unity as may create a certain bond between our experiences and within each of these experiences, at the time they take place. " My experience," he says, " would be as real *for me*, if, like the picture in the kaleidoscope, it changed completely at every turn, presenting some kind of coherence in the various parts of the picture which is for the moment in view."   On this point, we find him in agreement with some of Russell's theories.

Let us then have faith in pluralism ; it is the only way of preserving " the picturesqueness of the world, the worth of moral (æsthetic) judgments, the significance of our emotional and religious life, ay, and the very significance of our search after truth."

One of the distinctive characteristics of Bakewell's pluralism is that it sets forth a sort of theory of discontinuity, resulting from the mathematical studies of Peirce and from the ideas of James. The world of experience, he says, is " a world of gaps and breaks."   In his mind, pluralism and the theory of discontinuity are indissolubly linked together.

In spite of this belief in a radical discontinuity, as a disciple of Howison and Royce he conceives the world as a harmonious city-state. Nay, for this pluralism to be possible, this universal society must really form a whole, there must be a being capable of enfolding the whole in a glance, " an all interpreter," according to Royce's idea, a personal absolute. Here, too, we see pluralism presupposing monism ; this mutual implication of the two opposing doctrines, says Bakewell, is a law of the history of philosophy.

The further we proceed the more will the world of Bakewell, like that of Howison, of Schiller, and of James, become harmonised and unified. Will not this unification destroy individuality ? Bakewell says it will not. Does a great love, a religious bond, destroy individuals ? The saner the world becomes, the less will individuals imagine that they each possess it as their own and the more sociable will they become.

Overstreet, another follower of Howison, is bent upon showing how the perfect being can express itself in many ways and be entirely within each of its aspects ; how it can have several parts and be wholly in each of them ; how all quantitative conception must be replaced by a qualitative conception of personality in act ; how it is then possible to set up in a new way the metaphysic of " the many in the one " of which absolutists speak, and to believe in a deeper and more real qualitative duration than time, a duration which is a consciousness of values.

McGilvary, more of a monist than Howison, though still his pupil, conceives of the universe both as " one whole " and as " many wholes," and regards the teachings of Howison, James, and Royce as one. Afterwards he became more particularly attracted by the theory of knowledge, and we find his name amongst those philosophers who, starting from the different suggestions of Dewey and James, have contributed to form the empirical monism which is one aspect of neo-realism.

Lovejoy resumes the ordinary arguments against the philosophy of the absolute, a philosophy destructive of all life and reality. In an interesting fashion, this keen critic shows the bonds that unite pluralism and the affirmation of the irreducible existence of time.

The philosophy of A. Kenyon Rogers can be traced back to Royce, James, and Howison; from Royce he learnt the importance to be attached to the meaning of things; to James he is indebted for his love of risk and adventure, the idea of responsibility and the consciousness of co-operating in the active work of the world. But he obtains his pluralist theory mainly from Howison.

Assuredly he believes in the absolute, in the unity which binds all things, in continuity apart from which there is no real utility; a thing appears to be separate, he says, only when we no longer use it.

If the basis of reality is a single consciousness, at all events it develops by means of differences. The self, while possessing no real independence, while being an ephemeral appearance, the self, my self, is an essential element of reality. If it is only in the consciousness of God, at all events it can say to itself that God is social in essence, that he is not self-sufficing, " that he would not be God if I did not exist," that if I did not exist he would cease to be the absolute.

The different individualities into which the one reality is dispersed seem to return anew to this one reality, nevertheless this procession of spirits comes about from the development of each free individuality; not one can be conscious of the consciousness of its neighbour; all preserve for all time an indestructible personality.

Finally, if God is the goal of development, there is still always a certain interval to be crossed between his unity and the totality of individuals; God is distinct from ourselves, though containing us. Like the God of Rashdall, that of Rogers can become aware of our sensations and our feelings; he cannot experience them.

And so Roger's metaphysic is a combination of that of Royce and that of Howison; in it we continually perceive the original union of the idea of unity with a very keen sense of plurality.   At the time of writing, Rogers, who seems to have abandoned these problems, is mainly interested in setting in opposition to neo-realism another realism, the affirmation of unknowable objects and active subjects, a " critical realism " which Lovejoy also has embraced and of which mention will have to be made.

Like Rogers, Leighton is dominated by Royce as well as by Howison.   He also invokes German metaphysics ; as McTaggart interpreted Hegel in almost pluralist terms, so Leighton translates both Hegel and Fichte into a language that is almost pluralist.

Like Royce, Leighton takes the theory of knowledge as the starting-point of his philosophy ; as the foundation of knowledge, there must be a consciousness transcendental and immanent at the same time.   There is an absolute, but this absolute manifests itself in human individuals " who are compounded so variously and yet are not compounds," and who develop into a living dialectic.

This metaphysic, though tinged with pluralism, may perhaps seem at first very far removed from pluralism. Leighton, however, owing precisely to his Hegelian theory of the reality of relations, affirms against the neo-Hegelians the profound reality of time.   Relations between consciousnesses—and at bottom there are no other relations—have a metaphysical value.   And from the affirmation of their internality no deduction can be drawn as to their permanence.   Time is reintroduced into the universe.   It is even introduced therein under the form of a succession of discontinuities.   Time, he says as a humanist, cannot have more continuity than human plans have.   It is " a series of qualitatively in-dividual acts and never-to-be-repeated events."   There is even a plurality of heterogeneous times, as many times as selves, exerting and freeing themselves. Everywhere we see and perceive qualitative novelties, a continual epigenesis.

The reason why the world is in time, is a growing world, can only be owing to the existence of souls acting upon one another, of centres in relation. These souls are not lost in the absolute; the absolute exists only through them. It is a society, for the relation of beings in society is the most comprehensive mode of relation; here activities are both transcendental and immanent as regards one another.

The philosophy of Leighton had finally to return to an almost Hegelian idealism. Little of his original pluralism remains in his most recent work; spirits are centres wherein the nature of reality becomes aware of itself; reality is the expression of rationality; reality is a teleological system of self-organisation, a social and dynamic unity. He advances in the direction of a teleological and a logical idealism, while endeavouring to maintain the idea, within this totality, of a temporalist pluralism.

Can we connect with this school, as Thilly does, the psychologist and metaphysician, Trumbull Ladd? Ladd conceives the universe as an ensemble of finite beings, a kingdom of selves, of centres of related forces, a multiplicity of monads whose essence consists in action and which limit one another by their actions.

From the outset, however, the absolute plays so important a part in this philosophy, similar to that of Royce, that we can scarcely regard the metaphysic of Ladd as a pluralistic one.

To these American philosophers should be added two English thinkers who have sought inspiration, the one in Lotze, the other in Lotze and Martineau.

Galloway, who would above all retain the ethical and spiritual values, " the real qualification of the world," conceives the individuality as an absolute value, though below an omnipotent God. To him the world is an ensemble of monads in hierarchical order, acting for the triumph of the good. This, as Galloway himself says, is a pluralist philosophy, or at all events the outline of one.

Along with Upton, Rashdall, and others, he is one of the representatives of what might be called pluralist theology. We must note, however, that, beneath the diversity of things as beneath the duality of subject and object, he recognises a " supreme foundation," a universal will.

In the case of Upton, the influence of Martineau combines with that of Lotze. In addition, he finds in the works of James and the personal idealists of Oxford arguments favourable to his conception of the world. He wants a philosophy capable of making a reality of the relations between God and the human soul; in this metaphysic, as in that of James, evil has a place of its own. But for the existence of evil, the effort of the human soul would have no meaning. Freedom, the real freedom that Upton wishes to feel, more real than the freedom of the personal idealists whom he criticises, can exist only in a world in which great decisions are to be arrived at, in which there is evil to be fought.

For Upton as for Galloway the world consists of centres of energy that interact.

He is, however, more genuinely pluralist than Ladd or Galloway, even than Howison, Schiller, or James himself, for he sees at the end of evolution not a unified world but one of ever greater contrasts. He conceives the world as evolving by way of plurality towards greater plurality.

In order to give birth to the world, God tore himself

asunder.   It is this very sacrifice that makes the world so rich and so free.

While recognising beneath his pluralism a profounder monism, a dependence of all things, a perpetual unity, while regarding all things as related souls, Upton tells us that " pluralism lends infinite interest to nature and to human history."

Thus did the personal idealists, the followers of Martineau, the philosophers who took their lead from Schiller and Howison, endeavour to build up, by the help of pluralism—though they did not altogether succeed—a theory of human and of divine personality.

CHAPTER III

SOME TENDENCIES OF CONTEMPORARY PSYCHOLOGISTS AND LOGICIANS

In his *Psychology*, James shows the continuity of the stream of thought. But we have seen that he understands and allows for psychic discontinuities as well as for physical continuities.

Certain modern American psychologists go further than he had at first seemed to venture along this new path; they insist on breaks of thought, swift shiftings of ideas, outbursts of feeling. We have seen this in the case of D. Miller.

Colvin contrasts the psychic with the physical world, for he says the psychic world is the world of the discontinuous, of the indeterminate; in the psychic world, no deductive process is valid. When a state of consciousness is broken by the irruption of a new sensation, we can form no idea of the new state of consciousness that results.

Felix Arnold also notes gaps in our consciousness, and reproaches those who have emphasised psychic continuity for having thought only of visual sensations and neglected all the rest.

Perhaps these articles, along with those in which James sets forth his ideas on pure experience, may cause it to be imagined that the American psychologists, after insisting so strongly on continuity, feel that they must point out a certain discontinuity of psychic phenomena.

In studying the philosophy of James and Schiller, we have already remarked that metaphysical pluralism might terminate in a doctrine of the particularity of truths, the variety of systems, the multiplicity of realities, in a pluralist conception of the bond between truth and reality.

We have now to study a few logical theories which presuppose more or less a pluralist metaphysic.

H. M. Kallen, one of the philosophers whose thoughts can be traced back most directly to the influence of James, has insisted on the synthetic and truly creative character of propositions in a pluralist world. In the case of the pluralist, relations are not given once for all, as in the case of the monist; they are momentary, not essential. One thing, at a certain moment, is in relation with another; it is not so all the time. Hence it comes about, Kallen tells us, that while for the monist the " attribution," the judgment, is the enunciation of a tautology, for the pluralist it is a new truth. " For the pragmatist and pluralist, predication has a meaning," he says. " It would be a serious error to think we could read the writings of a pluralistic pragmatist as we read those of a monist; synthetic value and importance must be attached to all the propositions of the pluralist." A radical empiricism, as we feel it to exist in Kallen's writings, combines with a theory of creative relations.

Is the school of Dewey a pluralist school ? Is Dewey himself a pluralist ? While Peirce had great influence over him and afforded him, to some extent, a pluralist outlook upon the world, it must be remembered that Dewey started from the Hegelian school and always showed himself opposed to most of Schiller's ideas.

From a copyright portrait by the Keystone View Company

JOHN DEWEY.

[To face p. 240.

His love, however, for pure and changing experience prevents him from conceiving a reality, beneath phenomena, which subtends them; we must have faith, he thinks, in the power possessed by the elements and processes of experience and truth, to " warrant their own success."

Thus his metaphysic is a sort of phenomenalism, though a dynamic and shifting phenomenalism for which all things move and grow; above all, he loves " strife, the element of indeterminateness, the growing, unstable, potential element of the universe." Thought is conceived as a plan of action that is useful in the struggle.

It is not only a slow continuous growth that he recognises; in the world there may also be sudden changes, revolutions effected by consciousness in the nature of things, new starting-points.

This growth is never to end, and Dewey is one of those modern thinkers who insist most strongly on the incomplete and ever unfinished character of reality. He sees everything, as he says, not *sub specie æternitatis*, but *sub specie generationis*. He believes in a real time, in real potentialities.

Dewey never had the opportunity to broach directly the problem of pluralism and monism; it may be that his need of a certain continuity in experience keeps him away from pure pluralism. But in his vision of a disseminated and finite reality, in the teaching wherein he invites us to satisfy our appetite for the divine, the eternal and the complete, by fragmentary values enjoyed one after the other, he may be regarded almost as a pluralist.

A. W. Moore, one of the most interesting philosophers of the school of Dewey, of the Chicago school, tells us that pluralism is necessary, up to a certain point, for the logical doctrine of Dewey, of his friends and pupils.

Moore accepts from James everything that a follower of Dewey can accept : the idea of continuous generation and growth, of active relations.   Pluralism interests him in particular as being a temporalism, a theory of the shifting, the ever advancing.

When we conceive the universe, as do these writers of the Dewey school, to be a moving plurality of things in a state of struggle, the idea must be regarded as a useful weapon in this struggle, a means of attack or of adaptation, as the case may be, an essentially " prospective " element, according to one of the favourite expressions of these philosophers, a plan of action for the future, a promise of novelties in a world in process of incessant renewal.

And so we find ourselves confronted with a theory of creative relations and with one of shifting relations which are not unconnected with pluralism.[17]

But we have studied up to this point only one of the tendencies of pluralist logic.   There is another, which does not insist on the shifting character of thought but lays stress on the static universe of simple natures.   It is from this tendency and from the theory of external relations—united with some ideas of James—that neo-realism is to spring.   All the same, even in the case of neo-realism, we must take into account the ideas of the Chicago school, which at first might seem quite opposed to it and yet, for certain of these neo-realists, were a cause of reflection and inner development.

---

[17] It would prove a lengthy and difficult task to enumerate and study all those philosophers whose ideas can be traced back to pluralism : some in the importance given to time and the diversity of moments (Carl V. Tower, Woodbridge), others in the meaning and the love of individuality (D. Stoops, K. J. Spalding, Ph. Mason), others in the idea of different domains of reality (H. R. Marshall), and others again in the idea of empirical, piecemeal investigations (S. E Lang).

CHAPTER IV

NEO-REALISM

THE theories of G. E. Moore and of Russell are in some points very similar to certain of the pluralist theories we have investigated, though profoundly different in other respects.

Perhaps distinctions might be made between the way in which Moore arrives at pluralism and that in which Russell proves his theory; all the same, the starting-point of both seems to have been the philosophy of McTaggart, and their conclusions on the whole are identical; those of Russell, at least his earlier conceptions, are partially based on those of Moore.

To establish his theory, which is purely abstract and logical, Moore starts with the feeling that each man has of the individuality of his self. What, in reality, is this individuality? In myself I do not love my attributes, but the fact that I call them myself. On the other hand, do not all men say and think: self? I keep to my self only because it differs numerically from that of others. And so the pluralist logic of Moore affirms a numerical plurality, denied by the principle of the identity of indiscernibles. Every thing is what it is and not another thing: such is the epigraph of Moore's *Principia Ethica*. Hence the ideal of truth cannot be as represented by the absolutist schools, an absolute coherence of coherent truths. A proposition may be true apart from all other propositions ; we must pay more attention, says Moore, to the intrinsic truth of things than to certain external conditions of harmony. To seek for unity and system at the cost of truth is not the work of philosophy. *A priori* we can by no means affirm that truth will possess the unity and coherence we seek.

On the other hand, the study of moral judgments led him to affirm the existence of a world of universals. Thus we are confronted both with an empiristic and individualist realism and with a rationalistic and universalist realism. It is the same union of these two realisms that we find in Russell.

The theory at which Moore had arrived, starting from the study of moral questions, is reached by Russell mainly through reflection on mathematical data ; just as in the case of Moore morality cannot be understood without the affirmation of multiple terms and of relations external to these terms, so, without these terms and relations, mathematics, science in general, are incapable of being understood, according to Russell.

" The fundamental doctrine in the realistic position, as I understand it," says Russell, " is the doctrine that relations are external. This doctrine is not correctly expressed by saying that two terms which have a certain relation might not have had that relation. Such a statement introduces the notion of possibility and thus raises irrelevant difficulties. The doctrine may be expressed by saying that (1) relatedness does not imply any corresponding complexity in the *relata* ; (2) any given entity is a constituent of many different complexes." Thus, according to Russell, there are no elements in a term by virtue of which this term bears the relation it happens to have with another term. On the contrary, we must admit the existence of absolutely simple terms and purely external relations, of terms that contain no relations and of relations that cannot be deduced from the terms.

On the one hand, then, we have the neo-Hegelian doctrine of internal relations with its consequences : namely, that the knowledge of each part implies the knowledge of the whole just as the knowledge of the whole implies the knowledge of each part, that no truth can be regarded as completely true except when related to the whole, that in the last resort there is but one thing in the universe, that every proposition has a subject and a predicate. On the other hand, we have the theory of external relations leading us to believe that the knowledge of a part does not imply knowledge of the whole, that there are truths absolutely true, that there are many things in the universe, that there are propositions which cannot be reduced to the attributive form.

Now, the theory of internal relations has never been proved ; neither the doctrine of sufficient reason, nor the idea that a change in relations would bring about a change in terms, suffices to prove it. And it leads us to paradoxes from the maze of which we can find no escape. Every term in this theory would be infinitely complex. Again, is the nature of the terms, that is, the ensemble of their relations, identical with the terms ? If not, we must find out the relation between the nature of the terms and the terms themselves, and we are carried off into a *regressio ad infinitum*. If it is identical, we ought to find the nexus which makes the different predicates the predicates of a single subject; and, in fact, we can not. The axiom of internal relations, on the other hand, is incompatible with any real complexity, even with the idea of identity in difference, essential as it is to English monism. It is incompatible with the existence of asymmetrical relationships, such as those of the whole and the part.   Analysis and knowledge in general become impossible if the very fact of knowledge has to modify the being that is known.   Russell shows what difficulties we encounter if we accept the monistic conception of truth, *i.e.* if we think that the total truth alone is true and that all partial truths are more or less erroneous.   Finally, this theory is self-contradictory ; a philosophy which implies this monistic theory of truth is itself partially false.

Consequently we must reject the axiom of the internality of relations and refuse to speak of a nature of terms that is made up of relations, we must no longer believe that true judgments regarding a thing form part of that thing.   Indeed we shall be able to say that we know a thing without our knowing its relations, and that the knowledge of certain of its relations does not imply the knowledge of them all.

Thus Russell and Moore end in a kind of logical atomism and Herbartianism ; they believe in a world of independent realities into which all things can be decomposed.   Thus we come to the theory of terms as conceived by Russell.   " Every term, to begin with, is a logical subject: it is . . . immutable and indestructible." Each term, in itself, differs from all, before receiving any predicate, and though in a sense all are identical, they are different numerically, as Moore has shown.   Points in space also are identical to, and at the same time absolutely different from, one another.

" There is identity and there is difference. . . . We thus get a world of many things, with relations which are not to be deduced from a supposed ' nature ' or scholastic essence of the related things.   In this world, whatever is complex is composed of related simple things, and analysis is no longer confronted at every step by an endless regress."

Hence great diversity. "It seems to me," writes Moore, "that the Universe contains an immense variety of different kinds of entities. For instance: My mind, any particular thought or perception of mine, the quality that distinguishes an act of volition from a mere act of perception, the Battle of Waterloo, the process of baking, 1908, . . . etc., all these are contents of the Universe." We even see nothing but pure asymmetry everywhere; if, for instance, we take the relation of parts to the whole, we find, according to Russell and Moore, that it is impossible to produce the whole from any part by analytical methods, and that, on the other hand, the whole is not prior to the parts.

On these theories depend almost all the theories of Russell, prior to his behaviouristic phenomenalism of to-day. This philosophy is a realism: " it maintains that cognitive relations are external relations which set up a direct bond between the subject and an object which may be non-mental. . . . It considers existence as not depending on knowledge. . . . To know implies no community of nature whatsoever between the mind and what it knows." And so, because the relations are external to things and to the mind, we may believe in things separate from the mind and yet known immediately; for, by a sort of paradox, the intellectualism of Russell substitutes for truth conceived by the pragmatists as satisfactory mediation, as system, a world of immediately perceived truths.

Here realism and pluralism are closely linked together. " If we do not believe in the doctrine of internal relations, the question as to the number of things that exist becomes purely empirical." Logic does not solve the difficulty as to the alternative between monism and pluralism; experience alone can do that. Will it be said that from the consideration of what ought to be we may proceed to the affirmation of what is? But "very little can be proved *a priori* from consideration of what *must* be," and besides, logic does not tell us what must be but rather what can be; here logic merely supplies possibilities to our intellectual imagination; and when these possibilities are multiplied and our knowledge of what can be is increased, we can decide between these ever more numerous possibilities only by consulting experience. "Instead of being shut in within narrow walls, of which each nook and cranny could be explored, we find ourselves in an open world of free possibilities, where much remains unknown because there is so much to know." "Logic, instead of being, as formerly, the bar to possibilities, has become the great liberator of the imagination, presenting innumerable alternatives which are closed to unreflective common sense, and leaving to experience the task of deciding, where decision is possible, between many worlds which logic offers for our choice." Here, as in the case of James, we find ourselves face to face with endless possibilities.

Now, experience is of necessity haphazard. "We are reduced to studying the world in piecemeal fashion." And this experience gives us a world as haphazard and piecemeal as itself. "No empirical fact is more certain, if *a priori* refutations fail, than that many things exist." So the theory of external relations leads to empiricism and hence to pluralism.

But realism is connected with pluralism even more completely. Russell fully understood the pluralist nature of his philosophy: "I should prefer to call the philosophy which I advocate 'pluralism' rather than 'realism.'"

" The philosophy which seems to me truest might be called analytical realism. It is analytical, seeing that it maintains that the existence of the complex depends on the existence of the simple. . . . This philosophy is an atomic philosophy." Realism is but another name for pluralism.

And so Russell conceives a world of pluralities; the idea of numerical plurality, as conceived of by Moore, leads naturally to pluralism: " Numerical identity and diversity are the source of unity and plurality, and thus the admission of many terms destroys monism." Instead of conceiving " identity in differences," Russell sees " identities and differences," " a world of many things," a world in which evil exists, a world even nearer the world of James than that of McTaggart, a pluralist world in which there is absolute good and radical evil.

The philosophy of Russell is a pluralism because it states the existence of terms, it is also a pluralism owing to the way in which it states the existence of relations. If relations are ultimate and irreducible, neither monism nor monadism can be justified.

The Herbartianism of Moore and Russell admits of the existence of relations between terms, external and superficial relations in the sense that they do not completely attain the nature of the terms, but nevertheless real relations. Only at this cost can we escape from logical monism; no sooner do we attempt to reduce relations to mere adjectives than we deny them. Russell says that he has " accepted from Moore the pluralism which regards the world, both that of existents and that of entities, as composed of an infinite number of mutually independent entities with relations which are ultimate and not reducible to adjectives of their terms or of the whole which these compose."

Criticism of the predicative theory of propositions, *i.e.* of the affirmation that in every proposition there is a subject and a predicate, enables Russell to destroy one of the foundations of Bradley's doctrines. When real relations exist, there are possible propositions other than those which attribute predicate to subject. Besides, does not monism destroy itself ? Does not the fact that the absolute has predicates imply the proposition : " there are predicates," a proposition inconceivable to monistic logic ? Again, does not the very idea of predicate imply diversity in nature ? The predicate is an entity ; there is a certain relation between it and the absolute ; and the problem of relations reappears.

Russell's doctrine, realistic because it affirms the existence of particular things, is also realistic because it affirms the existence of general ideas. We know relations between things ; we know universals. " Relations must be placed in a world which is neither mental nor physical." Russell tells us that here he is maintaining the theory of Plato himself, though slightly modified in some respects. He arrives at the same time at a Platonic and at an empirical realism. Terms are something else than relations : such is the proposition that is the basis of his empirical realism. Relations are something else than terms : such is the proposition that is the basis of his Platonic realism.

Now, the only universals which ordinarily have been taken into account are those that are expressed by adjectives and substantives ; while those that are expressed by verbs and prepositions and attempt to translate the relations existing between a plurality of things are kept aside. This is why it has been thought that every proposition has for its function to attribute properties to a single thing ; it has not been seen that there are propositions which express relations *between* things, that the relations between things are themselves, in a sense, entities. Hence the erroneous idea that there is but one thing in the universe, or that, if there are several, there cannot be any interplay between them.

But, indeed, there are universals. Suppose, as the empiricists will have it, that whiteness is but an abstraction; at all events, a given whiteness must resemble our idea of whiteness, and so we can deny the existence of the idea of whiteness only on condition we admit the existence of the idea of resemblance.

These relations, too, are independent of our mind. All our knowledge of relations, as all our knowledge *a priori*, applies to entities which, strictly speaking, exist neither in the physical nor in the psychic world. If I say : " I am in my room," " Edinburgh is north of London," I exist, my room, London and Edinburgh exist, but where do the relations " in," " north of " exist ? They are not formed by my mind, for they may be true without my thinking them; they do not exist in temporal and spatial fashion. Likewise the act of thinking whiteness is psychic; but the idea of whiteness, unless it is to lose its universality, is external to my mind. Universals are not our thoughts, but the objects of our thoughts, and here Russell recognises the ideas of Meinong as akin to his own. The world of universals may be called the world of being. The world of being is immutable and rigid, in contrast with the world of existence which is fluctuating and vague, without plans or definite frontiers or arrangements. Although to the man of action only the world of existence is important, and to the mathematician only the world of being is of value, to the metaphysician both are real, both are important. Indeed, we know universals far more completely than those things *per se* which are the causes of our sensations.

On the other hand, as regards our knowledge, universals are far more independent than particular beings. The world of sense is subjective, whereas the world of abstractions is objective. And so, entities, atoms, are of two kinds : universals and particulars, concepts and the data of the senses.

But pluralism is true for both these worlds ; there is an irreducible multiplicity both in the world of relations and in the world of terms ; we have, as Russell says, a logical atomism and also a physical atomism.

After all, it was the same in the philosophy of James ; the pluralist outlook upon the world resulted both from the sense of the irreducibility of subjects and of that of relations ; it might be said that the one, in a more abstract and logical form, and the other, in concrete psychological form, express fairly similar ideas.

Perhaps the theory of time, as Russell presents it, seems at first opposed to the ideas of James. Russell, in some of his works, regards our world as an " unchanging world, a world at rest." But what he means by this is after all probably nothing more than discontinuity of time, and therefore here too we seem to find in him the expression, in static form, of what appears in dynamic form [18] in the philosophy of James. And now Russell seems to insist more and more on the " phenomenalist " aspect of his doctrine, approaching a pragmatist psychology in certain respects.

On the other hand, if we compare the logic of Russell with that of the Chicago school, we find certain identical beliefs in these two opposed theories which in some respects are both connected with pluralism. First,

[18] In *Mysticism and Logic*, Russell expressly admits the idea of " corpuscles of time." He denies the real permanence of objects and adopts a " cinematographic " view of the universe.

judgments are truly synthetic, whether formed in the concrete world of the Chicago school or in the abstract world of logistics ; then too, along with intrinsic and essential relations, there are more fleeting and shifting relations.

If the pragmatist logicians insisted less on the continuity and unity of experience than Dewey does, and emphasised more the temporal character of things than Russell does, they could reunite in logic—as has been the case in metaphysics—belief in the diverse character of things and belief in their temporal character.

What we find, in fact, are doctrines which aim at uniting certain of the teachings of James with certain of the teachings of Russell. It was natural, indeed, that an effort should be made to unite the affirmation of the independence of beings, based primarily on feeling and will as we find it in James, with the theory which is, in Schiller's expression, " the most consistent attempt to work out the notion of the ' independence ' of reality on intellectualistic lines."

These doctrines occasionally take into account the theory of consciousness which is essential to the functionalism of the Chicago school. In the articles of Woodbridge, and perhaps also of Montague, there was seen developing a monism of experience, shifting experience, the facts of consciousness being centres of action within this very experience, consciousness being a relation which cannot be separated from that moving context which things constitute. McGilvary endeavoured to unite James's idea of pure experience, Dewey's theory of functional consciousness, and Bergson's theory of images. Neo-realism, however, as it is to present itself, appears more particularly as a union of certain ideas of James's radical empiricism and Russell's theories.

We seem to find, in some articles by Sheldon which appeared in 1904 and 1905, an attempt, contemporary with the early attempts of the neo-realists, to bring about this junction between the two philosophies. We see here a study of universals, conceived from a pluralist standpoint. Why, he asks, should an isolated part of the universe lack reality because it is isolated or singled out ? Why should not the external world subsist, even though consciousness were suppressed ? Why, with the external world effaced, should consciousness lose its present characteristics ? Why, under the pretext that everything in experience appears in the form of a bundle, think that this bundle cannot be broken up ? Sheldon, asserting the existence of the abstract in the nature of things, invokes two essentially pluralist ideas : first, a theory of possibilities : Are there not, he asks, forces at work which may destroy this unity ? and second, a theory of external relations : Why should not one believe in the existence of multiple parts whose character would not be changed by the fact that they leave the whole ? Things may exist apart from their environment ; they may be constantly entering into new relations and leaving old ones. And so abstraction is based on nature, founded upon pluralism. Parts have a reality apart from the whole. Here we seem to see an attempt at a doctrine similar to neo-realism, and at the same time we discover what is to be one of the themes of Sheldon's interesting work on *The Strife of Systems and Productive Duality.*

" New realism " was already a current expression in American reviews between the years 1900 and 1904. Only by degrees did the word come to designate one of these doctrines, which was formed under the influence of Meinong and of Avenarius, of Russell and of James.

American philosophers of the present time are no

longer divided into pragmatists and anti-pragmatists, but rather into realists and anti-realists. Realistic theories have a dual origin—the one psychological, the other logical; the one, a doctrine of immanence, the other, a doctrine of transcendence; the one, James's theory of consciousness, the other, Russell's theory of relations. Perry was both the chief follower of James and the most important defender of Russell in the United States. We may say that the American Cambridge and the English Cambridge are alike opposed to monism.

This union of two doctrines so apparently different does not appear to us inexplicable; the theory of the externality of relations is seen very clearly in the writings of James. Radical empiricism is partly the affirmation of relations without internal foundations in the terms. It was natural that the pluralism of James, the more it unfolded its presuppositions, should prove to be fairly similar to the realism of Russell. James showed, Perry tells us, that there are relations other than those of logical implication and organic unity, emphasised by rationalism. No doubt this theory, to James, is not logical theory but observation : *there are* relations external to their terms. And so it does not deny the possibility, even the existence, of internal relations, such as are the relations between the moments of our mind ; this theory had not in the writings of James the rigidity which it had in some of Russell's. None the less did James, by emphasising the existence of " external " relations, open up the way to neo-realism.

In the second place, James admitted different domains of realities ; geometrical truths, for instance, exist in a certain way which is not that of the things of sense ; his realism is more and more emphasised. Above the solid existence of the concrete, he finds the coloured though vague existence of generality in thought (in which his conceptualism consists) and the definite though discoloured existence of generality in the realm of ideas (in which his realism consists). Perry speaks of the logical realism of James.

On the other hand, Russell and Moore are of necessity led into pluralism. Russell brings out in the *Journal of Philosophy* an article on the basis of realism : he says that he finds himself almost in perfect agreement with the realists of America. Pitkin declares that " the pluralistic objectivism " of Moore does not differ, as a whole, from the American neo-realism.

Perry notes that " pragmatism and realism are agreed in opposing both the narrowness of naturalism and the extravagance of idealism." The two doctrines of James and Russell are seen to be both pluralist.

Still, we must understand the differences between them, differences which have induced some of James's followers gradually to abandon certain of his theories. Pragmatism is a philosophy of life and of human thought ; it remains " anthropomorphic." From this point of view, it is not far removed from idealism. Realism is, above all, a philosophy of logic and fact. In opposition to the psychological and humanistic method of pragmatism he sets up a logical method. Pragmatism is an anti-intellectualism ; realism is an intellectualism. The one is a dynamic pluralism, the other a static pluralism. Russell says that in the theories of James the ideas of context, system, and mediation play a part which he looks upon as illegitimate.

American realists endeavour to reconcile, as far as they can, these various theories ; in particular, to unite the theory of immanence, as it appears in James, with the

From a recent portrait

BERTRAND RUSSELL.

[To face p 256

theory of transcendence required by the conception of relations which is common to James and to Russell. They assert both the immanence and the transcendence of the object.

While they believe in the independence of things with reference to our thought, the realists also believe in the immanence of things in our thought. On this point, again, they follow the lines of the pragmatism which, as a rule and more or less consciously, laid down both these affirmations alike. They think that in this way they are only making explicit the beliefs of common sense: "Primordial common sense believes that this same independent world can be directly presented in consciousness." Hence a new characteristic of this realism. "Modern realism," says Perry, "is closer to the monistic realism of 'ideas,' suggested by Hume, than to the dualistic realism of mind and matter propounded by the Scottish school." He speaks of an "epistemological monism." "The cardinal principle of neo-realism is the independence of the immanent" or the immanence of the independent, a principle which, in the last analysis, is based on the idea that "images"—to use the word by which Bergson expresses a theory which may possibly be compared with their own—*are*, but, strictly speaking, are not, in space. American realism is a "'new' or non-dualistic realism." The influence of Mach and Avenarius has not been alien to its formation. It is monistic, if you wish. Mention has been made of that "neutral monism" which characterises it. At the same time it insists on the idea of different realms of realities, and here we should note the influence of James and of Meinong, as well as that of mathematical speculation.

Like pragmatism, realism began by being criticism; in essence it is criticism. In various articles and books,

Perry has examined the most important theories in contemporary philosophies, endeavouring to explain the suppositions they imply. In his opinion, the most diverse doctrines seem based on a certain number of sophisms, chief of which are: that of false simplicity, which leads to the assertion that analysis has no value whatsoever; speculative dogma, *i.e.* the idea of the possibility of a concept which expresses the properties of each particular thing and is at the same time universal; the idea of infinite extension which is also infinite comprehension, which is at the root of crude naturalism as well as of absolutism, and which can itself be traced back to the sophism of pseudo-simplicity. We are also guilty of the sophism of pseudo-simplicity when we confuse unanalysed simplicity, that of Bradley's sensed totality or of Bergson's pure duration, with the true simplicity which remains, once the analysis is made, and is revealed by this very analysis. Realism is opposed to Bergsonism for the same reason as it is opposed to the philosophy of Bradley. It is opposed to all monism, to all monadism. Monism explains nothing; in order to explain the existence of relations, monadism must either be transformed into monism or into occasionalism; in both cases, it denies itself. To the realist, simplicity is not an immediate datum, it is the residuum of analysis. His indeterminism is based neither on a criticism of the intellect nor on a dynamistic conception, but rather on an analytical theory of the real. Indetermination is not the appanage of man; human actions are determined neither more nor less than other events.

And so realism is opposed to what these philosophers call romanticism, to the philosophies of continuity and indivisibility, of life and will, of the subjective and the mysterious and the one. " As a polemic, realism is principally concerned to discredit romanticism." It is a kind of new *Aufklàrung*.

Realism is an analytical doctrine, a scientific theory ; it insists on assimilating the work of philosophy with the work of science. Its aim is not to simplify experience by doing away with the object of experience, reducing it to a single word, such as life or consciousness. Its aim is to simplify it by making a complete analysis of it, not by retracing one's steps and returning towards the original unity, but by proceeding along the same lines as experience, and thus disclosing both the connection between the parts and the structure of the whole.

Therefore we cannot say that this realism is a rationalism, for rationalism is not necessarily a theory of analysis ; on the contrary, it is mainly as an empiricist that the realist is to attack the problems of philosophy. " A perceived truth is self-warranted "; truth lies in piecemeal sensations and affirmations, not in a coherent system.

There is one question which, for realists, dominates—and must be answered before—all others : " The ontological differences that separate such writers as Fichte and Berkeley, Mr Bradley and Professor Karl Pearson, are, for a realist, overshadowed by the epistemological error that unites them." Monism or pluralism, eternalism or temporalism, materialism or spiritualism, and even pragmatism or intellectualism, are to them problems which can be solved only after the one fundamental problem, that of subjectivism and realism, has been solved ; the main thing is to keep clear of subjectivism.

According to Perry and the realists, the idealistic argument is based largely on a sophism ; when we study knowledge, we find ourselves in a predicament we never meet anywhere else. We cannot, in knowledge, eliminate the self which knows; we cannot know what things would be if we did not know them. Some suggestion could be obtained from this observation only if things could be in but one context at a time; if, because they are united to spirit, they were to find themselves entirely in the context of psychical facts; and if, in the second place, this relationship were necessarily rooted in the nature of things. And so we see that the idealist argument rests on two presuppositions, both of which the realists deny—the error of exclusive particularity and the theory of the internality of relations, to use their terminology. The method of concordance can be applied: every object of which I am able to speak is known by a subject; but the method of difference cannot.

The theory of the externality of relations is not only logically necessary, it is exemplified in fact, implied in all the facts of change and evolution. The reason why certain ideas change without the whole of our knowledge being shattered, the reason why, more generally, there is change in the world, is because terms are independent of their relations. The fact is that terms in relations are not constituted by their relations: terms are what they are independently of the relations into which they enter.

If we recognise the theory of the externality of relations, then parts are not modified by entering into wholes, "simple entities are independent of the complexes of which they are members." We are able to conceive relations which "come and go," as Spaulding says, employing an expression of William James, and the cognitive relation is one of this kind.

Terms are irreducible to relations; they may be at the same time in one system and in another; they may change certain of their relations without changing them all.

Thus pluralist realism shows itself as the affirmation of the possibility of analysis, as the affirmation of particular " knowledges." Whereas the monist cannot possess any deep truth unless the whole of truth is known, whereas he regards any acquisition of truth as a sort of organic growth, transforming the whole of truth; the realist, on the other hand, is able to know particular truths, and besides, seeing that knowledge grows by a kind of addition process, fresh knowledge may be added on to the old without either transforming or negating it.

Like Russell, the realists are led by their logical theories to metaphysical theories, or rather their logical theories contain by implication—and are at bottom—metaphysical theories. Their essential determination is to free themselves from subjectivism. Besides, they believe, in Spaulding's expression, in the " unalterability of ' simples,' " in " Platonic realism." Along with Russell, Perry even tells us that the theory of externality, inadequate of itself alone to set up realism, is a proof of pluralism. They would establish a logical and at the same time empirical pluralism; for they consider that logic leads to the observation of the given reality just as observation of the given reality leads to logic. There are existences and there are " subsistences," an entire kingdom, both non-sensible and non-mental, of simple entities.

As empiricists, Perry and his friends consider that experience alone, the verification of reality, can inform us to what extent the world is one or multiple. Like the pragmatists, they think it impossible to solve the problem of unity by *a priori* arguments. There is even a presumption at the present time in favour of the hypothesis that the world, as a whole, is less unified than certain of its parts. " A loosely aggregated world, abounding in unmitigated variety, is a valid philosophical hypothesis." [19]   Or, to transfer this affirmation from the realm of experience to that of logic : " But *how few*," says Perry, " the fundamental propositions can be is not logically determinate. A universe that had as many postulates as terms, as many laws as events, would not be irrational or unintelligible. . . . There is no good reason, I believe, for supposing that every entity is related to every other entity."   In one sense, we may say that these intellectualists are irrationalists.

Do not the theories of Russell, like those of James, open up before our eyes a world of free possibilities ? The dual realism we find in Russell : that of universals and that of the world of sense, sets free our intellectual imagination.   But this increase of our knowledge of what may be is accompanied by an ever clearer consciousness of the decrease of our knowledge of what is.   Therefore we must observe things, not attempt to deduce them. Thus did the neo-realistic theory at first present itself ; as Russell has shown, from the fact that a thing is what it is we cannot deduce all its relations, and if we knew all its relations we could not say what it is.   Hence the need of empirical piecemeal investigation.

Nor can we say that there is one thing more representative of the universe than the rest. As Marvin says in his text-book (*A First Book in Metaphysics*) " We shall have to confess our ignorance as to what objects best represent the general character of the universe. . . . On the contrary, each thing is, as far as we know, representative of reality, each thing is a goal of existence."

That this world of ours is a world of multiple things

[19] Perry, *Tendencies*, p. 320.   See also *New Realism*, p. 33 ; *Tendencies*, p. 272 ; the realist affirms " the presumptively pluralistic constitution of the universe."

is affirmed by Perry and the neo-realists, as it was by James and Schiller, Moore and Russell.

This pluralism leads the realists to combat optimistic conceptions ; like James, they admit that there is such a thing as a root evil. " Realism recognises the being of things that are wholly non-spiritual, of things that are only accidentally spiritual, and of things that, while they belong to the domain of spirit, nevertheless antagonise its needs and aspirations. The universe or collective totality of being contains things good, bad, and indifferent." And each of the opposite terms, bad and good, may be defined in itself, each apart from the other. The victory of one of them depends on ourselves.

More particularly in Marvin's articles and text-book do we find clearly stated this tendency of realism to insist on the heterogeneity and the discontinuity of things ; whereas Spaulding remains a decided intellectualist, we find in Marvin's philosophy a kind of union between realism and certain irrationalist and evolutionist theories which, in the opinion of other philosophers of this school, are wholly opposed to it. Even science is not a unity ; Marvin by no means accepts the idea of the reduction of the various sciences to mechanics. " Each existential science brings in new terms and new relations that are either quite indefinable, or indefinable in terms of pure logic." And each part of each science brings with it new data. The nearer we get to experience, the more numerous are these irreducible propositions ; until we come to the particular entity given in experience " baffling all attempts to put it completely under any assignable number of laws ; and this means that each particular thing and event is itself a logical ultimate, or primitive." Marvin thereby concludes that general laws cannot be the full explanation

of any particular thing or event. " The world," he says,
" has an infinitude of ultimate and independent causes,"
and, again, " the world might be indefinitely different
from what it is in these particular propositions, without
requiring any change in the general propositions, and
the less general propositions might be different without
the more general propositions being false." Contained
in each fact, then, are certain propositions which cannot
be deduced, which are, as Marvin says, logically new.
Life, consciousness, are new facts which suddenly appear,
but they are only noteworthy particular instances of
that discontinuity which can be seen everywhere. We
find ourselves everywhere confronted with " unique individualities whose particular nature is logically ultimate ";
there are ultimate particulars just as there are ultimate
universals. In the mind of this logician, the individual
eludes logic. Besides, even when science explains things,
there remains a certain margin, a discontinuity between
the things and itself. Qualities are mutually heterogeneous, irreducible to one another, irreducible also to
their laws. And, finally, it may be that the number of
discontinuous facts with which we can become acquainted
will increase simultaneously with the number of continuous facts. On the one hand, then, we have the
universal causal laws whose existence Marvin does not
deny ; on the other hand, we have a " world of ultimate
individuals."

Indeed, Marvin looks upon the world as made up of
different levels or strata which perhaps correspond to
one another, though perhaps not to the full extent.
For instance, he asserts the importance of universal laws,
though at the same time he tells us that particular
entities do not obey these laws completely. He attempts
to combine the two characteristics of neo-realism, which

aims at being both logical and experimental; but the order of logic and that of experience, blended—given, so to speak—in each other in the opinion of other realists, are kept clearly distinct by him, as indeed they are by Russell.

To him, this essential difference, this individuality, is the very definition of chance. Chance is precisely the fact that " every particular thing or event contains particular propositions which defy deduction." This idea of an element of disjunction, of novelty, in things is manifest also in the works of other realists, *e.g.* of Perry. But it must not be thought that this indetermination is more essential to life or thought than to any other phenomenon in the universe.

Furthermore, each instant, as Marvin distinctly states, is logically primitive, introducing propositions which cannot be deduced from preceding propositions. Here we must insist on one of the strangest aspects of Marvin's doctrine; he attempts to assimilate the idea of creative evolution with ideas of neo-realism. " This doctrine that each stage of history brings with it logical ultimates may be called the doctrine of evolution or, more explicitly, of creative evolution." There is a growth of the world which expresses itself in a certain logical discontinuity.

Thus realistic intellectualism, which aimed above all at building upon science and analysis, at creating a foundation for science and analysis—and Marvin himself often strongly insisted on this idea—accepts the possibility of " romantic " and anti-intellectualistic hypotheses; here we have a fresh attempt to bring together the logic of Russell and the theory which Marvin calls that of creative evolution, while leaving them on different levels of reality. In short, by a final paradox, this doctrine, based on the unalterability of simples, seems to arrive at the affirmation that the world is infinitely complex.

Consequently, whereas certain neo-realists attempted to separate the realistic and positive elements of pragmatism from the romantic and irrational elements of the same doctrine so as to retain none but the former, Marvin tried to express these romantic elements in a sort of realistic, logical language. Moreover, did not Russell speak of the element of strangeness in nature, and Perry of its rich variety and the number of entities it demands ?

But on the other hand, and once more in a sort of contradiction both of itself and here of its inductive and pluralistic tendencies, the neo-realistic theory, as seen in Holt's *Concept of Consciousness*, ended by asserting the possibility of a deductive and monistic conception of the universe. Holt looks upon nature as a seething chaos of contradictions, but in this book at least he also thinks that some day we shall learn that being, as a whole, is one infinite deductive system in which the whole of variety is developed deductively, starting with a relatively restricted number of fundamental propositions.

And so neo-realism seems to split up and give birth, now to a sort of dynamic and qualitative monadism, now to a monistic and purely deductive theory wherein idealist and materialist affirmations become strangely blended together. The different tendencies which had combined to form this realism became distinct from one another. The logical tendencies of Russell, after uniting with the empiricism of William James, now united with certain ideas of the Bergsonian philosophy on the one hand and with certain revived conceptions of Spinozism on the other. New " blendings " of ideas were formed.

And after prolonged wanderings, while Russell seems to be tending towards a sort of behaviourist phenomenalism, American neo-realism would seem once more to be treading the path of monism from which the pragmatists wished to keep aloof, or of that evolutionist romanticism to which the realists were at first opposed.

CHAPTER V

PRAGMATIC REALISM: THE BEGINNINGS
OF CRITICAL REALISM

SEVERAL writers in the *Journal of Philosophy* have set forth particular forms of pluralism which are mostly based on scientific observation. Though always trying to keep in touch with scientific realities, they are none the less difficult to follow at times, and their metaphysics are often very complicated in their form and expression.

In Boodin, as in almost all the pluralists we have studied, we find the inclination towards finite experience, the vision of the fragmentary or piecemeal. His method is empirical; he attacks problems one after the other in piecemeal fashion. He takes account both of unity and of multiplicity; he recognises only relative constancy in the universe.

He knows that truth is not a unity, that we can build up the world in different ways. Wherefore should not truth be a "checkered mosaic"? Why, he said in a delightful letter to Carus, published in *The Monist* of 1908 (pp. 299–301), should we not ask: Who is your favourite philosopher, just as we ask: Who is your favourite poet? Once they are quite convinced of these truths, says Boodin, philosophers can become humorists.

The causal process has nothing in common with a logical classification. Because we believe that like alone can act on like, we remain insensible to the complexity of reality, to its variety of nuances. Both Boodin and Peirce claim that there may be different worlds of experiences capable of acting upon one another; there may also be non-thinking things which act upon the designs or schemes of thinking beings. And so, instead of insisting on the unity of matter, we shall be able to break up the universe, deal with it in each part and not as a whole, recognise chaos where there is chaos, unity where there is unity, see diverse qualities everywhere. Though things encroach upon one another, they are none the less essentially individual. The unitary forms of space and time cease to be, or at all events are mere ciphers in the opinion of the consistent pluralist. Unity of energy—as well as unity of substance—falls to pieces in our hands.

We no longer find anything but a scattering of discontinuous activities.

Boodin's pluralism has its completion in a certain moral idealism, in the idea that we can create new universes of worth, and, willy nilly, introduce portions of them into the world of reality. Indeed, the world is rich in possibilities; incessantly shifting and new, it may be interpreted in different ways.

More recently, Boodin has endeavoured to build his theories on the observation of scientific results, and to establish a realistic theory of knowledge.

Sellars, like Boodin, is a realist and also a pluralist. He says that the idealist mainly insists on the temporal nature of things, the realist on their spatial character. Hence the realist is led to conceive a pluralism; space introduces differences and complexities into the universe. But the pluralist does not regard time as disappearing, according to Sellars, who would make the relations of permanence and change more fluid than ever; he arrives

at what he calls a plastic naturalism. " I cannot be you "
must be one of the fundamental propositions of philosophy.
And monism offers us but one aspect of things.

Strong insists firmly on the individuality of minds.
Each consciousness, if it would conceive anything else
than itself, must make a leap, an irrational saltus. His
world, consisting of unconnected Platonic ideas, is a
discontinuous world; to deny discontinuity, in his
opinion, is to deny the Platonic—the ideal—element of
things. Therefore he would seem to answer pluralistically
the question he propounded at the end of *Why the mind
has a body*, regarding the one and the many.

By degrees only, and in certain respects at all events
in opposition to neo-realism, Strong and Sellars, along
with certain other philosophers we have just studied,
though sometimes starting with very different ideas,
found themselves naturally in favour of a doctrine which
they call critical realism. Whereas neo-realism, following
the main trend of the ideas of James on this subject,
mostly insisted on the immanence of the object in knowledge, the critical realists insist on this saltus between the
idea and the object which some of them, Strong, Santayana, Pratt, have illustrated, and which James had com-
mented on in certain passages. For neo-realists, things
may exist without our knowing them ; for critical realists,
they do exist—without our knowing them *as* existing.
These philosophers draw a very clear line of demarcation,
as Drake had also done, between knowable essence and
affirmed but unknowable reality. They insist on the
existence of mind, of minds, and they define this mind in
terms of action. A new blend of ideas is thus effected.

Several of them are bent on being Platonists and
naturalistic evolutionists at the same time. Santayana
combines with his rationalism the idea of the development

of reason, of the slow growth of the tree of knowledge on the soil of life ; for the most part, in spite of the incisive criticisms some of them have levelled against pragmatism, they recognise the importance of the idea of action, and in Strong and Sellars we even seem to find distinct traces of the ideas of the Chicago school as to the " biological " *rôle* of thought, as well as of Bergson's ideas on the *rôle* of the body and the brain. They believe in immediately perceived essences ; in this we see both a theory of neo-realism and the Platonism invoked by Santayana and Strong. They believe in the reality of minds, and we can well understand that such personalistic philosophers as Lovejoy and Rogers are to be found in their ranks.

A multiplicity of minds that know, a multiplicity of essences known, perhaps a multiplicity of existences unknown : these appear to be some of the ideas of this critical realism, as far as we can see at the present time. Whereas the neo-realists insisted on the immanence of the object in knowledge, whereas it was their tendency to deny the subjective element of knowledge, the critical realists maintain the existence of subject and object, or rather of subjects and objects, of subjects which themselves affirm, beyond essences, the objects they do not know. This is a theory of the transcendence of the object, a theory of discontinuity. It is a claim for the independence of objects and the reality of subjects. These philosophers start with a threefold criticism of neo-realism, from the standpoint of the history of knowledge, the reality of the subject, and the transcendence of the object, in order to affirm, it would appear, the existence of things in themselves and of active noumena.[20]

[20] For the recent ideas of these philosophers, see Strong's *Origin of Consciousness* (London, 1919), the articles of Sellars (*Mind*, 1919, p. 407), A. K Rogers (*Philosophical Review*, 1919, p 228), Durant Drake (*Philosophical Review*, 1920, p. 172).

Perhaps they will find—in certain ideas of Russell, in the realistic agnosticism he seems to have expounded in dealing with the world of common sense known only " by description," in his theory which regards our affirmations as a kind of instinct, in the ideas of Whitehead, who sets up a world of objects beyond the world of events conceived by Minkowski—suggestions which will make their theories more definite.

We need not study this " critical realism." Still, its existence had to be noted, seeing that it develops in a novel way certain ideas found in the works of James and Russell, ideas which had not appeared in neo-realism. Here, too, we are confronted with a metamorphosis of doctrines or rather the formation of a theory which, like personal idealism, like neo-realism, seems as though it must end in pluralist metaphysics.

CONCLUSION

I

It may have been advisable to study the pluralists in this patchwork, piecemeal fashion, to use an expression dear to James.

Pluralism is not a system created by one philosopher and developed by others. It is a " democratic," a social philosophy, one attempted by a great number of thinkers in co-operation.

As a matter of fact, there is not one pluralism, there are pluralisms.[21] These pluralisms vary according to the temperaments, the conceptions of individual souls, according to the very changes in each of these souls. Now it is morality, the desire for freedom of action, now it is religion, now æsthetic feeling, or, again, the observation of the results of sciences, or sometimes logic, that produces pluralist ideas.

Speaking generally, pluralism is a metaphysic of pragmatism ; though pragmatists cannot hold the monopoly of this metaphysic. It is usually associated with a realistic tendency which is particularly strong in the United States. But, on the one side, the realists do not monopolise pluralism ; on the other side, the profound theories

[21] A. D. Lovejoy, who wrote an article entitled " The Thirteen Pragmatisms," might perhaps discover at least as many pluralisms. " A revival of pluralism in more than one sense of the term," he writes in the *Journal of Philosophy*, 1909, p. 75. See also Tawney, *Journal of Philosophy*, 23rd June 1904.

of the English realist, S. Alexander, are certainly not pluralist at bottom.

Therefore, if we would define pluralism, it might be necessary to try to give, not a theoretical and abstract definition, but one akin to the individual soul, as James wished.

1. The pluralist is opposed to the monists, especially the English monists who, after 1870, were dominated by the philosophy of the Hegelian school. His theories are a protest both against Hegelianism and against Spencerianism ; their aim is to maintain the rights of personal minds and also the personality of God. In many cases, they may be partly explained by religious aspirations and beliefs. If we do not see how neo-Hegelianism, after assuming the form of theism, seemed to assume that of pantheism and then of atheism, if we do not study this particular monism which was perhaps exaggerated and misunderstood by its opponents, we cannot altogether explain the power and extent of the pluralist movement.

When, on the other hand, we observe the influence exercised upon pluralism, we see that most of the philosophers by whom it was inspired form part of a great movement against the teaching of the Hegelian school.

It was by making use of these foreign philosophies that the English spirit as well as the American spirit, with their instinct for the concrete and the practical, rebelled against what might seem to be the spirit of German philosophy.

The monist, say his opponents, desires to find his soul's rest in an abstract and general unity, the pluralist seems to insist lovingly on distinctions and differences.

2. The pluralist is also opposed to the monadist, as he calls him ; to him the world is not a static system

of individualities. Temporalism asserts the profound reality of duration, along with the idea that the world is endlessly finishing itself and remains ever unfinished. To the pluralist, the world is a great incomplete thing going on incessantly completing itself, without ever being completed.

In opposition to the monadist and the monist alike, the pluralist asserts that there is a " root evil " in this world, that this is something atrocious and inexplicable, which we must not try to understand but to destroy.

Individuals alone can do this; they alone, piecemeal and gradually, can save the world.

3. It is just at the moment when the idea of time thus steps, so to speak, into the idea of plurality, when monadism is transformed by temporalism, that there appears real possibility and freedom and pluralism.

Pluralism, in a general way, springs from a disposition to see the world in all its flux and diversity, to see things in their state of disorderly struggle and in their free harmony. To this pluralist temperament there responds a philosophy. Speaking generally, we might say that pluralism is a philosophy which insists by preference on diversity of principles, in opposition to monism, and on the mobility of things, in opposition to " monadism." It asserts both the diverse character and the temporal character of things, and it asserts that both these characters imply each other, without indeed any prejudgment that they will always remain real, without necessarily denying its rights to the unity towards which the world may appear to be tending, and which, at this moment, is already, it may be, immanent in its diversity.

Pluralism, thus defined, naturally leads to two complementary moral beliefs : moralism and meliorism. On the one hand, man uses his liberty in fear and trembling, to satisfy the requirements of the ideal, to struggle against the forces surrounding him on all sides.

On the other hand, he knows that the world, though not good, is not irremediably bad, that it may improve; and this belief comforts him just as much as the other belief, though elating him, caused him to tremble.

In logic, we have pragmatism endeavouring to envisage truth in concrete and particular fashion; " polysystematism," which enables reality to be constructed in various ways; " polyrealism," a belief closely connected with this latter and asserting several independent " bodies of reality " : these are all consequences of pluralism.

Two of the most important developments of contemporary logic—on the one side, the instrumental logic of Dewey and his school; on the other side, the works of G. E. Moore and of Russell, the study of logical terms and relations—may be traced back to pluralism, upon which they simultaneously react. The former emphasises the element of diversity in things, the latter the element of temporality.

In the religious domain, pluralism has been favourable to a renaissance of theism, a special—perhaps strictly Anglo-Saxon—theism. Rashdall, Galloway, Upton, who approach very close to pluralism, are the true successors of Martineau. Sturt proceeds from the criticism of absolutism to a philosophy of religion. Schiller reverentially stops short of treating particular along with religious problems, though he advocated a personal God. James fought on behalf of theism as well as of polytheism.

Polytheism is a natural complement of pluralist metaphysics; in maintaining it, the pluralist asserts that those very individualities that are apparently disunited by its teachings come together anew in a great society, a world republic. We have seen that the idea of metaphysical collectivism, of a grouping together of lives in the universe, is the natural complement of pluralist individualism.

A new philosophy of individuality and striving, a metaphysic of " fellowship," a call to action, a " revelation of nature in its own native character of richness and malleability ": this is what pluralism appears to be at the outset.

Perhaps certain of these characters are at first scarcely perceptible in some of the works of the neo-realists. And yet they are not absent even there, and a belief in the plurality of principles and essences enables them to affirm the reality of worth and of the ideal, the reality of the struggle needed to bring about this ideal.

II

To study the development of pluralism in English and American philosophy at the end of the nineteenth and the beginning of the twentieth centuries is to see how the forces of feeling and will revolted in English and American minds against what appeared to be an abstract and empty monism, a purely intellectual doctrine. The attractive element in pluralism is the vision of a multiple and moving world made up of clashing wills, the negation of rigid unity, the negation of the abstract, and the negation of a lifeless eternity.

There would seem to be, one might say, at first, a new conception of philosophy in the works of the pragmatist philosophers. Here the philosopher thinks not with his thought alone but also with his feeling and his will. He also discovers new horizons. The books of Schiller manifested a seductive youthfulness and boldness of thought.

James combined in original fashion a theory of the will, an irreducible empiricism, and a mysticism; the visions of Hume and Carlyle, the influence of philosophers as different as Emerson and Renouvier, puritanism and romanticism, were all blended together in his mind.

Pluralism does not seem to us to be a " solution " of the problems of metaphysics; it propounds problems, and it insists on certain problems remaining propounded, on their not being solved, *i.e.* finally annihilated in the absolute. The main reproach it brings against monism is that the latter, in transforming certain ideas, destroys them. If evil is a lesser good, if error is at bottom a truth, if freedom is a sort of determination, then there is no longer any such thing as evil, error, or freedom. Pluralism is the affirmation of negation, of contradiction, of effort. The pluralist believes there is an Everlasting Yea, but he also believes there is an Everlasting No.

Consequently pluralism is the affirmation of the irreducibility of certain ideas and certain things. The interpretation of things and ideas by the monist always detracts from their purity; he obtains unity only at the expense of unicity. The pluralist would like to apprehend things in themselves, to find in them particular characters which would separate and absolutely isolate them from one another. To him there are really such things as root evils, absolute errors, pure freedom. To him the given is that which resists, that which is outside of ourselves. The possible is that which is only possible, that which is to no extent given. Time has nothing of eternity; belief, nothing of knowledge; diversity, if he is a consistent pluralist, must have nothing of unity. The theory of the externality of relations is an expression of the idea that a real definition is not a putting of things into relation. The distinctive quality of an idea, feeling, fact, can be thought only as the negation of all that is not this idea, feeling, fact. But it would not be legitimate to see only this element of opposition; this very opposition is thought only as expressing a position. From this standpoint it may be said that pluralism is a realism; it is this profound realism that asserts the irreducibility of phenomena. A complete enumeration of the relations which a thing has with its neighbours by no means exhausts the essence of this thing, and there is always an interval remaining between the essence and this conceptual enumeration. Thus it is possible to explain that pluralism is both closely akin to Platonic realism, to the realism of the Scottish philosophers, and to empirical -realism, in so far as each asserts the irreducibility of one domain of the world to the other.

Such a realism necessarily leads to empiricism, to that profound empiricism which believes that being should not be conceived as a generality or as a totality, that there are only pieces of being. If multiplicity is here and unity there; if there is continuity on the one hand and discontinuity on the other; then the world must really be a piecemeal world, a mosaic universe. The idea of purity leads to the idea of multiplicity. Pluralism is a theory of separate essences. "As to the monistic view, the *all*-relationship, the relation of each to all is definitive; according to pluralism, it is accidental," says Perry.

But while the empiricism of the pluralist may thus be defined as a philosophy of the fragmentary, the piecemeal, the patchwork, the mosaic; on the other hand, it opposes the old forms of empiricism by insisting on the aspects of continuity and of totality of experience. The empiricism of Hume was a doctrine of decomposition;

that of James insists on concrete continuity. The old empiricism generally reduced qualities to quantity; the new empiricism emphasises the original and irreducible element in quality. Thus empiricism tends to become more deeply empirical; it is striving towards a fuller experience, it would rid itself of a host of theories of whose Cartesian and rationalistic origin it is more or less vaguely aware.

In particular it will be pluralist. By reason of this conscious or unconscious character it will always be opposed to rationalism; even if the world is one, nothing would stand in the way of it being many. The empiric does not feel within himself a need of unity; to him the intelligence of things is not connected with the unity of things. True intelligence is, above all else, a craving after the concrete and the particular.

Such an empiricism is easily united in the minds of its exponents with a voluntaristic romanticism. And we may rightly say of pragmatism, of pluralism, as of many other contemporary philosophies, that they are a sort of empirical romanticism. To the pluralist, experience is romantic; facts are hard, strange, threatening; in the second place, we find within ourselves the testimonies of a creative will, and the will we feel to be real *is* a real force. We find also within ourselves mystical states. And so this romanticism contains what might be called a "Gothic" element, a voluntaristic element, and a mystical element, all of which appear within experience itself; it is observation, fidelity to what the pluralist sees and feels, that we see at the origin of these romantic theories, of voluntarism, of temporalism, of the conception of vaster consciousnesses absorbing consciousnesses of a lesser span.

III

If we would inquire into the importance and value of pluralism, we first find ourselves confronted with certain contradictions, of whose solution, perhaps, it is not impossible to obtain a glimpse. But afterwards we are confronted with fresh contradictions, and these, we think, reveal internal lack of coherence in the doctrine, as it has so far been expounded, and compel the mind to transcend it. Let us examine the former.

On the one hand the pluralist seems to deny, and on the other hand to affirm, the existence of substance. He denies the existence of substance because, for him, substance is a word, an abstraction, and to affirm substance is actually to begin the process which will cause the world to melt away in the idea of the all, it is to deny the profound reality of time ; moreover, observation never offers us anything but sequences of phenomena ; and James, studying in his *Psychology* the idea of the self, indicates therein a sequence of thought-pulses which die and are reborn in eternal renewals.

At the same time he would seem to affirm the existence of substance, for this incessantly disappearing Ego is still a creative Ego ; on this vanishing Self, this hardly perceptible *Fiat*, the universe hangs.

Pluralism asserts the existence of substances : in the case of James, because he affirms the activity of the person and the concrete character of things ; in the case of Russell, because he asserts the externality of relations ; to the externality of relations with reference to terms should correspond the internality of terms with reference to themselves.

When we recognise the irreducibility of terms with reference to relations, the irreducibility of objects with reference to the definitions we give of them and to the mental images they evoke within us, are we not affirming substance ? And the affirmation of this substance, says the pluralist, is not a step in the direction of monism ; on the contrary, it is because there are substances thus absolutely separate that monism is impossible.

But perhaps there is here no contradiction at bottom. A pluralist like James, even, it may be, one like Russell, denies the one infinite substance, but he affirms the self-creative substances that, at every separate moment and in disseminated points throughout the universe, pulsate and act. James affirms it, not because he is able to name it, but rather because he cannot do so ; and mainly, less because it is necessary to thought than because it is present in action.

We should also find apparent contradictions in the conception of continuity and discontinuity. James appears to see in the self nothing but a succession of distinct phenomena " welcoming " one another ; freedom does not manifest itself to him in the continuous development of the voluntary act, but in the instantaneous *Fiat*. This is a purely phenomenalist conception remaining as far as possible within the confines of the instant. This conception, however, seems kept in check by the idea of the continuity and the indivisibility of psychological phenomena. And so, right from the time he wrote his *Psychology*, two tendencies appear to have been clashing together in the mind of James, two ways of understanding psychological life, two ways of regarding time.

Again, whereas William James the psychologist affirms the indivisibility of the psychological phenomenon, William James the metaphysician defines his empiricism by saying that it is an explanation of the whole by the parts, a patchwork philosophy. Just now, instantaneous vanishing phenomena appeared before us as subsequently extending over the entire psychological life and over the whole world; now, undergoing a contrary tendency, the totality first affirmed is split up into elements; continuity breaks up into discontinuities.

Here again it might be possible to attempt to find a reply in certain theories of James, in the idea of indivisible "blocks" of duration or in that of "drops" of time: ideas whereby he attempts to reconcile continuity and discontinuity. Or else he has recourse to anti-intellectualism; and *A Pluralistic Universe* is an attempt to solve the problems now propounded to him by the idea of the composition of mental states, an idea he had hitherto combated, but which his anti-intellectualism enables him now to adopt.

: Nevertheless, we soon find ourselves faced with contradictions at whose solution we can no longer guess. For instance, how are we to reconcile the idea that there is a universal participation of things in one another, that starting from any one point of the universe we can go to any other point, with the idea formulated in the "Principle of Absence," that there are things which have nothing to do with certain others? Radical empiricism aims at being a philosophy both of the distinction between and of the "confusion" of things.

There would seem also to be opposition between James's affirmation of external relations and a certain conception of his regarding the internality of relations. The idea of the possible, at first justified by the theory of external relations, was explained finally by the affirmation of internal relations like that existing between our thoughts and our acts. James wavers between a purely logical theory and a purely psychological theory of the possible. However it may be, the idea of the possible can only with great difficulty form part of a philosophy of radical empiricism. His theory of knowledge, too, in so far as it ends on the one hand in pragmatism and on the other hand in realism, seems to involve a contradiction ; his pragmatism goes so far as to assert that the details of the world are not independent of our thought, that our thought and the world form a whole ; his realism even denies the necessity of regarding thought as acting on things.[22] Sometimes he tries to represent beings as placed alongside each other, sometimes he pictures them as being transformed into one another, and the contraries as being metamorphosed into their contraries. At one time, truth is a useful and definite orientation ; at another, it is a way of taking things for what they are " known as," and, we might say, " felt as."

Again, to set forth the same contrasts in another way, James tells us on the one hand that between external things and our thoughts of these things there is nothing but a difference of context, and on the other hand he believes in the specific activity of the mind. At one time we find that the tendency under his conception is the desire to set all phenomena on the same plane, at another he wishes to retain the distinctive character of psychological facts along with the reality of the object. Now, the psychic is mere change of environment ; then again, it is something irreducible.

Do we not see a consequence of this wavering attitude when he tells us in certain passages, as we have remarked, that pluralism and pragmatism imply each other, and in other passages that they are independent of each other ? And, again, we have guessed at all the problems which would originate in the affirmation of

[22] Bradley notes the contradictions in the reasoning of James as regards the conception of relations in *Essays on Truth and Reality*, pp. 151, 241

different " bodies of reality "—those bodies which are now external and now internal to one another.

If we consider other elements of his doctrines, for instance, his conception of deity, we again see that at one time God is transcendent, and at another time he is a vaster consciousness, immanent, so to speak, in our own consciousness; now, James is very near to the transcendentalism of Emerson; now, to what he calls a crude supernaturalism. Many problems would also be raised by the idea of the existence of evil and by the idea of creation.

Various conceptions of realism, even those that have contributed to the formation, one, of neo-realism, another, of critical realism, and again another, perhaps, of the particular and profound realism of Hocking—a way of criticising ideas which is now wholly intellectualistic and then again welcomes and adopts mystical conceptions—the value of the principle of contradiction affirmed at the outset and during the larger part of his philosophic course, and finally, the negation of this value, at least in certain respects : these are so many theories which it is very difficult to unite completely from James's standpoint.

We have seen that there is in his mind a conflict, not only of intellectual determinations, but also of sentimental tendencies. The craving to be assured that there is something won for eternity, the idea that the world is progressing towards unity, the affirmation that we shall " finally " be delivered from evil, seem as though they could scarcely be harmonised with what he tells us of the pluralist temperament. Along with a need of that which clashes and is difficult and painful—whereon we have specially insisted—there is a desire that things should be " easy-going," a manifest desire, in his earlier

as in his later writings, that our aspirations, both towards
the unity of the universe and towards a universe in which
we should not feel ourselves out of place, should meet
with satisfaction.   Now, we find him thinking that we
must feel, as it were, " cabin'd, cribb'd, confin'd " in
the world, and then again, that the universe must be
full of breathing-space, of air, of freedom, and ease.
The philosopher, James tells us in certain pages, must
above all be able to moderate, to arrest the natural
expansion of his ideas ; in others, he tells us that these
must be left free.   Now the term, mystic, is a reproach
levelled against monistic doctrines ; and again, mystical
experience is regarded as the most profound of all.   At
one time, religion adds an element of danger to the
world ; at another, it ensures our security.

And so we should be tempted to apply to this thought,
which cannot be content with or confined to its own
affirmations, the phrase which James, following on Blood,
applied to the universe: " Ever, not quite."   Thus
we are led to the impression of a sort of dialectic
in the thought of James, a kind of—Hegelian—play of
contradictories.

James seems to proceed from Hegel to Hegel, as an
Hegelian would say.   He had first been attracted by
what, later on, he was to regard as the mirage of unity ;
finally, he returns to this idea of unity, translating it, as
he says, into empirical terms ;   he no longer thinks it
necessary that the universe should be subject, as Renouvier
had taught, to the laws of contradiction and the excluded
middle.   At times his ultra-empiricism is one with
Hegelian ultra-rationalism.   Aided by the ideas of
Bergson, he sees the process of dialectic at work in
experience itself, as did Bradley.

At the same time, he endeavours to combine with

this new empiricism certain ideas of Russell which he regards as somewhat similar to some of his own. He wishes to retain both the idea of a perpetual flux and that of a conceptual kingdom.

The more he tries to go deeper into his own ideas, the more he feels his outlook upon the world, however contradictory this may appear, similar to that of Hegel, to that of Bergson, and, in certain respects, to that of Russell, and yet all the time to that of Renouvier. The philosophies of Renouvier, Hegel, Bergson, and Russell seem to him, each one of them, increasingly true. Hence his apparent syncretism—if by this term we mean the effort to bring together, without destroying or perverting them, the truths of the various doctrines into radical empiricism.

Or rather, under pluralism we find monism, and under monism we again find pluralism; neo-criticism leads him to Bergsonism, whence he goes back once more to certain theories of neo-criticism. And so this is not the simplistic philosophy, by any means, which it is sometimes thought to be. In James an Hegelian vision of things underlies the empiricism of John Stuart Mill, but this Hegelian vision is itself perhaps no more than a veil set over a neo-critical empiricism. Thus beneath each affirmation of James we seem to find another very different affirmation. May it not be a sort of empirical dialectic whereby each conception simultaneously deepens and fades away?

Will it be said that James sought a *via media*, that to this end he often set forth his philosophy as an effort to reconcile the various tendencies of the human soul, that he wrote: " Radical empiricism and pluralism stand out for the legitimacy of the notion of *some*: each part of the world is in some ways connected, in

some other ways not connected with its other parts."
He appeals to the moderation of common sense ; things
are partly joined and partly disjoined.

There is in him, it may also be said, a sort of " balance "
of different tendencies, a co-existence of those elements
which were about to separate.

These different elements, however, cannot thus be
durably united, or even perhaps " balanced." All the
less is this so because James mostly does not seem to be
following that middle path to which he sometimes
points ; because he goes to extremes in one direction or
in the other ; because in his later works, as we have
seen, he appears to be very near to the neo-critical
philosophy at one time, at another to the neo-realistic,
and at another to the Bergsonian philosophy.

While we may note this wavering and hesitation in
the mind of James, Schiller disclaims whatever was
radical in his pluralism. The pluralists had promised
philosophers a new world and new horizons. But when
the road had to be pointed out, the masters hesitated.

And the disciples were divided. Do not the antinomies
we noted in the doctrine of James explain this division
among the disciples ? Undoubtedly Dewey's pupils
continue their work, keeping above all to their idea of
the immanence of thought within reality, which is its
origin and material and end. But some philosophers
rally to the Bergsonian philosophy and adopt a sort
of empirical monism ; whereas others, in greater numbers,
combine certain conceptions of James with the ideas of
Russell and attempt to build up an intellectualistic
empiricism, an empirical Platonism.

This dialectical development of which we have been
speaking is so strong that it would be very difficult to
speak of pluralism—appearing, now as personal idealism,

and again, as objectivist realism—if we wished to take these two tendencies equally into consideration. At first, pluralism seemed to be an affirmation of the self, a negation of general ideas and of the extra-temporal; but when it assumes the form of neo-realism, it seems to be an affirmation of general and extra-temporal ideas and a negation of the self. At first, pluralism was a personal idealism; in a second stage, it appears as an impersonal realism. The tendencies that had endeavoured to exist together become separate.

But the neo-realists themselves, as we have said, cannot get at a completely coherent philosophy; they are both monists and pluralists; and neo-realism in its turn is split up into incompatible elements.

Critical realism opposes neo-realism; it also develops, in its own way, certain suggestions found in James, and some ideas of personal idealism.

If we studied the history of the various forms of realism, resulting from the clash of mathematical speculations, the functionalism of Dewey, and the theory of consciousness of James, we should find that they tended, either in the direction of an absolute idealism, or in that of a realism akin to the realism of the Platonists, or again in that of an agnostic realism.

At the same time, we see a kind of mystic realism shaping itself, and the monistic thinkers expounding anew their philosophical conceptions more powerfully than ever.

IV

We may say that the development of contemporary English and American philosophy is bound up with the development of the problem of the externality of relations. By following the evolution of this problem we shall

19

best understand the course of this philosophy. There are no external relations; there are no simple juxtapositions of terms; and the basis of the relations is within the terms themselves. This is the thought of Leibniz and of Hegel that is now being resumed, and it is the very essence of the dialectic of *Appearance and Reality*.

The terms in Bradley's philosophy disappear within absolute unity; relations are abolished, negativity is denied. This threefold negation of terms, of contingent relations, and of negations, really constitutes only one negation; these three ideas being but three aspects of one and the same idea: the term is the negation of that which is not itself; relations can be contingent only with respect to terms; contingence presupposes the idea of the possibility of negation; and negations are relations.

We understand how the ideas of pragmatism may issue from such a doctrine and at the same time be opposed thereto. They issue from it; for if there are never any but internal relations, thought is bound up with reality; on the one hand, reality gives birth to thought; on the other hand, thought transforms reality. Indeed, we readily find affirmations of distinctly pragmatist tendencies in the writings of the absolutists, especially in those of Bradley. And Dewey was at first an Hegelian. But, at the same time, against the theory of the internality of relations, which at bottom annihilates both relations and terms, pragmatism emphasises the existence of terms of contingent relations and of negation. For the world of relations and terms is not only a creation of the intellect, as Bradley says; it would seem also to be an affirmation of feeling and will. Through its very denying of the possibility of a theory of terms and relations, through its obstinate criticism of it, absolutism brought it into being.

If we would conceive dialectically the trend of English and American philosophic thought, pragmatism may be regarded as the moment of the terms (especially of the subject), of the " also," of the " no," and of relations, as distinct from terms.

But while in our knowledge there is an external relation between subject and object, certain pragmatists are naturally induced thereby to set up a theory of terms and of relations as external to mind ; this is still a philosophy of terms, but instead of insisting, as he did at first, on the term which is the subject,[23] the philosopher will insist on the term which is the object ; the subjectivist form is succeeded by an objectivist form of the doctrine. There are objects ; there are domains of objects.

We may say that in pragmatism there are at least three different conceptions of what is called radical empiricism. As a radical empiricist, the pragmatist tells us that experience is absolute fusion, an indissoluble blend ; he asserts the internality of relations ; the experience of which he speaks is akin to that of Bradley or to Bergson's theory of pure duration. As a radical empiricist, he affirms that we must take our mental states for what they are " known as," and so restore reality to our feelings of freedom and of negation ; and he arrives at the conception of a world of doubts, of terms whose position is their mutual opposition, of negations, of decisions and contingent relations, and this is what might be called subjectivist pluralism. And again, as a radical empiricist, he endeavours to set up a philosophy of entities in rela-

[23] The idea of an objective reality seems to be essential to pragmatism, and this is what makes comprehensible the possibility of passing from pragmatism to realism, though pragmatism mainly regards things from the side of the subject, and emphasises the subject.

tions, whose tendency will be objectivist and no longer subjectivist, which will be akin to the empirocriticism of Mach and Avenarius or the realism of Russell, and will constitute an objective pluralism. And so radical empiricism is now the affirmation of moving, continuous and indivisible experience, now the affirmation of the will, and then again a conception of distinct bodies of reality.

The thought of James was vast and airy enough to comprehend and gather together the various forms of pluralism. But pragmatism was only a momentary grouping of ideas. Subjective pluralism seems to have constituted a simple " moment," the protest of terms against the attempt that would have annihilated them in the absolute. Whereas monism, by the negation of relations, made up the absolute, the one reality ; pluralist pragmatism, on the other hand, by the affirmation of relations and terms, relations and terms in motion, relations and terms mainly considered from the standpoint of the subject and from a dynamic point of view, denied the absolute. This antithesis is succeeded by new conceptions, one of which, under the influence of Bergson, denies the externality of relations, while the other sees relations and terms from the standpoint of the object, sees them as static, and ends in a realistic conception quite opposed, in certain points at least, to that of pragmatism.

Still, as we have also seen, this latter theory, in spite of appearances, does not seem to have been built up in a permanent and definite fashion.

Over against it appears critical realism, the " rehabilitation," partly at least, of the unknowable ; whereas neo-realism was a " rehabilitation " of knowledge.

On the other hand, a profound and brilliant metaphysician, Mr Hocking,[24] sets in contrast to these conceptions, whether subjectivist and voluntarist or intellectualist and analytical, a new conception which is at the same time a mysticism and an intellectualist philosophy, an objectivism and a voluntarism. Intelligence and sensibility are eager for objectivity; they are essentially our love of objectivity, though not of that conceived by Russell. What they want is a concrete one, that of an object which is a subject, an objectivity which is divine. In a somewhat different domain, in the profound studies of von Hügel on religion, do we not find similar ideas? "God," says von Hügel, "is absolute Over-Againstness."

And so we have an intensive and mystical realism over against the extensive realism of Russell. After the moment of the subject, after the moment of the objective object, we have now reached the idea of that which is object, because it is subject; a philosophy which attempts to contain within itself what constituted the worth of pragmatism, though with the element of arbitrary creation and pure subjectivism eliminated; a philosophy which seems at certain points to be inspired by the idealism of Royce. We then witness a return in the direction of monism, a mystical monism.

V

1. A history of English and American philosophy would show us a perpetual union and a perpetual dissociation of ideas. Thus we might see the influence of philosophers like Fechner, on the one hand, Avenarius and Mach, on the other hand, meeting for an instant, and then

[24] In a prior phase of his thought he might, it would seem, be classed among the pluralists. See *Journal of Philosophy*, vol. ii, p. 477, etc.

again separating violently.   Blendings and combinations of theories ; then sudden separations and oppositions.

2. This philosophy of the England and America of to-day is a sort of experience and adventure in thought, as indeed is any important phase of reflection.   To attempt to reflect, apart from the commonly accepted solutions, to yield to the most diverse influences, to satisfy the requirements of the feelings and aspirations within us, however contradictory they may appear ; the feeling of a creative power in man, the feeling of external forces limiting his activity, the feeling of a superior force in which, it may be, the various souls become blended ; the affirmation of the finite and the affirmation of an indefinite evolution; intellectualism and anti-intellectualism, phenomenalism and substantialism—all these tendencies and intuitions struggle and blend together, doubtless only to separate and disunite anew.   It is a philosophy which departs from traditions, and in which at the same time all thoughts and all traditions meet, from those of Heraclitus and Pythagoras to those of Renouvier and Bergson.   Here we find the strangest combinations of usually contrasted doctrines.

On the other hand, never have the different philosophical tendencies appeared in so absolute a form ; never, for instance, has there been greater insistence on the perpetual and complete transformation of things ; nor ever, it may be, has there been a philosophy that conceives the world more clearly as a static world.   In order to characterise one of the fundamental tendencies of these doctrines, Professor Lovejoy had to invent the word temporalism ; while a few years later, Kallen spoke of the "staticism of the new realists."   On the one hand, the absolute affirmation ; and on the other hand, the absolute negation of time.

3. Within each of these philosophies we should discover that constant effort of thought whereby it completes itself, whereby it denies itself. Each of these philosophers, the contradictor of another, is also the contradictor of himself. Everywhere we find the same vortex of thought, whether we study Bradley, or James, or again the neo-realists. Monism appears behind pluralism; or pluralism behind monism.

And so it seems as though we could rationally build up the development of contemporary English and American philosophy, just because this thought, in its desire to apprehend reality, only succeeds each time in bringing forward a partial aspect of this reality, and consequently, when it has done this, is constrained, as it were, to bring forward a different aspect.

We may say that the succession of doctrines is perhaps more rational than at first appears, that within this disorder an order may be discovered. But we must always realise, on the one hand, the element of personal irreducibility, the " vision," as James says, of each philosopher, and the relation between his doctrine and this " vision "; and, on the other hand, the fact that the historical order of doctrines is not so important as the relation—extra-temporal, so to speak—between them.

VI

After this, looking at the matter from the centre of pluralism itself, can we not ask ourselves whether the works of the pluralists, their contradictions and their antinomies, may not be the origin of a dialectic which would take us beyond the limits of pluralism ?

Pluralism, because it is a philosophy of the purity and the separation of things, seemed to us, an instant ago, as though it were to become a kind of eclectic philosophy, proceeding by juxtaposition of ideas. There are leaps or saltus in our consciousness, and a moment before there was a continuous flux which afterwards begins again. But does not James himself manifestly wish to express certain discontinuous phenomena in the language of the continuous? For instance, if we hear a clap of thunder, we hear not only thunder but thunder-breaking-upon silence; and so James attempts to reinstate discontinuity into the continuity of the psychic life. On the other hand, did he not, in his later works, regard all life as a series of distinct moments, of discrete or discontinuous drops, of quantities which fall one by one? Does not then all continuity appear to overlay a discontinuity, all discontinuity to overlay a continuity, just as beneath the continuity of space we presuppose atoms and have presupposed ether beneath the atoms, and sometimes further continuities beneath the ether?

The ideas of discontinuity and continuity mean, we may say, in pragmatist terms, that we can pass, now smoothly, now after a certain shock, from certain parts of an object to certain other parts. These qualities exist with reference to ourselves and our action; the object in itself is neither continuity nor discontinuity, and this is why it is for us both continuity and discontinuity. The fluctuations of the philosophy of James might be explained by this fact: he advocated both neo-criticism and Bergsonianism because at every moment the object eluded, perhaps, both the theories of the neo-criticists and those of the Bergsonians. But then we see disappear one of the characters we had remarked in this philosophy, to which we have given the name of eclecticism and the philosophy of juxtaposition. In radical empiricism we recognised this philosophy of the *auch* of

which Hegel spoke ; there is continuity and there is also
discontinuity. But from what we have just seen, this
empiricism should be transformed and should signify :
the object is continuous, and it is discontinuous as well ;
or rather, finally, it is neither. No longer will there be
juxtaposition in space ; juxtaposition in space becomes
dialectic in thought.

The given, as we have said, is, for James, that which
resists us ; but it would not be given us if it were that
alone. On the other hand, the given is our idea, our
representation ; and James may even occasionally say
that it is nothing but our idea of it. The given, on the
one hand, is an obstacle to our thought ; on the other
hand, it is our thought itself.[25] Thus we find in the
theory of James both extreme realism and extreme
idealism. The object is immanence and transcendence
at the same time. There is absolute unity and complete
difference between itself and our idea. Does not this
again mean that we endeavour to think that which
finally cannot be thought ? The relation between subject
and object is no longer finally thinkable, since it would
continually require fresh subjects ; here, strictly speaking,
there is no relation, there is a presence.

Likewise, we cannot have certain objects that are one
and certain others that are many, as James says. We
must not simply say, in opposing this affirmation, that
there may be multiple unities, as the English monists
express it, but that the only unity is the unity of diverse
things, and the only diversity is the diversity of the one
thing. Because they have not really united unity and
diversity, the pluralists have been led to add on to their

[25] And, in order to account for the pragmatist theory, we must add
that our idea is also a progress towards the given. The given is both the
goal and the obstacle for our idea, as well as our idea itself.

pluralism *de facto* a monism *de jure*. Schiller in particula
—and James also in certain passages—believes that th
world is making for—aspiring after—unity.

It may be that the pluralists have also formed a some
what erroneous idea of the opposition between th
absolute and the relative. When we examine th
criticisms they level against Bradley, we may see tha
belief in the absolute and belief in the relative impl
each other. What they object to above all else ii
Bradley's doctrine is not absolutism ; it is, on the contrary
relativism. And it is the relativism of the pluralist
which enables them to believe in absolute values, ii
ultimate realities. The fact is that the absolute and th
relative not only oppose each other, but posit each other
To admit that the universe is not a whole is to admi
the possibility of wholes, of " particular absolutes."

But if we say in this manner that our ways of livin
and our beliefs are *absolutes*, we are using the word ii
a sense which is neither that of the monists when the
admit the absolute nor of the pluralists when they den
it. It is not an absolute that contains all facts and al
qualities ; it is not an absolute that absorbs somethin
given outside of itself. The " relative " when sensed
that is the absolute.

Between the absolute and the relative, the infinit
and the finite, the eternal and the temporal, there is no
that opposition which is imagined by the pluralists. W
have seen that the affirmations of the pluralists are, a
a rule, accompanied or followed mentally by contrar
affirmations. But here the contraries cannot be th
ones alongside of the others ; they inevitably permeat
one another. The idea of irreducibility on which th
pluralists insist implies the idea of opposition, anc
between such terms opposition can be nothing els

than union. There are affirmations that cannot be set alongside each other without necessarily uniting. After this we leave the quantitative sphere in which the problems of pluralism and monism are being discussed. The opposition between monism and pluralism does not now appear to us so important as it seemed at first. Empirical pluralism is generally an analytical philosophy ; now, an analytical philosophy is one which, in the name of smaller wholes, protests against absolute totality. Synthetic and analytic philosophies are both quantitative conceptions and not so strongly opposed as at first seemed to be the case.

Pluralism calls itself a philosophy of the parts ; monism is a philosophy of the whole. But we do not know if there is a whole, and therefore we do not know if there are parts. A "mosaic philosophy" is at bottom a philosophy of unity. On the other hand, this philosophy of Bradley's, in which all the facts must find their place, is a philosophy of parts, a mosaic philosophy ; Bradley's conception is often nothing but a philosophy of the *auch*. The ideas of whole and of parts have no meaning except through each other. By identifying philosophy of the particular with philosophy of the parts, James took his stand on the plane of quantity. There are only elements ; several things exist in the world, he says. These affirmations have their value, but the contrary affirmations also are important ; if there are elements or constituent parts, then there is a whole ; there is a world in which things exist. Here also pluralism and monism evoke each other and one cannot exist without the other.

Therefore we must endeavour to think the idea of the particular without thinking of the idea of parts, and we must combine it with the idea of the concrete. James, by an intellectual method, criticises the idea of unity.

He says that there is nothing more sacred in the number one than in any other number. The fact, however, is that unity is not a number, an abstraction, to the neo-Hegelian whom James is attacking; it is the very way in which the diverse unites in him; it is sensation, feeling itself. It is not abstract unity; it is concrete totality.

The pluralist says: the parts are more important than the whole. But that is affording too simple a solution of the problem; for there are two kinds of parts, and while a being is part of the universe, it is itself a whole as regards its elements or constituents. To the pluralists, the being appears more important than the universe, but he will not, as a rule, allow that the parts of a being are more important than this being. The universe on the one hand and atoms on the other hand are abstractions; the idea of elements is no less abstract than that of the whole; the real is the concrete totality.

The concrete is the particular seen as a whole. The particular as imaged by the pluralists, and the general, are both abstractions, they both represent phenomena spread out by the side of one another or subsumed under one another in a sort of intellectual space. The concrete is the particular which closes upon itself, which becomes a separate life.

And so the antinomies and oppositions we have observed, continuity and discontinuity, realism and nominalism, externality and internality, bring us to see in pluralism a dialectic which leads us to transcend pluralism itself; while we must remain fully aware that even these antinomies are the very manifestation of a thought which would apprehend things in their deep and solid reality, that they must not be simply absorbed, resolved, transmuted, but also kept intact, and that they are not merely the sign of the inadequacy of thought as compared with reality, for they at the same time diminish and impoverish reality and make it richer and of greater significance.

VII

Whilst the pluralists were developing their theories, the thinkers whom they had undertaken to oppose were pursuing their work. Bradley, Bosanquet, and Royce continued to celebrate what the pluralists call the perverse cult of unity.[26] Let us open their writings and see what they bring us and what we needs must take exception to. We shall discover that unity, as they conceive it, is not that empty, dead unity for believing in which they were blamed by the pluralists. Like the world of the pluralists, it is rich and moving; it is not given to the mind which would passively receive it; the mind must live it and create it within itself. Confronted with the pragmatism which dissociates itself, the absolutists have drawn up anew their philosophical constructions. Bosanquet in his *Gifford Lectures* and Bradley in his *Essays on Truth and Reality* again take up their formerly expounded theories, though now perhaps they give them a more concrete, living, and thrilling character. They attempt to prove that individual effort does not lose its importance in their doctrines, that their monism leaves room for everything concrete, finite, and tragic that there is in things. When we return to the writings of the monists, of Bradley, Bosanquet, and Royce, after reading the works of the pluralists, we are struck by the

[26] Ward frequently, in his interesting works, comes near to pluralism. Andrew Seth Pringle-Pattison in his last admirable volume, *The Idea of God in the Light of Recent Philosophy*, endeavours, by way of pluralism, to join up with monism. It would be interesting to trace out, in this book and in different articles, the way in which the latter stands related to Bosanquet.

difference between the simplified appearances of these philosophers, as presented by their opponents, and the complex reality of the philosophic mind, so difficult to grasp and yet so definite in Bradley, so rich in Bosanquet, and so supple and large in Royce.   Bradley, in bold dialectic, proceeds from a theory of immediate experience, very similar to those of James and Bergson, to one of absolute experience : he has a very keen sense of the particular and at the same time of the inadequacy of the particular.   Bosanquet possesses the sense of the concrete ; to him the world is a unique work of art, full of infinite meanings.   Royce sees the world as a totality of contrasted lives, known by a single mind ; he fully appreciates what is individual and free.

Royce proceeds from psychology and epistemology to a kind of universal sociology.   His philosophy, the result of the blending in a unique personality of influences as diverse as those of Browning's poems, of mathematical speculations, of the German romantics and of Le Conte, is an instance of that incessant transformation and interpretation of the past into the future, of which he himself has spoken.   He ever attempted to fathom the depths of his own thought by bringing himself to contact different minds, like Peirce and James, who also were able to welcome and interpret the ideas of others.   None the less did their individuality remain all the time—if not opposed—at least altogether distinct.   In Royce's thought, is not the world made up of individuals who, both in and by their resemblances and in their contrasts, become more and more individualised ?

Here unity is always to be seen.   It is that of a mind eager to reveal itself to itself in order that it may reveal itself to others, eager to grasp its widest and most definite meaning, which combines the utmost frankness with the intensest effort towards the most profound thinking, which is at the same time tradition and renewal. Here, too, Royce appears as one of those monads, with open windows, of the " Roycian " world.

His philosophy culminates in these two great ideas of loyalty and community, the loyalty of the individual towards a cause, but also towards that " cause," that " meaning " which is himself—his most personal and most universal self. And so, since the " cause " is the meaning of the individual, these two forms of " loyalty " combine at the same time that, here as later on in the work of Hocking, community and personality become identified.

The very tendency of all our ideas towards objects regarded as external makes us feel that we are ourselves moving within a subject ; thoughts free and united, words uttered and words heard, ever more and more thoroughly investigated and worked out : all these diversities merge into a vaster Thought, a more living Word.

Are not, on the other hand, the theory of the undivided continuity of experience of which Bradley speaks, and the conception of that finite centre which he tries to make felt, ideas akin to those reached along other channels by James and Bergson ? As James indeed says, Bradley starts from the same continuity of experience as Bergson, and this negation of relation, for which he is blamed, is nothing but the affirmation of the irreducibility of being to discursive thought. Bradley starts from the experience of radical empiricism and proceeds towards the experience of the absolute, an experience which might be called religious ; both in him and in James mysticism and empiricism are united.

The very idea of transmutation and of degrees of truth is nearer to ordinary experience than the pragmatists and pluralists imagine. Are not our feelings, our sensations and ideas, capable of being deepened and transformed according to the degree of tension of our consciousness ? Can we not, as Bosanquet remarks, give a new and a richer meaning to our former ideas and feelings in proportion as our experience itself becomes enriched ? This idea of transmutation is the affirmation of the incessant renewal and deepening of thought.

Absolutism, says Bradley, is " a hard doctrine." Employing the method of a dialectic in constant contact with experience, he proceeds towards a unity he does not know. In his desire to comprehend things, he winds his way towards that which comprehends all, but that which comprehends all is what a finite mind cannot comprehend. To save all appearances, he must abandon them all. Both in the practical and in the religious domain, Bradley seems to disdain, perhaps more than James ever did, that coherence he seeks in the order of theory ; in the last resort, our sense of the value of things determines our ideas, and the ideas it adopts, even if they are mutually self-contradictory, even if they are contradictory in themselves, are in some degree true. For practical needs, he thinks, there is something higher than theoretical coherence. A man can believe both that there is perfect goodness and that nothing is more intensely real than action performed in order that the good may be realised. My will must count, while, on the other hand, the good is actually realised. We must believe in struggle in the world, we must believe in the peace of God. Uncertainty and certainty, ideality and reality, immanence and transcendence, must be united. Often we have the impression that it is in the name of coherence that pragmatists criticise absolutist theories.

In consequence of the unstable and uncertain element

in pluralism, shall we have to be thrown back upon the doctrines of idealistic monism ? We must see if these doctrines, particularly that to which Bradley and Bosanquet have given the most definite form, can satisfy us.

It has been said that the monism of Bradley may appear as more concrete than that of the German philosophers; but the reason Bradley pays attention to facts is mainly in order finally to transform them. There is nothing given, he tells us, which is sacred : metaphysics cannot accept any element of experience unless it is absolutely forced to do so.

According to Bradley, reality must correspond to the postulates of thought. In Bradley there is a sort of speculative hedonism; nothing must resist his intellectual passion. But it is not only with postulates of thought, it is also with postulates of the heart, that reality must fit in. I could not rely upon a truth, he writes, if I were forced to regard it as odious. He would have our deepest needs all satisfied, and the moving principle of his dialectic is the axiom that what must and can be necessarily is.

He is certain that reality may thus be transformed into a harmonious whole; all progress may be regarded as already attained in reality; there is enough matter, he affirms, in the finite centres to supply harmonious experience in the absolute. Perhaps we might think that there is even too much matter, that conflict may result; but conflicts, to Bradley's mind, must necessarily in the end disappear in the One Absolute Whole.

This absolutism ends in a radical relativism. All idea and all feeling are inadequate; no appearance or value at all can satisfy us. Absolutism prevents us from understanding error on the one hand, but on the other hand it prevents us from affirming truth.

No longer is there affirmation, for there is no longer negation and contradiction. Negation implies the reality of the individual will ; contradiction requires that contraries be retained in all their purity. No longer are there autonomous details in the universe, no longer is there any self-sufficing element.   Life and struggle and victory are indeed useless if the absolute ensures the triumph of the good.

To Bradley, as to the eclectics, any affirmative judgment he makes is true and any negative one false ; of reality nothing can be denied, for what is denied of it must be included in a larger one. But, it may be objected, is not this reality a paler reality than the partial ones from which we started ? How do we know that it is the larger but apparently necessarily discoloured reality that is the truest, and not the more vivid and perhaps deeper partial truth ?

All truth becomes essentially relative, it is truth only in so far as it is contained in the whole of reality.   But can we not say that any affirmation of value, any judgment is at bottom even a negation of this total reality ?   Can we not think that there is more in these judgments than in the reality into which they are transfigured ?   Can they be transformed without losing that element of exclusive affirmation which constituted their nature ? Can we not think that there is more in the finite centres than in the total reality which is said to contain them ? For in them there is the particular individuality and the particular will.   This individuality and this will, according to Bradley, must be found in the absolute ; but how could that be ?   We cannot conceive an individuality as contained in a whole without placing itself outside that individuality and for that very reason denying it.

The element of internality in each of us disappears finally in this doctrine along with the disappearance of the idea of externality.   There is for it no such thing as private feeling, as deep, exclusive individuality.

There is no irreducible subject, also says Bosanquet ; substantiality and individuality are no more than qualities susceptible of degrees. All affirmation and negation, all internality and externality are destroyed The transmutation mentioned by Bradley finally appears before us as the negation of that which it transforms.

In spite of his efforts, in his doctrine the world seems to lose all trace of a tragic character. Bradley has not, as James had, the dramatic sense of realities in contact and of resistances, of possible defeats, of victories to win. The absolute gives rest to the world.

How should action be possible, pluralists will say, if such philosophy is accepted ? With time, possibility and freedom disappear.

Morality and religion seem no more than inadequate forms of thought, illusions. The absolute is outside of morality. No longer is there evil or good, beautiful or ugly, its opponents will say ; everything is justified, everything is true and beautiful and good to some extent ; everything is imperfect except the all, and the all justifies everything that is imperfect.

Shall we take refuge in contemplation of the absolute ? But of the absolute we can say nothing except that it is each thing we know, mysteriously transformed into a totally different thing and united to all other realities, however contradictory to it they may seem.

On the other hand, the subjective element, the finite centre, externality, the temporal process remain incomprehensible. Bradley entitled his great work *Appearance and Reality*, and his last volume is called *Essays on Truth and Reality*, but according to him it is impossible to state what are the exact relations between each of these ideas, if indeed we can speak of relations at all. We can say nothing about the relations of truth and reality ; we cannot say how it comes about that there is both union and opposition between them. He even tells us, a pluralist will say, that there is no reality whatsoever except in appearance ; and yet appearance is but illusion.

" Higher," " truer " : these terms count on the whole in the universe as they count to us.   Bradley says that the dogmatistic " to be sure " is followed by such expressions as " somehow," " in one way," " on the whole."   This is an agnostic dogmatism ; problems must be—are— solved ; there are no problems, but the solution of problems is itself a problem.   What matters it to reason, Bradley seems to say, how it is to be satisfied, since reason knows that it will be ?

We are thus led to ask ourselves if the arguments used by Bradley to effect a transition from the idea of perceived experience to that of the absolute can be accepted.

For instance, on what is his criticism of qualities, essential to his criticism of pluralism, founded ?   On these two postulates : that all separation implies an action which consists in separating, and that we cannot think quality without thinking distinguishing characteristics.   The first postulate is the affirmation of what we have to prove ; the second perhaps shows us that the intellectual conception of qualities implies the relation of quality with other quali- ties, but does not prove the non-existence of qualities. Will it be alleged that, even to perceive them, they must be brought in relation one with another ?   But such a rapport, a perceived rapport, a felt relation, as Bergson expresses it, seems in no way contradictory *per se*.

It is also at times on wholly abstract and intellectual arguments that he bases his monism : negative relations imply an inclusive unity.   No doubt if we say that blue is not red, it is because we compare them, because both are colours and both objects of perception.   Still, as a pragmatist would rightly ask, what can such reasoning really teach us as to the nature of the world ?

Or again : all truth external to its terms, he says, is not true of its terms ; but this is taking for granted a certain conception of truth, of truth interior to reality, a conception, indeed, by which he cannot abide, since on the other hand, in a sense, if truth were interior to the terms, it would no longer be truth to him, it would become reality.

This intellectualism also, on which he partially bases his refutation of pluralism, might be criticised. The words " here," " now," " I," he says, resuming Hegel's criticism of our sensible world, cannot bring the certainty of feeling into the domain of thought, for the mere fact of naming them gives them a place in an intellectual series, and certainty no longer exists. But is an idea necessarily a term in a series ? On the other hand, are there not series perceived in immediate experience ? In addition, does not Bradley tell us that all idea is a designation of a particular reality ? Hence is it not permissible to make use of ideas, not to go farther and farther away from immediate experience but to draw nearer and nearer to it ? The answer to this question would also be the answer to the question asked by James in the words : " Bradley or Bergson ? "

Bosanquet's theories appear in more concrete form ; for instance, he attempts, comparing the world with a work of art, with a great picture, to show that expectation and despair do not disappear in the absolute, that these feelings give a certain tint to hope and satisfaction, just as the qualities of the sketch must be recognised in the finished work.

Dissociation itself and the partialities of experience enrich the whole with significance. So the previous failures of the artist are present in his very success. Here we have an attempt to explain certain ideas of Bradley by tracing them back to our loftiest experiences. But it is no less true that expectations and despairs, when transmuted, cease to be expectations and despairs.

If we note the way in which Bosanquet criticises pluralism, we find the same tendencies and ideas as we found in Bradley. This is the case in his criticism of the idea of finality.

Like Bradley in his denial of " fleeting ideas," Bosanquet is led to deny one of the fundamental conceptions of pluralism, that of reality as incessant effort. The neo-Hegelian, ever seeking the inner connection of terms, can conceive of change only if he has a reason, and this reason can be found only within a whole which does not change. Is not this employing one of those wholly intellectual arguments which pluralism condemns ? Is it not also opposing a static conception to the dynamic conception of the pluralists ? Because all change depends on certain determinate conditions, Bosanquet conceives change in general and the very development of the world and of thought as depending on certain given conditions ; change is then only a circumstance within a motionless whole. A plan or design, after all, says Bosanquet, is nothing but a need, a lack, or at most an object we miss. Or again, an effort is always relative to some special type of enjoyment. Thus, subordinating will to the object of this will, subsuming will under its object, Bosanquet apparently sees here in creative activity itself nothing more than the present and absent object towards which it is turned ; hence he is perpetually brought back to the idea that a plan can never be essentially anything but a partial element of a logical whole which " stretches into time." *De facto*, the whole appears to be stretching out into time ; *de jure*, there is nothing but the extra-temporal and rational whole.

It is the same intellectualism that we appear to find at the root of the affirmation that the ideal is not something to come, but something which is present inside the whole, and which we see when we view things in their totality.

By the idea of plan and will, we try to single out, to emphasise certain aspects of the whole. But, to the mind of Bosanquet, all must be withdrawn into the heart of the absolute. Hence this compact view of the world, this opposition to all philosophy which conceives of discontinuities, of sudden births, of new plans. We are simply confronted with the active form of totality within a certain mass of content. The individual is no more than " a living world of content," and as this content is not strictly individual, the idea of the individual as distinct from other individuals finally disappears ; there is a universal implication of things in the absolute.

Although Bosanquet desires to retain in his universe the sense of the tragic which, in his opinion, is one of the loftiest feelings of the finite being, the tragic worth of life seems finally to disappear, as with Bradley. By the idea, somewhat analogous to that of Höffding, of " the conservation of values " in the universe at large, by the use of terms similar to those employed by Bradley (" on the whole," " on principle ") he expects to solve the problem of immortality.

Nor does it seem astonishing that the sense of the tragic should disappear, if it is connected with the idea of the self, the effort of the self.

Perhaps it may be said that Bosanquet, with his idea of negativity, leaves room for all the contradictory and negative elements of the world, for evil and error ; but this negativity of which he speaks, instead of being the negation of harmony, is a possibility of union, an appeal to harmony. Negativity is not contradiction, but rather contradiction loosening and easily dissolving away into a higher harmony.

The world, such as it is, is declared perfect. Although not morally good in the ordinary sense of the expression, still it is perfection itself, the criterion of all goodness and all worth.

Again, the pragmatists might say that the final result of Bosanquet's profound theory of evil, the germ of which may be found in Hegel and Green and Nettleship, must finally be the annihilation of the difference between good and evil; for him, the ultimate logical structure of suffering and of evil is the same as that of good and satisfaction. The distinction between them is only one of degree. There is no evil desire in the vilest human life or the basest human action which with certain additions or readaptations might not be incorporated within a Self which is good; there is nothing in evil which might not be absorbed in the good and might not contribute to the good; its primitive source is the same as that of the good and the valuable; and its ends are the same. Consequently good contains evil, somehow as truth contains error. Distributed and systematised in a new fashion, evil reappears in the good.

The absolute is victorious from all eternity, just as beauty, for those who worship it, if it would overcome ugliness, has but to make evident the triumph which its very essence ensures for it. Perfection is present from the outset, and alone makes progress possible.

And in what can progress consist ? Simply in the fact that we shall more and more completely apprehend the whole. That is what " the future, the future of the race," reserves for us.

We reach a purely æsthetic attitude. To Bosanquet, the contemplation of a work of art is, it would seem, the nearest approach to the absolute. For in religion there is something which must be widened out and softened down. Besides, in religion as in morality, we are confronted with an antagonism between good and evil, an antagonism necessary in practical life but which must be transcended if we are to attain to the absolute. Even when religion endeavours to transcend it, it is still affected by this opposition; now, in the absolute not only must oppositions be overcome, they must have wholly disappeared.

And cannot we finally criticise the very way in which Bosanquet in certain passages seems to conceive the absolute? Progress seems to present itself in quantitative form; the self draws to itself and appropriates as much matter as it can. It is the superabundance of this material that shatters the envelope of the self, the individuality in so far as it is negative.[27]

We have no wish to deny the beauty and the elements of very profound truth in these conceptions, in these ideas we have just examined, in this affirmation of an absolute totality, of an infinite comprehension, now and at all times present, and which we can incessantly reveal to ourselves. But we had to recognise that which, in these ideas, cannot be assimilated or absorbed by a pluralist theory, a theory of diversity and time, or at least that which would need to be interpreted and—as these philosophers express it—transmuted. And we had therefore to single out and to emphasise certain conceptions which, admirable though they are and full of deep truth, appear to be objectionable from the pluralist's point of view.

VIII

Nevertheless, in spite of these oppositions, do there not seem to be certain common ideas between the

[27] The same conception is found in Nettleship's *Philosophical Lectures*.

philosophy of Bradley and Bosanquet and that of James ?
First, their mistrust as regards the abstract; their condemnation of intellectualism regarded as an abstract
explanation of reality.   We cannot understand the world
if we start from general laws; true universality, says
Bosanquet, true particularity, says James, is that of the
individual.   And the ordinary discursive intellect cannot
comprise the individual.   No doubt, neither of these
two philosophies keeps within the limits of this conception.   James has long tended to disintegrate, so to
speak, individuality, and to regard the self as a sequence
of momentary volitions and ideas.   Bosanquet comprehends the selves in order to make one whole individuality.
Still it is no less true that their teaching may, at a definite
moment in the process of their thought, seem to coincide.

Their starting-point, the theory of pure experience,
is identical.   Sometimes also, the two philosophies
" coincide " in a thought which may be called transcendentalist, although in reality it is an affirmation of
immanence.   There are moments when Bosanquet and
Bradley, in order to think the absolute, raise themselves
above the logical numerical category of extension, and
even above that of comprehension, although this latter
comes much nearer to a really metaphysical thought.
It is the same frequently with James's conception of
personality.   Thus they see that beyond the logic of
quantity there is a logic of quality which denies it,
that the essential thing is not the discussion between
pluralism and monism, that experience is no longer
additive but intensive, that the absolute gets itself
revealed in an act of our thought.   In *A Pluralistic
Universe*, certain expressions resemble those of Bosanquet.
Indeed, all the time there persisted more or less strongly
in the mind of James the transcendentalist idea of an

Emerson : in the very phenomena the absolute reveals itself ; they are of infinite depth.

Thus we see the endeavour made by James, and by Bradley and Bosanquet, to bring together the ideas of transcendence and immanence. Bradley and Bosanquet tell us that experience ever tends to transcend itself and yet that all is immanent in experience. James insists on the externality of God with reference to ourselves, and on the other hand he regards us as a consciousness which is one, so to speak, with divine consciousness. And he tells us that he has reached an empirical philosophy of identity ; in this philosophy the affirmations of the juxtaposition of the elements of experience and of the fusion of these same elements are united. In this empirical philosophy of identity, James seems to be departing from pluralism, just as Bradley, in his theory of the finite centre, goes beyond monism.

We might still find a " coincidence " in certain moral conceptions ; for Bosanquet as for James, the higher joy is born of despair and contains despair within itself. The will to regard life tragically is the same in both.

The conceptions which seem to have succeeded those of these two philosophers appear in some respects still to " coincide " with them. For instance, the neo-intellectualism of Hocking is quite different from intellectualism as generally conceived. And the neo-realism which seems a revival of intellectualism in its most abstract element is nevertheless based on what might appear a mystery, since it affirms both the identity of our thought and of its object, and the independence of the object as regards thought. This is what has been called by Perry the transcendence or the independence of the immanent. Hocking also, though from quite another point of view, shows us the equal necessity of both affirmations. And do we not find them in various forms in the many philosophies we have examined ? Recognition of the transcendent and recognition of the immanence of the transcendent : such are these philosophies.

No pluralist has insisted more distinctly on individuality, on the separate existence of the selves, than McTaggart has done in certain passages; on variety of meanings and purposes, more vividly and boldly than Royce; on the infinity of the individual, more deeply than Bosanquet or Bradley. Just as the monists necessarily make room in their universe for elements of diversity, so the pluralists, James, Schiller, Howison, like those by whom they have been influenced as well as those who have followed them, have made room for unity and for a kingdom—we might say for kingdoms—of the eternal.

Perhaps the centre of this vortex of which we were speaking is everywhere the same, certain truths flash out at the heart of this perpetual movement of reciprocal negations.

Still, these affirmative elements, these " coincidences," should not be looked upon as absorbing or as eliminating the negative elements on which pluralism has insisted. Such a conception as we should wish to be propounded should not be a negation of pluralism, it should recognise the irreducibility of phenomena, be both dialectic and realism, maintain both the presence of the object and the creative act of the mind, be able to retain, from the pluralist doctrines, that sense of the concrete particular, that empiricism, that voluntarism, and that mysticism which mostly characterise them and to which they owe their lasting value.

APPENDIX I

SOME DEFINITIONS OF PLURALISM

1833. The following sentences are to be found under the heading *Pluralismus* in Krug's philosophical dictionary : " The word pluralism may be interpreted either in a psychological, a cosmological, or a theological sense Psychological pluralism claims that, apart from the particular mind, the self, there exist other independent beings, spiritual beings, or souls, and that the various souls cannot be regarded as mere parts of a universal cosmic soul. Cosmological pluralism is the belief in the plurality of worlds inhabited by rational beings as expounded by Fontenelle, or again the belief in various systems of bodies (the Solar System, the Milky Way). Theological pluralism is nothing else than polytheism."

1879. Eisler defines pluralism : " The conception of being composed of various essences." Pluralism, he says, may be an atomism or a monadology. It has for its synonym : individualism.

1902. Dewey defines pluralism in Baldwin's dictionary as " the theory that reality consists in a plurality or multiplicity of distinct beings." (Baldwin, ii, 306)

1903. Marvin says of pluralism : " The difference between the pluralistic conception and the monistic conception is that of the intellectual interpretation and of the ethico-religious interpretation of the universe."

1905. Höffding sees in pluralism " the tendency to emphasise the multiplicity and the difference of phenomena "

1906. Fullerton writes : " Pluralism is meant to cover the various doctrines which maintain that there is more than one ultimate principle or being in the universe." He contrasts it with " singularism."

1907. One of the best definitions of the pluralism of the pragmatists was propounded by Goldstein : " If I insist on the plurality and the distinction of things as it is given in experience, as well as on their unity, if I regard it as impossible that a single law should traverse all the various domains of being—if I do not believe in an absolutely rounded unity and the shut-in character of reality—if I believe in a world still partly incomplete and apprehended in its very becoming, a world that man, within certain limits which experience alone will determine, can model in accordance with his ideas and his ideals—if I keep always within a sphere of reality in which there are such ideas as 'on one side' and 'with,' so that I see the world, as James says, as something like a limited company—then, I am a pluralist" (*Frankfürter Zeitung*, 8th September 1907, "Litteraturblatt").

This definition is narrower than the others, in so far as it binds the notion of time to that of diversity, and wider, in that it speaks neither of beings nor of principles. The definition to be given of pluralism, especially the pluralism of the pragmatists, will necessarily come somewhere near that definition.[28]

1909. Murray tells us that pluralism is " a theory or system of thought which recognises more than one ultimate principle."

In the *Vocabulaire Philosophique*, pluralism has been defined by M. Lalande as a " doctrine according to which the beings that make up the world are multiple, individual, independent, and must not be regarded as simple modes or phenomena of an absolute reality."

---

[28] It is to be remarked that certain American writers have used and misused the word "pluralism." In the case of Marvin (see *An Introduction to Systematic Philosophy*), pluralism ranges from atomism to hylozoism (*Introduction*, p. 223); in the case of Miss Calkins, the world is peopled with pluralists; Spinoza is studied in a chapter entitled: "Monistic Pluralism" (*Persistent Problems*, v, also pp. 411, 412). Similar remarks may be made on Leighton's classification in *Field of Philosophy*, pp. 75, 263, 268, where Plato, Leibniz, and Hume are cited as pluralists. We have already considered the many meanings attributed to the word at the present time (see note at end of Book II). For the use of the word "pluralist" in recent controversies dealing with the nature of the State, see M. P. Follett, *Philosophical Review*, 1919, p. 588, and N. Wilde, *Journal of Philosophy*, 1920, p. 316. See also the article of Mrs Parkhurst, *Philosophical Review*, 1919, p. 466, on æsthetic pluralism.

APPENDIX II

THE WORDS "PLURALISM," "MELIORISM," "MORALISM"

The word "Pluralism"

THE word *Pluralismus*, says Eisler, was used for the first time by Wolff. Kant employs it in his *Anthropology*. It is for him the conception of the world as an assembly of citizens.

In England and America, according to Murray, the word "pluralistic" precedes the word "pluralist." Winchell uses it in *Science and Religion*, 1881, vol. ii, p. 40 : "The later Eleatics were pluralistic." In 1884, continues Murray, the word "pluralistic" is used in the translation of the *Metaphysik* of Lotze (i, 443).

The word "pluralism" seems to come direct from the *Metaphysik* of Lotze ; it does not date from 1902, as we might imagine from Murray's article, nor even from 1887, as Dewey thinks in his article in Baldwin's dictionary. Bowne uses it in his "*Metaphysics*" : The ultimate pluralism of spontaneous thought, p. 132, 1882 edition. And Bowne does not use it incidentally as we might infer from Dewey's article ; even in the *Philosophy of Theism* it is found a number of times (pp. 47, 87, etc.). At all events, it was a commentator, a disciple and friend of Lotze, who seems to have introduced the word into the English language.

The word made rapid progress. "It is argued," said Fullerton, "that we should have some word under which we may bring such a doctrine, for example, as that of the Greek philosopher Empedocles." [29]

The word "Meliorism"

The word "meliorism" was used by George Eliot (Her Life, edited by J. W. Cross, vol. iv, pp. 183–187, Leipzig, 1885).

[29] Fullerton, *An Introduction to Philosophy*, p. 205.

319

Murray defines meliorism as " the doctrine intermediate between optimism and pessimism, which affirms that the world may be made better by rightly directed human effort." [30]

The word " Moralism "

Murray does not give a definition of the word " moralism," which applies to the moralistic view of the world in the case of James. All the same, under the heading " moralistic," he cites a passage from J. Grote, in which the words seem to be used in a sense which is not very far from that of our contemporary pluralists.

It may be remarked that the father of William James had brought out a pamphlet entitled : *Moralism and Christianity.*

[30] The word " meliorist " has been in existence since 1858 (J Brown). *Cf.* also McGavin Sloan on Meliorism, in the *Free Review*, 1895, pp. 171–183. See also Frederic Harrison's *Memories and Thoughts*, published by Macmillan, London, in 1906, where we find the expression : " Meliorist at last."

INDEX

PRINTED IN GREAT BRITAIN BY NEILL AND CO. LTD. EDINBURGH.

Lightning Source UK Ltd.
Milton Keynes UK
UKOW06f1936240913

217871UK00008B/92/P